How to Become the Restaurant of Choice

A Fresh Look at Service, Hospitality and the Bottom Line

Bill Marvin
The Restaurant Doctor℠

Hospitality Masters Press
Gig Harbor, Washington

Library of Congress Control Number: 2013913018

ISBN: 978-1893864-01-6

ATTENTION ASSOCIATIONS AND MULTI-UNIT OPERATORS:
Quantity discounts are available on bulk purchases of this book for premiums, sales promotions, educational purposes or fund raising. Custom imprinting or book excerpts can also be created to fit specific needs.

For more information, please contact our Special Sales Department
Hospitality Masters Press, PO Box 280, Gig Harbor, WA 98335
e-mail: bill@hospitalitymasters.com
Phone: (800) 767-1055, Fax: (888) 767-1055
Outside the US and Canada: (253) 858-9255, Fax: (253) 851-6887

Cover: Kitty Hoynes Irish Pub, Syracuse, New York
Photo Credit: Wainwright Photography

Contents

1
A Note From the Doc

A Note From the Doc

Life Is Like a Jigsaw Puzzle

Have you ever done a jigsaw puzzle? A pile of seemingly disjointed pieces turns out to create a cohesive picture. Life is like that, too!

Over the years you do whatever it is you do and collect puzzle pieces – experiences, ideas and such – usually without a clear idea of what the finished picture (aka your life) will look like. But you still make up a picture in your head of what you *hope* it will be, show up every day and do the best you can, always with the best of intentions.

If you're paying attention, after awhile you might start to notice a few of the pieces fit together. You may even identify edges and corners as the puzzle starts to take shape. But you still don't know exactly what it's going to look like when it's finished ... and you're sure some of the pieces you have can't possibly be part of the same puzzle.

With luck, one magical day you suddenly get the finished picture ... and it's a little different from the one you'd been imagining. In a flash *all* the pieces fall into place and you see they were all necessary parts of the whole. It is an awesome (and humbling) experience.

Puzzling It Out

I started collecting pieces to my own professional puzzle at fourteen when I got my first job: a minimum wage summer position washing dishes (by hand!) in a small restaurant on Cape Cod. Except for the getting paid part, it wasn't a particularly pleasant experience. Little did I know it would be the start of a career!

In the 50+ years since then, I earned a degree in Hotel Administration from Cornell, managed about every type of foodservice, developed and operated my own restaurants, wrote over a dozen books, spoke before audiences all over the world and advised clients on everything from new concept development to profit improvement.

Along the way there have been triumphs, tragedies, dead ends and U-turns as I collected pieces to the puzzle of my life. In retrospect, all these learning experiences were essential pieces of the finished puzzle and brought me to the understanding I wish I'd had when I started. (I couldn't see it at the time, but I probably learned more from the things that *didn't* work than from those that *did!*)

This Book is Another Puzzle

I have written books, articles, newsletters and such for the hospitality industry for more than twenty-five years now. Of necessity, each addressed a fairly narrow topic area and, at the time, was my best effort at offering something of value on that subject.

In the course of writing this, my 13th book, I discovered that some elements from my past works were actually pieces to yet another puzzle, one called *How to Become the Restaurant of Choice*. So in some ways, this book might be a bit like a "Greatest Hits" album! Who knew? Longtime readers may even recognize certain passages. If so, consider them a refresher to emphasize a slightly different point.

[Note: typos and grammatical errors are intentional. Some folks enjoy looking for them and I try to please as many readers as possible!]

The Dilemma

Our industry has many moving parts that all must mesh smoothly, each discipline affecting and influencing the others. For example, you can't talk about effective marketing without addressing how you'll deliver on the promises you make to prospective patrons.

The ability to effectively create an memorable foodservice operation depends on your vision, professional expertise, concept, ambience and menu along with the staff you select, how you develop their talents and how (and where) you lead them. But that's not the end of it ...

The ability to stay in business hinges on the ability to maintain reliable profitability, a totally different skill set. All these elements impact on your guests' experience of the service you provide ... and so it goes, round and round. I can't adequately cover one area without straying into another. So the hardest part about crafting a book like this is deciding what to include, what to omit and when to stop.

The teacher in me wants to explain the rationale behind everything, but even if this evolved into a multi-volume set, there would still be massive amounts of information left unsaid. Maybe there will be more books or seminars exploring each idea in minute detail. We'll see.

I suspect there are likely three possible reactions you could have to the material I present in this book:

"Well, I knew that!"
If everything I say is new to you, I'd be concerned. The odds are you've been in and around the industry for awhile and picked up some basic understanding of how it works. But if any of what I say turns out to be information you already know ...

Does your staff know it?
I was always surprised by the things my staff didn't know! After years in the biz, there are things that have become so intuitively obvious that it never occurs to you someone else wouldn't know them. So the parts that are old news may give you language that will help you pass a concept along to your team.

But there is perhaps a bigger question:

If you already know it, are you doing it?
In my seminars, I'll often ask how many in the audience have ideas they know would make their business better, yet they still haven't done them. Most of the hands in the room go up!

"That will never work!"
Do you say that because the idea challenges the way you do things, the way you think things ought to be – what you "know" – or is it because you don't operate a full service restaurant?

If an idea irritates you, it means the notion hits close to one of your blind spots. We all have blind spots, we just don't know what they are ... which is what makes them blind spots! I won't ask you to agree or disagree with anything I say, just to reflect on it and see if you can't validate the *principle* from your own experience.

Foodservice operations are diverse. Most share the same operating principles but one size will not fit all. If you think an idea wouldn't apply to your unique situation, ask yourself how the underlying principle or idea could be adapted to meet your particular needs.

"That's a great idea!"
If it's a great idea, will you actually implement it? All the great ideas in the world won't put a dime in your pocket. The Universe rewards action ... and you have to take some to reap the rewards.

Although I've done my best to present my case in a cohesive manner, I expect each answer I offer may trigger another question. Chapter 11 addresses a few "Yeah, but" type questions that often arise after I first introduce these principles. I also include additional resources to help explore any particular area in more detail.

They say a wise man learns from the input and experience of others. With that in mind, I am indebted to my good friend Ed Manley for asking me to organize my thoughts on service and hospitality in the first place and staying on me until I got it right. The finished product is much better for his insights and tough love.

Thanks go to Karl Spangler and Jeff Simmonds for wading through the original manuscript and offering brilliant suggestions on how to make this effort more meaningful. My hat is off to Danny Meyer and Union Square Hospitality Group for proving to the world that hospitality is also a profitable business practice. Finally, I am eternally grateful for Sydney Banks, George Pransky and Robert Kausen. Their wisdom helped me appreciate the power of a quiet mind and understand what makes people tick. Those insights changed everything.

This is my latest attempt to organize the perspective gained (so far) from a lifetime of lessons. I suggest you read the material at least twice and allow time for reflection between readings. The first time through you'll get the overall flavor, but the insights gained in later chapters will help you understand earlier chapters in a much deeper way when you re-visit them. It's more work perhaps, but if you're after a fresh way to understand what you do, I promise it will be worth your time.

The next 256 pages offer powerful principles and uncommon ideas. Some will validate what you've always suspected, some may irritate you, but they all should cause you to re-think what you "know" ... and that will make all the difference.

My hope is some of these notions will become valuable pieces in your own puzzle, perhaps even ones that help you see a larger picture for your business ... and yourself. Let me know how that comes out.

Now let's get to work!

Bill Marvin
The Restaurant Doctor℠
Gig Harbor, Washington

2
The Restaurant
of Choice

The Restaurant of Choice

What Do We Mean?

The Restaurant of Choice is an establishment guests patronize over and over again because they WANT to ... and they gladly pay full price. It is their favorite place, an important element in their quality of life. Here's a perfect example of what I'm talking about:

Steve and Nancy Butcher own the modest Nutcracker Family Restaurant in Pataskala, Ohio ... a typical small town diner and gathering spot, seemingly nothing special. One weekend in 2005 they had an electrical fire and the original restaurant burned to the ground.

On Monday morning, their neighbors showed up to help them rebuild. The community simply felt the town wouldn't be the same until they had the Nutcracker back in their lives and took it upon themselves to make that happen. The new restaurant was built ... and Steve was elected town mayor!

Do you think there would be the same level of community urgency and support if a national chain restaurant burned down? More to the point, would YOUR patrons instinctively show up to help rebuild YOUR place if such a tragedy struck? They would if you were truly their Restaurant of Choice.

When you are their Restaurant of Choice, they think of you as THEIR place. They feel a personal connection to you and your staff. They trust you to always be working in their best interests. They know the names of most of the crew and the staff knows theirs. They feel comfortable, like old friends when they come in.

9

And even though they often seem more like family than paying customers, they know you will never take them for granted and consistently work hard to earn their continued patronage.

Becoming someone's Restaurant of Choice is a lofty goal to shoot for and you usually don't simply get picked. Sure, random good fortune will happen from time to time and we're quick to claim credit for the good fortune fairy when she randomly shows up and picks us.

The thing is, the good fortune fairy has to pick someone and from time to time you get lucky, but counting on that to happen is just a version of waiting and hoping, not a plan.

A plan involves steps that are largely under your personal influence and control. A plan involves the hard, dreary and often difficult work of a thousand brave steps, of connecting and caring and bringing generosity when you don't think you have any more to bring.

This book will give you ideas and approaches that can help you do all that ... and it will increase your chance of being chosen ... but only if you're willing to **Do the Work!**

Becoming someone's Restaurant of Choice is a high honor ... but it takes more than completing a checklist. It takes a combination of consistency, passion, seamless service and personal caring ... in other words, the experience of heartfelt hospitality.

The expectations someone might have of an upscale restaurant are quite different from what would be appropriate in a military dining facility, a country café or at a fast food drive-up window, but ...

The principles that lead to the experience of hospitality are universal

So this book is less about what to do (specific actions) and more about why it works (the principles that might make a particular action appropriate). As we develop these principles, I will offer examples to illustrate how they might be applied in real-life situations to help you see the simple beauty of it all.

Validating the principles of service and hospitality from your own experience (and owning them as your own) will serve you far better than if I simply presented a long Do and Don't list.

That would just clutter up your head and you'd never remember it all anyway. But there are some basics to be aware of as we begin to explore service, hospitality and the bottom line.

The Magic in the Mix

Since its start in the late 1950s, McDonald's Corporation has grown from a single concept in San Bernardino, California to more than 34,000 restaurants employing more than 1.7 million people in 119 countries, all embracing Ray Kroc's core principles of QSC&V – quality, service, cleanliness and value.

In the years since McDonald's first burst upon the US dining scene, there have been countless industry surveys looking at the factors most important to diners when choosing a restaurant.

The relative importance of the various factors shifts from year to year and often varies with the concept. For example, speed is a much more important factor in a limited service restaurant [fast food] than in a fine dining establishment. But regardless of the type of eatery, quality, service, cleanliness and value are always the top items in any diner satisfaction survey. Ray Kroc was definitely onto something.

Let's look at some of the factors that figure into a diner's experience of the meal, whether they are eating at a food truck, in a cafeteria or seated in an upscale restaurant.

Speed

Lunch is a timed meal. Most people have only an hour to eat, so guests usually need faster service. At lunch, slowness leads to poor satisfaction ratings.

A more leisurely pace is appropriate in the evening. In general, the higher the check average, the less overall dining time is a factor, but whatever the timing, the pace of service must always be responsive to the needs of the guest.

When guests decide they want something, they want it as soon as possible. If they have to wait longer than they originally expected – and who know where they get their expectations? – it negatively affects their experience. In most cases, guests are more interested that the service be at an appropriate pace rather than just fast, but the pace of service is an important element in guest gratification.

11

Food Quality

As my colleague, Phyllis Ann Marshall so neatly puts it, "It's about the food, stupid!" Restaurants that serve bad food won't be in business very long (although it seems restaurants with famous name chefs can fool the public awhile longer than most!)

Food quality is more than just great recipes, properly prepared using painfully fresh ingredients. That is important, of course, but in evaluating overall quality, you must also consider quantity (are the portions the right size?), consistency (does it taste the same every time?) and presentation (do guests have a "WOW" reaction when the plate is presented?)

Service Quality

No guests are happy when they're treated rudely or feel rushed. It may seem obvious that services must be performed in an accurate and timely manner and that guests will not be satisfied when service is haphazard, but too many restaurants take it for granted.

Diners have dozens, even hundreds, of meal alternatives and they will often switch to a different restaurant – or simply stay home – if they experience indifferent or mediocre service. Although other factors certainly influence guest satisfaction in the service industry, it's hard to find any more important than whether a guest was served responsibly and respectfully.

Cleanliness

Cleanliness is not just a legal requirement in our industry. How the business (and the staff) look important to most guests. This comes under the category of image – how appropriately a service-oriented business presents itself to the public.

For instance, if a guest goes to a restaurant and is greeted by dirty floors and unkempt employees, it might not matter how good the food tastes. A bad first impression can lead the guest to expect poor service, leading to low satisfaction, even if the service was actually performed adequately.

Likewise, a positive appearance can push guest satisfaction over the top or help turn a mediocre service experience into a good one.

Communication

Ease of communication (or lack of it) can greatly color a guest's overall experience with a restaurant. How easily patrons can communicate with, and relate to, the members of the service staff influences their overall satisfaction.

When they can establish personal connection ... when a name and a face are attached to a business ... diners naturally feel more engaged with the operation.

Furthermore, when patrons personally connect with those providing them service, they are more likely to feel positive about the meal experience. Ultimately, ours is a one-on-one business and experience proves that people are more loyal to people than they are to places. ("Yes, it's a great place, but I go there because Mary Ann always takes such good care of me.")

Value

Consumers want to get their money's worth, whether they're spending several hundred dollars in an upscale dining room or grabbing a taco on the run. As the price goes up, so do expectations, so a good value means not just what you pay but whether you get more than you expected for the price.

"More than you expected" doesn't equate to the size of the portion or the number of courses (although it could). Rather, it is the sum of all the elements that make up the dining experience. That includes the ones we have just discussed as well as any personal preferences or pet peeves.

Seamless Service

All these elements are critical to the success of a foodservice operation, of course. Of those on the list above, this book will limit its focus to the critical factor of service: what it is (and isn't) and how to consistently deliver a memorable service experience to your guests.

As you'll quickly learn, effective guest service involves much more than just having a system and following a script (although most chain restaurants apparently haven't figured that out yet!)

Another eye-opener: much of what people lump under the general category of service really involves something far deeper than the mere mechanics of the interaction. If you grasp the lessons in these pages, you will always have an edge in the marketplace, much happier guests and a more engaged crew of workers.

Seamless service describes an experience that flows smoothly from beginning to end; where all the guests' needs are met at the proper pace with no snags

Seamless service is almost invisible, supporting the dining experience – whatever that may be – in a way that never intrudes on the reasons the diners gathered in your establishment.

The goal of this book is to get you to understand – not just how to get it right and how to put those ideas into practice, but more important, the principles that cause your guests to feel well-served or not. Success in the service game is not measured by your actions but rather by the delight of your guests. When you (and your staff) understand the principles that drive this dynamic, you will always know what to do.

Terminology Traps

As you proceed through the book, you may notice I don't use some of the words you might expect to see. I also use some terms that may sound different to you. Here are some examples of what I mean:

Customer

The word customer suggests a relationship based on the transfer of money and is less delight-oriented than using the word "guest." Customers are just people who walk in the door and buy something. They all get the same treatment. On the other hand, guests are special individuals to whom you extend hospitality and offer an experience tailored to their particular needs. Think about it.

Employee

Employee is another word based on the transfer of money. I prefer the word staff although many companies use crew member, team member or associate with good results. Team-oriented words help contribute to a more empowering work climate.

Good Service

The concept of good service can be dangerous because it is too easily defined just from the perspective of the service provider. ("I can't understand why Table 6 is complaining. I gave them good service") The quality of the service experience can only be determined and evaluated from the guest's point of view.

Good service, like good food, is the price of admission in the foodservice business. Every restaurant says they have good food and good service. If they don't, they won't be in business very long. So just having good food and good service is not enough to make you stand out from the herd of competitors.

Even "satisfaction" isn't powerful enough – it only means guests got what they expected. Merely meeting expectations won't make you a legend in today's market. At the least you must deliver more than they expect, to provide the pleasant surprises that make them think, "Wow!" Doubletree Hotels, for example, wants to provide service that "astounds" you.

Play the word game. Focus on "gratifying" or "delighting" your guests instead of simply serving them. You'll like what happens!

Manager

If you call someone a manager, they may think their job is to manage other people. This can be dangerous because I don't think most people like to be managed. You can lead them, inspire them and train them, but when you start to boss the crew around, it can lead to micro-management and manipulation and totally destroy their initiative.

I much prefer the word "coach." I feel it better represents the model for effective leadership in a restaurant. A manager looks for problems to fix; a coach looks for strengths to develop.

Waiter, Waitress, Server

Similarly, these job titles may cause your crew to think their job is to wait or to serve – a very costly misunderstanding, both for your operation and your guests.

Consider the possibilities if you called the position as Sales Manager, Service Manager or Ambassador. Their role is truly to manage the process of making sales and delivering an experience of personal caring to your guests.

What if you called the position Storyteller? This could fit as well because your staff can best help build relationships and long term sales by telling guests stories about your operation, menu items and what makes you better or different – stories your guests, in turn, are likely to pass along to their friends.

Whatever direction you take here, give it some thought. Words are powerful and the ones you use unthinkingly may contribute to many of your problems in the service arena. If you want to change your results, start by changing your choice of words.

A Business of Details

Hotelier James Nassikas coined the term "monumental trivialities" to reflect his obsession with details. He built one of the most respected hotel experiences in the world, the Stanford Court in San Francisco, on his passion for attending to the little points that he knew were important to his guests.

Industry observers note the distinguishing feature between legendary operators and mediocre ones lies in their absolute belief in mastering the details. Many failed restaurateurs learn this lesson the hard way.

What Makes Trivialities Monumental?

To understand how the little things can destroy your guest' experience (and your business!), you must first understand why people have a good time and why they don't. The answer is not as obvious as it may appear. It is, however, surprisingly simple.

You know from personal experience that when you are having a bad day, everything looks like a disaster! Conversely, when you feel great, the whole world just seems to work more easily for you. The events of the day don't change, but their impact on you changes significantly depending on your mood.

It works the same way for businesses. If you enter a business that has a depressing environment, it starts to bring you down. In your lower mood, minor events take on more significance. You tend to be less trusting of people. You are more likely to find fault and complain. You can become more touchy and harder to please.

Because they are unaware of the importance of the atmosphere they create, many businesses foster an environment that almost guarantees their guests cannot have a pleasant experience. Think of the last time you went to the Post Office or the average bank! How likely is it that anyone will feel well-served if called in for a tax audit?

Fortunately, restaurants have a natural advantage over many other types of businesses. Because people go to restaurants expecting to have a good time, they usually arrive in a pleasant mood. Their higher state of mind predisposes them to enjoy themselves.

You see, people will have a good time anytime they are in a high state of mind; anytime they feel good. When they're in a good mood, they are more forgiving and more generous. They spend more. The food tastes better. They are more open to your recommendations. They tip better and are more likely to tell their friends what an exciting restaurant you have!

For the most part, if you handle the basics of the job well (quality, service, cleanliness, hospitality and value), you just need to maintain an atmosphere where people will stay in a good mood and they will usually have an enjoyable experience. It almost seems too simple!

Minutia Becomes Monumental

People enter your restaurant focused on having a good time. Anything that snags their attention can be a distraction and distractions change a person's mood. Every distraction, every minor irritant that affects your guests, is like tying a small weight onto the helium balloon of their good mood.

As these weight of these little annoyances adds up, it creates more of a downward pull on your guests' sense of well-being. As the mood drops, their thoughts become more negative. Their level of security goes down. They are more critical and abrupt with your staff. They become more difficult to please.

In turn, your staff can easily become less responsive to these "suddenly" impolite people. The experience can spiral down quickly for everyone. When a guest is in a lower mood, even the finest food and service will draw complaints. You can't fix it – that's just the way people view the world when they're in a low state of mind.

It's simple: Guests inevitably experience an increasingly worse time as accumulated distractions drop them into lower states of mind. Things they'd hardly notice in a good mood become intimidating at lower levels. Yet, without the weight of these distractions, people are likely to remain upbeat and enjoy themselves. This is how minutia destroys your business.

The tough part is that many of the distractions that impact the mood of your guests are seemingly insignificant items like a dirty menu, dead flies on the windowsill or lipstick on a water glass, details that are all too easy for the staff to overlook.

17

In my book, *Restaurant Basics: Why Guests Don't Come Back and What You Can Do About It* and its recent update, *Restaurant Basics Revisited*, I identify about a thousand of these minor annoyances ... and I add to the list every time I eat a meal away from home!

Picky, Picky, Picky

The first step in solving a problem is always to realize the nature of the problem. No one who's ever been in the business would deny that foodservice is a game of details. The price of success in our industry is attention to the small points.

A few details are obviously sudden death. For example, if you send guests to the hospital with food poisoning, don't expect to see them back as patrons. If your staff embarrasses a corporate executive in front of clients during an important dinner meeting, she is history.

For better or worse, most of the trivialities that savvy operators watch are not as terminal as that – they're more like minor distractions or petty annoyances. But remember the idea of weights on the balloon or the straw that breaks the camel's back. If you want to be a legend, you can't afford to dismiss anything as too insignificant.

Trivial details turn out to be monumental in the minds of guests who don't return.

Why Guests Don't Come Back

I mentioned that the overall feeling of value comes from exceeding the guests' expectations. It may help to think of the quality of your guests' dining experience as a game.

Because people expect to have a good time when they go to a restaurant, you start this game with a relatively high "score," say 90-100 "points" that equate to the diners' expectations. As guests approach the building and progress through their meal, you gain or lose points depending on what they notice and experiences.

Most of these distractions are things for which you will lose points when they happen but you won't necessarily gain points if they don't. On the plus side, personal, unexpected touches can gain points and improve your score. It's not fair, but it's the way human nature works.

There's no particular point value to anything other than the value arbitrarily assigned in the mind of the guest

For example, something one person might not even notice could cause someone else to walk out in a rage! This happens because people's perceptions are a function of personal preferences and the mood they're in at the time. The lower the mood, the more serious and threatening something appears to them in the moment and the more points it carries.

Your guests are not aware of it, but they keep a mental score. As they leave, they assign a subconscious value to their experience. The more positive their experience, the higher your score. When the final result is equal to or greater than their expectations going in, you win big!

Your point total also has relevance in comparison to your competition. If you provide a 75-point experience when your competitors are scoring 70, you'll have an edge ... but let a competitor rack up 80 points with a guest and you'll be in trouble. Remember, too, that people have higher expectations of a $150 dinner than they do of a fast food lunch ... and they should!

Exceeding expectations creates delighted guests. If you score higher than people expected, they will love you, at least for the moment. If you score less than they expected, no matter how good a job you do, you won't make their A List.

Worse yet, if you are inconsistent – good one time and sloppy the next – your guests won't trust you. When people mistrust your restaurant, you must score higher to reach the same level of guest satisfaction. For every person (in relation to every individual restaurant), there is a score so low it will cause them never to patronize the place again.

What You Can Do About It

It is hardly reasonable to expect you can operate error-free 100% of the time. Nonetheless, you can significantly reduce minor lapses through true caring, professional awareness, conscientious staff selection and continual training. Passionate attention to detail is one way you and your staff show respect and concern for your guests' well-being.

It is critical that patrons see your entire operation focuses on their delight and that you're making a sincere effort to identify and correct any shortcomings. This level of focus and caring creates and maintains an environment where guests will have a high sense of well-being.

Personally, I appreciate when an error is swiftly and skillfully corrected. It often shows me more than if the mistake never happened in the first place. Perhaps it is the human frailty and personal concern shown. If your heart is in the right place, you will not usually lose points for occasional oversights.

(Don't get me wrong – I'm not advocating making mistakes just so you can correct them. There are plenty of opportunities to blow it without doing anything intentional!)

The Soul of Service

So far we have talked about service in fairly typical terms based on the actions performed (or not) and the results they produce. But there is another critical dimension to the guest experience that has been largely taken for granted: Hospitality.

It always seems ironic that the competitive element most responsible for success in the hospitality business ... and the piece most visibly absent ... is hospitality itself!

You can be adequately fed and reasonably well-served in most food-service outlets, but how often do you experience the warm feeling of heartfelt caring and personal connection that shows the staff is delighted you're there and your enjoyment really matters to them?

My mission for the rest of this life to fix that – to make hospitality the rule rather than the rare exception and show independent restaurants how they can operate with effortless excellence.

Most operators say the word hospitality but talk about service. They seem to think the words mean the same when in reality, the two are quite different. Understanding the difference will elevate your game in ways that will astound you, your guests, (and your accountant!)

Here's a start on how to understand the difference:

20

SERVICE IS ...	HOSPITALITY IS ...
Procedural Service is the technical delivery of the product, a series of actions you can identify, plan out, organize, train and educate. It's serve from the left, clear from the right, don't spill wine on the table. It's about temperatures, timing and how to process credit cards. All these actions are important parts of the overall service sequence and you must execute them accurately and well.	**Personal** Hospitality is how the delivery of that service makes the guest FEEL. It is a human equation, a personal gift of caring. It's me taking care of you ... because it's YOU, not because you're one of 75 people coming through my station tonight. You don't serve 75 people anyway. You serve one person at a time in 75 different scenarios and it is the quality of those individual interactions – the level of hospitality you provide – that determines how successful you will ultimately be, both professionally and financially.
Monologue Service is one-sided. You can flawlessly deliver all the elements of the service sequence without the guest needing to get involved in the process at all.	**Dialogue** Hospitality, on the other hand, must involve the diners. It is an exchange of energy at some level between the staff and the guests ... a dance of sorts.
Executing The measure of service is how efficiently the service staff performs the steps and functions of the service sequence.	**Embracing** The measure of hospitality is how guests FEEL about what you do for them; that "warm fuzzy feeling" that lets them know it actually matters to you they are there.
Systematic Service can (and should) be organized into a replicable series of steps so that the staff (and guests) know what to expect at each point in the dining experience.	**Organic** By its personal nature, hospitality doesn't lend itself to structure. Comparatively speaking it is messy – an organic process that must be conceived (and only exists) in the moment. This is why chains can't deal with it that well ... and what makes it such a powerful force in the market for independent operators.
Doing Service is about what you DO.	**Being** Hospitality is about how you ARE.

IN A NUTSHELL ...

SERVICE is efficiently doing what is EXPECTED.	HOSPITALITY is spontaneously doing what is UNEXPECTED ... and uniquely personal to that guest in that moment.

We will explore both the service and hospitality experiences more deeply in later chapters. For now just be aware that the overall guest experience that draws your guests back is made up of two separate aspects – what you do and how you do it – that often just get lumped under the broad title of service.

The competitive edge belongs to those who understand and appreciate the distinction between service and hospitality.

Once you grasp (and internalize) the principles that govern human behavior, you will instinctively know the appropriate actions to take, regardless of the situation

3

Play a Bigger Game

Play a Bigger Game

Know Where You're Headed ... and Why

This is the part that few would-be leaders will ever take the time to do ... and why most will never build world-changing organizations. Lofty goals and flowery mission statements are not enough to make you successful or earn you a reputation for service.

Whether their lack of effort results from ignorance, short-sightedness or simple laziness, the end result is that they will work harder than necessary to achieve lower results than they might otherwise see.

Many businesses never create a Mission Statement. Too often, those who do write rambling, self-serving documents that nobody can possibly remember, let alone embrace. Because they are essentially useless, they confuse the staff and make management seem like they are just giving lip service to their grand plans.

They start off with something like, "To be the leading purveyor of ___ in the _____ area," enumerate a laundry list of what they want to get and talk about how they plan to make it all happen. Here's a typical example I snagged at random off the Internet. See what you think:

MISSION STATEMENT FOR MAMA'S RESTAURANT

"To be the absolute best at what we do and to make Mama proud in so doing."

Our mission is to be the restaurant of choice because we have honored the legacy of "Mama". We will strive to exceed our guests' expectations and provide a warm, pleasing dining experience just as Mama once did for her family. To achieve this end, we must hold ourselves to the highest possible standards of excellence for service and food. We will dedicate ourselves to these values and principles. We will be committed to developing leadership skills and to encouraging empowerment of our employees, like Mama raised her kids. We will embrace the challenge of constant self-evaluation to improve our performance as both the restaurant and employer of choice.

Our goal is simple: TO BE THE BEST AT WHAT WE DO.

There's nothing wrong with the sentiment here (perhaps other than a shallow – and incorrect – notion of what would actually make them the restaurant of choice). But how likely is it that every staff member will personally remember and own all these elements to the point where they actually guide daily activities?

The wording speaks only to what the *business* plans to do, and while these goals are all worthwhile, the Mission Statement still does not address the *really* big question:

What's the Point?

The sad truth is that nobody in your market gets up in the morning with a burning urge to come down and give you money! (Sorry about that!) As a consumer, I really don't give a rat's patootie what *you* want. I will patronize you (or not) based on how well you satisfy needs of *mine* and support causes that make a difference to *me*.

Define Your Purpose

I believe all people – at least the sort you want to associate with – really want to be part of something bigger than themselves. To illustrate what I'm getting at, let me share an old story with you. There are examples of this tale going back more than 5,000 years, so you've probably heard it in one form or another. Still, it is the best way I have yet found to make an important point.

> Several thousand years ago, a traveler was walking down a dusty highway and came upon three men chipping rocks by the side of the road.
>
> He asked the first man, "What are you doing? The fellow looked up at him with a scowl and snapped, "I'm chipping rocks. What does it look like I'm doing?"
>
> He asked the same question of the second man, who wiped the sweat from his brow and said with a sigh, "I'm squaring up these stones. They're going into a building or something."
>
> The third man smiled with pride and said, "I'm building a cathedral."

All three were chipping rocks ... except one guy, maybe not so much.

- Which worker do you think showed up in the morning with more sense of purpose?
- Which was most likely to leave every day with a greater sense of accomplishment?
- Which one likely found more satisfaction in his work?

The difference among the three was not in what they are doing but how they thought about what they were doing

Without a sense that what you do is meaningful, your whole life just becomes about cranking it out – doing it, doing it, doing it – the same things over and over again every day. After awhile that really grinds on you and can ultimately kill your spirit.

The role of the leader is to provide this meaningful context for the work to be done and keep the group engaged in the pursuit of the larger purpose, a dream that is not only important but represents an end result none of them could hope to accomplish on their own.

Putting Purpose Into Context

I didn't create my business for the purpose of providing you with a job. That was not my motivation when I did it. So if you come to me looking for work, we first need to talk about the cathedral.

You must understand what we're here to do and, more essentially, you must want to become part of making it happen. If you don't embrace our larger purpose, a job here just won't work out well for either of us, regardless of your skill set.

You could have a great work ethic and be excited about getting a job but if you want to build kayaks ... well, that's just not what we're about. The world needs kayak builders, though, and if that's where your passion truly lies, somebody in the kayak business would surely love to talk to you. But your kayak-building talents, no matter how exceptional, will not be a good fit in my organization and can only impede progress for both of us.

To pull off a massive task like building a cathedral, you must assemble a team of artisans dedicated to the task. Being totally clear on your purpose for doing what you do helps you identify the talent you must recruit and lets you separate those who want to make it happen from those who just want a paycheck. In the end, everyone is happier.

Purpose and Goals

We've discussed how people often talk of service and hospitality as if they were the same. Similarly, the words "goal" and "purpose" are used interchangeably, but they too have quite different meanings.

27

Goals are the steps you take
Purpose is why you take them

To illustrate the difference, think of a long stairway climbing up the side of a mountain and disappearing into the clouds, so long you can't see how many steps it takes to reach the top.

Purpose is where the stairway is going and why it is worth making the climb. Purpose answers the question, "What's the point?" The role of the leader is to define the company's purpose.

Each step on the stairs is a goal, a necessary task to complete in order to make it to the top. Goals answer the question, "What's next?" The role of the coach (manager) is to recognize the next step and help the team accomplish it successfully.

Clarifying Your Purpose

A strong Purpose is impersonal. That means it's not about what's in it for *you*. Instead, it focuses on the greater benefit others derive from your doing it. Purpose deals with what you offer to others rather than what you want to receive from them.

Clarity doesn't come from asking, "How do we do this better?" Rather, it starts by pondering whether you are doing the right thing in the first place and asking, "What larger contribution could we make?"

Getting clear on your purpose takes reflection, not struggle, but it won't happen overnight ... which is probably why most independent operators think they're just too busy to do it.

Yes, it takes time to get it right, but I contend the process of reaching clarity will ultimately save more time (and make you more money) than anything else you can do. When you get clear on what you are on the planet to accomplish, it provides a standard against which you can evaluate everything you do as you move forward.

A clear, impersonal Purpose is incredibly compelling. It gives you energy and a reason to go to work each day. It will draw followers to your cause. Perhaps best of all, it will change the way your team feels about what they are doing. They will stop simply chipping rocks and become engaged in building a cathedral ... together.

I can't tell you what your Purpose should be. One size does not fit all. But the process is painless. First quiet your mind and allow yourself to slow down to the speed of life. Reflect on the needs in your neighborhood or community. If you could wave a magic wand, what "impossible dream" would transform the quality of life for everyone?

There's nothing to figure out. Just quiet your mind and wait for something to strike you. It's like standing beside a river watching ideas float by like leaves in the current. When you see something that catches your imagination, grab it and see if it grows on you.

Hint: If you know how to achieve your dream in this lifetime, it isn't big enough. Just keep asking yourself, "What's the point?" until it becomes so huge it scares you. Then get busy!

What Does Purpose Look Like?

Just in case this whole idea may still seem theoretical, here are two examples of how seeing a larger Purpose played out in the real world.

#1: In 1984, I was hired to take over the foodservice department at the US Olympic Training Center (OTC) in Colorado Springs. In the interview I was told they really didn't know what Olympic foodservice *was*, but they were sure what they had wasn't it! My job was to invent it.

My predecessor had a background in military foodservice. He ran the place like a 1960's Army mess hall because that's what he knew. **He saw his job as putting out 2000 meals a day for the lowest cost possible. Period.**

In addition to uninspired food, he was only open two hours for each meal. This meant the various sports we hosted had to build their training schedules around meal hours. Athletes could only come in once during each meal period and the hours were strictly enforced.

I heard stories of athletes running down the sidewalk, looking at their watches, obviously trying to get there before closing, while a foodservice employee ran across the dining room to lock the door in their faces, pointed to their own watch and shook their head!

Not surprisingly, when I took over, foodservice was the #1 source of athletes' complaints about being in training — we generated all the hate mail! The standing joke was that when you came to train at the OTC, you could always get something good to eat any time of day ... at the Taco Bell across the street!

In contrast, **I saw the role of OTC foodservice as supporting the training of Olympic hopefuls. I wanted to become their restaurant of choice ... even if they didn't have a choice!**

That meant finding out what was really needed and wanted, then working backward from there. I met with my staff, the athletes and the coaches over coffee, asked a lot of questions and started making changes.

We served from 6am to 9pm. (Why not? We were there anyway!) We cleaned the place up, added some color and laid it out in a more convenient way.

In the past there had been no money for premium items like shrimp, but there was plenty of money for strange dollar-a-pound yellow bologna that nobody would eat.

Since my reimbursement was based on the number of meals served not dollars spent, we upgraded the menu. The more we gave athletes, the more they patronized us and the lower our cost per meal became.

Noticing that the interaction between my staff and the athletes was strictly task-related ("Do you want green beans?"), I blew out the front of the sneeze guards, turned the spoons around on the line and let athletes serve themselves.

They could come in as often as they wanted and take as much or as little as they chose. The line attendants' job was now to keep everything looking good and the interactions became more personal ("Is your knee feeling better?") Throw in warm chocolate chip cookies every night at 8:30 and everybody was happier.

Within two months we had become the #1 source of compliments. Within six months, the number of times athletes came in had gone from 1.3 times a day to 2.5 times a day. My food cost per meal went down 25% with a better-quality menu. Labor cost per meal dropped by a third and staff turnover went from over 300% to 25% ... with no change in wages.

Oh, and the Taco Bell went out of business!

#2: I was talking about Purpose in a seminar at the International Pizza Expo a few years ago. A young man in the audience came up to me after the session almost in tears and said, "The economy in my area has been in the tank for years and my town is dying. I believe my pizzeria can be the best part of living in [my town]. We can be the reason people won't want to move away and the one thing they'll miss most if they do. My pizzeria can save my town."

Unfortunately, I didn't get his name so I have no way to know how that turned out for him, but I'll guarantee when he returned to his shop he was playing a bigger game than just selling pizza. It surely changed the way he approached his work ... and, I suspect, the way he was regarded (and supported) in the community.

No matter how modest your initial inspiration, it can be expanded by continually reflecting on each potential purpose and asking yourself, "What's the point of *that*?" Here's what this expansion process might look like for my unknown pizzeria friend:

Purpose	Activities
Sell as many pizzas as possible	Standard pizzeria menu, build sales with coupons, door hangers, mailers, discount-based offers
"What's the point of that?"	
Bring families together over a shared meal	Family-friendly menu, children's play area, beer & wine, spreading the word via sponsored events for families and school tie-ins, no discounts
"What's the point of that?"	
Re-vitalize the community by bringing neighbors together to solve common problems	Everything immediately above plus coordinate fund-raising events for schools and community causes, organize clean up of blighted areas, host community meetings, market via "Buy One, Give One" (donate a pizza to a shelter for every one purchased), sponsor a Little League team

The bigger the dream you see, the more it will stretch your thinking, the greater sense of excitement you will have about what you're doing and the more followers you will attract to your cause.

Profit Is Part Of Purpose

An impersonal Purpose is about the good you do for others, but that doesn't mean you operate like a charity.

To be sustainable you must execute the basics of foodservice well and have a viable (profitable) business model

You'll accomplish your Purpose through what you do and how you do it in the restaurant, so if you fall down there, you're out of the game. But if you aren't making money at the same time, you won't be able to stay in business to meet your goals or pursue your Purpose.

The bottom line is important, but it becomes the way to keep score on how well you are serving your Purpose and your guests rather than a single-minded obsession and reason for being.

This means you need to create systems and procedures that will allow you to do several things:

Offer Solid Value

To maximize profitability, take the long term view. People who are seeing their profits erode often ask me the best way to maximize profitability. My response? Stay in business a long time!

It's easy to think of profit with a short term mindset -- "How much did we make tonight?" I think the smarter approach is to make a little less money and make it for a lot longer.

Don't try to take every penny from your guests' wallets tonight. Leave them a little change so they can patronize you tomorrow. Under-promise and over-deliver. Do more than you have to. Give them something for nothing.

I could give you a 5% food and 5% labor cost, but it's ugly and you would be out of business in a week! You bank profit and pay bills with dollars, not percentages. Give more, make it better rather than cheaper, and you will reap the rewards ... year after year after year.

Within limits, patrons are less interested in how much they pay than they are in what they get for their money. The average operator tries to see how little they can spend and how much they can charge for it. Carried to extreme, this approach will only destroy your value proposition ... and your credibility.

Instead, figure out the profit you need to be sustainable and work backward to determine what sales level you need and how much you can spend on food, labor and such. Then focus on achieving the necessary sales and see how *much* you can offer while still hitting your cost targets.

NICKELS AND DIMES

Ten years ago I attended a conference at a five-star resort in Florida. It was definitely a top class property with an amazing and historic physical plant. There were multiple bars, excellent restaurants, pools, golf, a beach club ... the works. So what memories did everyone at the conference take away after four or five days in this amazing place?

They remembered six bucks for a beer, $12 for a margarita and ten bucks a glass for the house wine. They remembered being charged five dollars to drop a prepaid FedEx package in the pickup box. They remembered three people expected a tip just to get the bags out of the car, into the building and up to the room. And so it went.

People are free to run their operations any way they want but the result of these policies was to cause most of the attendees to steer clear of the hotel's bars and to one-up each other with tales of even greater extortion. People always remember (and repeat) these kind of stories.

I know that this is what people remembered about the property because it was the leading topic of conversation during the conference! Could the attitude behind these policies have been part of the reason the hotel lost their five-star rating shortly afterward?

Charge Fair Prices

You are your own worst enemy when it comes to raising prices. In my experience, operators are more reluctant to raise prices than the market is to accept them, so do what you need to do when you need to do it ... but consciously and in a way that respects your guests.

What kind of memories are you giving people? Do you have little add-on charges guests don't expect like an extra dollar for blue cheese dressing? When the market tightens, moves like this may seem more attractive, but while a "nickel and dime" approach may produce some marginal income, it carries a steep long term cost.

Charge a fair price so people can afford to give you their business now and raise prices when you must to avoid the need for surprise extra charges later. In the long run, you will stay in business longer, and that will be far more profitable.

Monitor Your Operation

In Chapter 9 I talk more about the numbers you should be watching, but for now remember that hope is not a business strategy. You must know where you are financially every day so you can make the right decisions at the right time for the right reasons.

Keep Accurate (and Honest) Books

Ours is still largely a cash business. I know taxes are a pain, but your restaurant is a business, not a personal piggy bank. Aside from the fact that it is illegal and unethical, skimming cash from the till or taking unaccounted-for product home effectively gives your staff a mental justification to do the same things.

An additional complication is that when you want to sell, the value of the business will be reduced because sales will be understated (or costs overstated) with no way to adjust them.

Keep your books in accordance with the *Uniform System of Accounts for Restaurants*, the standard industry accounting format. It will help you make sense of your numbers much faster and allow you to compare your operating ratios to industry figures.

Seek Alignment, Not Agreement

The most powerful force on earth is a shared vision. As the leader, you are the chief dreamer, resident compass and traffic director. It is not realistic – or necessary – that everyone in the organization agrees on how everything is done. You will do it in a way that works best for you. So will I and so will everyone else on the team.

In life, there are many right answers

Each of us will approach a task in slightly different ways. We'll likely never have total agreement on one "best way" to do anything ... but we don't need it. As long as everyone is headed in the same direction, focused on achieving the same end result to the same standards, individual preferences are hardly significant.

In his book, *Corporate Culture*, Allen Kennedy wryly suggests the basic challenge of leadership is to get the whole herd moving roughly west! I often borrow this line in seminars and it always gets a chuckle ... but it is also a real-world metaphor. It speaks to the two biggest roles that leaders have: 1) determining which way is west – which direction the company should move and 2) keeping the herd moving that way.

Within the parameter of "roughly west" you will have people headed straight west at a dead run and you'll have some who seem to be milling around. Some days you'll move faster than others, but if the general movement of the organization is toward the west, that's about as good as it gets in the real world.

Your job as the leader is to determine what direction is "west" for your company (the Purpose), clearly communicate that direction to the staff and direct traffic to help the company move that way. Your role is definitely NOT micro-management or enforcing a set of rules to get everyone to do things exactly the same way you would.

Periodically you'll have a staff member who wanders off to the north. Now north is a good direction. There is nothing wrong with north, it's just not the direction your herd is moving.

When someone in your west-bound herd wanders off toward the north, ride out there and find out what's going on. If they're lost or disoriented, give a little course correction and point them back toward the west. If they're truly northbound, put them in touch with a northbound organization. Everyone will be happier!

The Key to Alignment

Without a shared Purpose, you can't create alignment. This is why it's so important to be clear on the company's Purpose when you bring new staff members aboard ... and why that will give you an advantage over competitors who think that process is "too much work."

The important thing is that everyone understands the leader's vision and embrace it as their own personal quest, at least for the time they are with you. This is the "west" I spoke of earlier and it is what assures the group will continue their progress toward a common outcome, even if the leader is struck down.

You will never have 100% alignment, of course, but you can definitely stack the odds in your favor. Even those who are on board with you initially may wander away as years pass.

There is a time for everyone to head off in their own direction. Your job as an effective leader is not to fight that urge, merely to channel it in a productive manner for as long as you choose to travel together.

Creating a Cohesive Culture

With the clarity that comes from Purpose, you always have an innate sense of where you are headed. You may not always be clear as to how best to get there, but once you know you want to head west, you will always have a sense of where west is.

You become a compass that unerringly keeps the efforts and energy of the company focused in the right direction regardless of outside conditions.

This clarity of direction comes from owning your Purpose, having a clear vision – a dream if you will – of a larger possibility for the company and your community.

Without Purpose it is easy to get lost. Like a small boat in a storm, leaders without a Purpose are tossed about on a chaotic sea of swirling problems and pressures, switching direction depending on prevailing winds, behaving more like a weather vane than a compass.

Absent the steadying effect of Purpose, would-be leaders tend to get confused and freeze up in a crisis. They either try to enforce an arbitrary set of rules to preserve their illusion of control or simply disappear and leave their team floundering in heavy seas.

The inevitable result is that everyone in the organization becomes lost, discouraged, stressed and ultimately unproductive. Some will jump ship rather than continue to work in such chaos.

Be in Alignment with Your Guests

Alignment within your organization is critical, of course ... and it is just as important to be in alignment with the needs of your guests. After all, they are the ones you're out to serve. If you are not doing things that are meaningful to them, they won't support you.

If your patrons are looking for a pleasant experience and you're just focused on how much you can sell them, the relationship will not endure. However, if you are passionate about being known as a Place of Hospitality – about making their day, every day – the relationship will be effortless and mutually beneficial. They will patronize you more often and order more of your products ... because they *want* to.

Alignment is not at odds with profitability, but the money comes because others feel good about supporting you rather than because you were clever at prying money from their clutching fingers.

So while the typical approach to suggestive selling may produce short term results, I seldom see it make guests feel warm, fuzzy and anxious to return. If you get the sale tonight but lose the patron forever as a result, it is the most costly sale you can make.

Do you have a larger Purpose that is in alignment with what your market needs and wants? Can you clearly put it into words? Does your staff know it? Does it drive every decision you make?

Your reputation (and your legacy) will be determined by what you do for others

4

Cook Up
Seamless Service

Cook Up Seamless Service

> *"The best way to find yourself is to lose yourself in the service of others."*
> —Mahatma Gandhi

Service is Efficiently Doing What is Expected

Your staff cannot efficiently do what is expected until you determine (and clearly communicate) what you expect. Then you need a process that enables the consistent delivery of your plan ... and have a way to monitor its progress so you can either reinforce their progress in the right direction or make course corrections as needed.

In working through the logic of how to actually deliver a consistent level of service, I saw a clear parallel with what it takes to consistently prepare exceptional food. See if this analogy works for you:

Anyone in the food business knows there's a clear process to follow to produce consistent, world class products:

1. **Start with a great recipe**
2. **Use high quality ingredients**
3. **Prepare the dish properly**
4. **Observe proper sanitation**
5. **Give it some WOW**

All five elements must be handled properly or you cannot consistently produce outstanding products, right? You can use the same model to cook up seamless service.

1. Have a Great Recipe

You can't effectively teach the steps of service until you have determined what they are ... and just like the recipes in your kitchen, your service recipe is one of the things that can set you apart from your competition.

39

This means creating a blueprint – a Service Sequence – that outlines every direct interaction between your staff and your guests. The Service Sequence specifies who is responsible, what you want them to do, when it should happen, your standard for the action and the result the action should produce. You could also create a sequence for the interactions between the kitchen and the dining room.

Getting your service act organized in this way creates consistency for your guests. Because it is specific, it also provides real structure for your training program and allows you to bring your service staff up to speed in stages, feeding them information at a pace they can absorb.

It is important that every guest feel treated as an individual rather than a number. That's the difference between being well-served vs. efficiently processed. Structuring service is not about producing "do-it-this-way-or-else" rules, but to provide guidelines that make it easier for your team to learn how to deliver a consistent experience to every guest, every time.

> "The beautiful choreography of service is, at best, an art form, a ballet. I appreciate the grace with which a table can be properly cleared. I admire the elegance when a bottle of wine is appropriately opened and poured. There's aesthetic value in doing things the right way.
>
> "But I respond best when the person doing those things realizes that the purpose of all this beauty at the table is to create pleasure for me. To go through the motions in a perfunctory or self-absorbed manner, no matter how expertly rendered, diminishes the beauty.
>
> "It's about soul – and service without soul, no matter how elegant, is quickly forgotten by the guest."
>
> —Danny Meyer in *Setting the Table*

Stages of Table Service

The appropriate stages of service will depend on your concept and the day part (meal period), of course, but here are the various sequences you might expect to find in a full service restaurant. You may want to add others or break some of these into sub-steps to better fit your needs and the organization of your staffing.

First Impression
What should happen when guests first walk in the door?

Managing the Wait
What is the procedure when guests can't be immediately seated?

Seating
What should happen as guests go to the table and get seated?

Engage the Guest
How can the staff make a friend when they first initiate contact?

Beverage Service
What are the standards for drink orders, delivery and refills?

Taking the Order
How should it be done to be a merchandising and educational experience rather than simply order-taking?

Starter Service
How do you want to present appetizers and samples?

Salad Service
What are the specific procedures for presenting the salads?

Wine Service
What should guests expect in ordering, service and follow-up?

Entree Service
What is the sequence of activities when the meal is served? How about follow-up?

Support Service
How do you want peripheral activities like refilling water, clearing tables, and such to be handled?

After-Dinner Service
What happens after the main meal plates are cleared?

Settlement
What are the steps in settling the check?

Memories
What final impressions you want guests to have when they leave?

Other Operating Formats

The sequences that apply in other foodservice settings usually involve fewer steps than these, but they are no less important to organize.

All operators must think about creating a first impression, handling waiting guests, how the guest will get their meal, support service while guests are eating, how they will receive payment (or document meal attendance in the case of a subsidized operation) and what impression they want their patrons to have when they leave.

A quick service operation may have to think through how things are handled at the drive-up window. A cafeteria will want to structure the interaction between guests and those behind the line.

Fill In the Blanks

To give you an idea of how to go about creating your own service blueprints, the following pages contain examples of how you might plan out the first few sequences on the list. These are not the "right" way to do it, merely the way I might set it up in a mid-scale restaurant. Feel free to adapt any or all of it to your own particular requirements.

Here are the steps:

Who and What

First, break each segment of the meal service into baby steps. Who is responsible and what specifically should they do? This is about as far as most restaurant training programs go ... and I think it's the reason that service levels are so sporadic across the industry.

As you probably know by now, just telling people to do something isn't enough to make it happen consistently. If this is all the training you have for them, you will likely find yourself constantly having to nag and follow up, resulting in frustration for all parties.

Spelling out *what* people should do is merely a suggestion ... a possible starting point from which they can improvise their own approach. As we discussed, everyone has their own best way to accomplish almost any task. The only requirement here is that their actions comply with your standards and produce the desired result.

When

Then decide when you want each step to happen. Is there a timing goal or should they take their cue from what is happening at the time? Responsive service is all about having the proper pace to the meal so the whole experience flows smoothly – seamlessly – from beginning to end. Timing is something you can monitor.

Standard

The next step is to specify the standard that applies to each action. What can your guests expect from you every time? Good service is not doing things exactly the same way for every guest. Rather, it is providing a consistent *experience* every time.

What it takes to do that will vary with the mood of the guests and the specific reason they chose to patronize you. What constitutes a good time at a business lunch is quite different from what you want when you are out for a romantic evening.

What's the Result?

Today's workers won't do something just because you say to do it. They want to know *why* you want things done that way ... or even better, the end result you're after.

When you hold people to your standards, specify the results and don't get too hung up on exactly how they have to achieve those results, it leaves your staff free to interpret their jobs in a way that works for them. That not only makes your service experience more personal, but minimizes the need for supervision, simplifies performance appraisal and improves productivity.

If people respect your standards, achieve the desired results and don't break any laws in the process, do you really care exactly how they do it?

Get Your Staff Involved

People don't argue with their own information, so when you get your staff involved in developing and refining the service sequences, they are far more likely to own the final results. That make implementation much faster and easier.

I suggest you develop, train and implement one stage at a time. That will give your crew time to get used to any new procedures – and develop the muscle memory of how to do – it without cluttering up their heads with too many new things to remember.

Also, since all aspects of your service program need to work together seamlessly, the gradual approach will let you make adjustments and improvements as you develop each new stage.

Reverse Engineer Your Systems

The Service Sequence is the end result you commit the company to achieve, so to make that possible, you must set yourself up to win. Work backward from the results and design every aspect of your organization to make it as easy as possible for those results to occur.

It means writing staff schedules, designing operating procedures and creating menus that make it easier for your crew to meet the timing standards. It means establishing policies that support the guest experience you are committed to achieve. It means consciously creating your organization so it will excel.

WHO	WHAT	WHEN	STANDARD	WHAT'S THE RESULT?
Floor Manager/Greeter	Acknowledgment	Within 30 seconds	Smiling eye contact, no distraction	Positive first impression
Floor Manager/Greeter	Warm welcome, use name	Within 60 seconds	Different for each guest	Greeting is always fresh and sincere
Floor Manager/Greeter	Identify reservation		Give benefit of the doubt	Guests never feel in the wrong
Floor Manager/Greeter	Verify size of party		Don't use numbers	Identify a table the guests will enjoy
Floor Manager/Greeter	Determine seating preference		Suggest area w/available seats, balance station loading	Identify a table the guests will enjoy
Floor Manager/Greeter	Advise of wait time, provide an accurate time quote, ask their agreement to wait	When can't seat immediately	Smiling eye contact, no distractions, sell the wait, accurate quote = five min. less than actual wait time	Reduce anxiety, be hospitable, show that you respect their time
Floor Manager/Greeter	Note party, table and quote	When guests agree to wait	Let them see it being done	Reduce anxiety
Floor Manager/Greeter	Offer to call other restaurants	If they can't/won't wait	Be smiling and helpful	Be on their side, make a friend

WHO	WHAT	WHEN	STANDARD	WHAT'S THE RESULT?
Floor Manager/Greeter	Provide an accurate quote	When can't seat immediately	Actual is 5 min. less than quote	Reduce anxiety
Floor Manager/Greeter	Find a seat for waiting guests	When they agree to wait	Be smiling and helpful	Make the guest feel good about wait
Floor Manager/Greeter	Initiate service	When seated	Offer cup of coffee/glass of wine	They feel like guests in your home
Floor Manager/Greeter	Give them a menu, explain specials, answer questions			Give them something to do, make decision faster at the table
Floor Manager/Greeter	Monitor the wait & check back	Halfway through quoted time	Be smiling and helpful	Reduce anxiety
Floor Manager/Greeter	Advise of imminent seating	When their table is being reset	Be smiling and helpful	Allow guests to make mental transition

Implementing Service Sequences

Anytime you introduce something new into the work flow, slow and steady wins the race. Let each crew member work at their own pace and don't turn them loose until they have the tasks mastered.

This may mean you need to adjust the size of their stations in the dining room at first or assign personal trainers to help those who are having trouble picking up the new procedures. Don't move to a new section until the crew member has a full grasp of all that came before.

Seating

WHO	WHAT	WHEN	STANDARD	WHAT'S THE RESULT?
Floor Manager/Greeter	Record seating time	Just before getting guests	Neat, legible, accurate	Compare actual to quote
Floor Manager/Greeter	Advise of table availability	Upon reaching party	"I have a great table for you"	Reduce anxiety, create anticipation
Floor Manager/Greeter	Escort to table		Move at the guests' pace	Personal connection
Floor Manager/Greeter	Market research	On the way to the table	Casual & friendly vs. task-oriented	Data to evaluate marketing
Floor Manager/Greeter	"Is this your first visit?"			New guests need more info
	(Yes) "How did you find out about us?"			Learn source of referral
	(No) How long since you were here last?" (listen) "We've added some interesting features since your last visit." (explain)			Date for marketing, give returning guests something new to talk about
Floor Manager/Greeter	Assist with seating	Upon reaching table	Pull out chairs for ladies	Common courtesy
Floor Manager/Greeter	Present menu	After all guests are seated	Open and hand to guest	Common courtesy
Floor Manager/Greeter	Inform of specials		Enthusiastic, smiling, sincere	Guests have something to talk about
Floor Manager/Greeter	Recommend a dessert		Enthusiastic, smiling, sincere	Pre-dispose them to order dessert
Floor Manager/Greeter	Make transition to next step		Inform of what to expect next	Keep level of certainty high
Floor Manager/Greeter	Record market research info	Upon returning to host stand	Neat, legible, accurate	Identify sources of biz, repeat %, etc.

It's not just that practice makes perfect (it does!), but only *perfect practice* develops the flawless muscle memory that will correctly create a new habit.

Needless to say, never start training a new procedure during a time of peak demand. Pick a slow day, role-play through the steps and work out timing. Start slow and gradually ramp up to full speed.

Observe them in action under real-world conditions. Open a dialogue on what went well and discuss which areas they should concentrate on. If the coach remains firm, positive and patient, everyone will gain more confidence moving forward.

2. Use High Quality Ingredients

You wouldn't serve a sandwich on moldy bread, would you? Would you be famous for your chili if you made it with spoiled beef? Of course not. These questions sound silly because it's obvious even the greatest chef can't produce quality food from substandard ingredients.

In a similar vein, who would deny that foodservice is a people business? Think of your team as the raw ingredients in your service recipe. The quality of your staff determines your level of guest service and produces your sales volume. It also determines all your principal operating costs. Yet many operators still try to produce a quality dining experience with substandard staff.

It will not work with people any more than it will work with chili. Operators don't intentionally assemble a team of slackers, of course, but few would deny they could (or at least want to) do a better job when it comes to staff selection.

Find the Right People

It's time for a good rant. I, for one, am getting sick of hearing operators whine about the labor situation. "There are no good people out there," they whimper. "I'm forced to hire to a lower standard just to fill my shifts ... if I can even do that." So it's a little harder to find good people. So what? Is the labor market running your business?

Don't get me wrong. I understand that it's difficult to find the sort of people you need to give your guests the consistently excellent products and service you want them to have ... but so what? This just means your old methods of staffing don't work anymore. Instead of griping, change the way you staff the joint!

Can you imagine a professional coach, losing game after game, sitting quietly in the locker room hoping the talented player he needs will accidently drop by looking for a job? That's absurd! If you want talent, you have to go out there, find it and recruit it. The super stars are already employed!

You know the sort of folks you need. Are you actively seeking them out? Can you recognize them when they walk in the door? Can you identify those who will do an exemplary job from the ones who just "give good interview?"

Good people are everywhere ... but the odds are they're not out wandering the streets looking for work. They may not be excited about what they're doing at the moment, but they're not likely to show up on their own.

One of the best (and cheapest) recruiting tools I know of is simply your business card. As you go about your life and run into someone who impresses you with their service attitude, hand them your card with a comment like this: "I'm really impressed with the way you handle yourself. If you know of someone *like yourself* who might be looking for a fresh opportunity, ask them to call me."

Half the time, the person who received the card will drop by. But even if they're happy where they are, good people tend to hang out with good people and slackers tend to hang out with slackers. People who impress you are likely to have friends who share their values.

So even if the person you meet isn't looking to move on, they may know of a friend who is ready for a move. This indirect approach also keeps you from actually soliciting someone in their place of work. Most operators really resent such poaching.

Remember you're looking for the attitude – you can train the job skills. That's why it's always best when you can observe attitude in action.

I know a multi-unit operator whose VP of Operations is a woman he found working for a dry cleaner! He was so impressed with her service ethic he made her an offer she couldn't refuse. She took him up on it, learned the business and is now running his company.

Where else can you look for potential super stars? Here are some suggestions:

POTENTIAL RECRUITING SOURCES

1. Present staff (internal promotion)
2. Online job boards (Craigslist, Monster, etc.)
3. Newspaper classified ads
4. Restaurant guests
5. Telemarketing
6. Culinary schools
7. Computer bulletin boards
8. College bars
9. Radio ads
10. Youth groups (Boy Scouts, Girl Scouts)
11. Workshops and seminars
12. Exchange with competitors
13. Work release programs
14. Police and firefighters (moonlighters)
15. Military bulletin boards
16. Disabled organizations
17. Fraternities, sororities
18. Referrals from present staff
19. Personnel agencies
20. Direct mail

(continued overleaf)

Build a Better Mousetrap

Compared to what we do for a living, most other businesses are deadly boring. With a population as into "experiences" as ours, don't you think you could find a few folks in your area who would trade boredom and a dead-end job for a little excitement and a chance to have more say in their lives? They aren't going to knock on your door without an invitation.

What was that? Give them more say in their lives? That, too. You won't attract super stars to an oppressive environment (or at least you won't be able to keep them there once they figure it out!)

Even super stars need direction and coaching, but once you're sure they understand the game, you must give them the opportunity to excel on their own terms.

Relax a little more. Train a LOT more. Be willing to achieve results you want in ways other than the ones you would have chosen. If you give people the latitude to be great and believe in their innate ability to shine, you'll rarely be disappointed. The good people demand this freedom ... and they deserve it.

Do the Right Thing

To attract and retain great people, sometimes you have to pay more. The law of supply and demand requires it. "But I can't afford to pay more," the whiners chorus. Am I the only one to hear strains of "the sky is falling" in this?

48

The sky is not falling, it's just that you might have to pay more for top skills ... but you have never been able to attract the talent you need by paying minimum wage anyway! So what? Are wage rates running your business?

Then they whine, "But if I pay more I'll have to charge more and I'll lose all my customers." Well, if you don't take care of your guests, you will lose them anyway.

In my experience, we are more reluctant to raise prices than our guests are to accept increases. Besides, they have been expecting you to bump prices for months now! And if your prices increase a bit, so what? Are menu prices running your business?

If you are in a market that will not recognize, appreciate (and pay for) a higher quality experience, you're in trouble anyway, no matter what the economic conditions. Do what you have to do to deliver to your own standards and charge what you have to charge for it.

[Hint: make sure you educate guests about what you are offering and what makes it better/different so they understand its worth. If you can't create points of difference, you must compete strictly on price.]

Do the Work

If you want the results that others are not going to get, you have to do the work that others are not willing to do

The basic game hasn't changed, only a few of its ground rules. Your choice is to acknowledge reality and change with the times or become a statistic to your own stubbornness. The universe rewards action.

The fact that you never had to do any of these things before is no excuse to sit there complaining while your restaurant slowly collapses around you because your guests stopped putting up with substandard products and services.

If you want to be successful in this business, you have to earn it. Who cares if it's tough? Of course it's tough. So what? The ability to prosper in spite of outside conditions is why you get to call yourself a professional. So stop complaining and start doing what you know you need to do ... or is your ego running your business?

Effective staff selection is critical to your success. "My guests are the most important assets I have," says WC Wells, longtime restaurateur in the Pacific Northwest. "I won't risk their patronage by placing them in the hands of just anyone. Hiring warm bodies is an injustice to me and my staff and a disservice to my guests."

He's proud that it's difficult to qualify as a member of his staff. "The real value is to our guests – the one who really receive the benefit of our commitment to select only people who demonstrate a service attitude. With most of our staff oriented toward delighting our guests, we create stability and consistently high standards. We think this helps good workers become excellent workers."

Shannon Foust, former CEO of Damon's, put it rather nicely when he said, "It's always easier to find gold if you're looking for it."

Making It Easier

Staff selection is arguably the most important aspect of guest service, but in the real world of foodservice operations, it seems there is never enough time to do it right.

Did you ever think this probably happens because managers spend too much time cleaning up the messes made by the last marginal workers they hired ... the ones who are only there because there wasn't enough time to spend in staff selection?

You know warm bodies make for lukewarm business, but how can you break the cycle? If you were a human resources expert, that would be one thing, but who has the time to study personnel theory when there are meals to get out and deadlines to meet? Just staying on top of labor laws and regulations can be a career!

There are many excellent books on interviewing and hiring, but no matter how well-crafted, I always had two problems with books of that ilk: they weren't specific to the needs of the foodservice industry and they all required the information be further interpreted and adapted before I could use it.

So as an operator, I always hoped for a more effective way to select quality staff. Finding a better (and easier) way to pick the right people the first time became a personal project. Since nobody was offering what I wanted, I had to create it myself.

I took the best ideas from the most practical sources I could find and combined them with the experience and trade secrets I'd learned during my foodservice career. Then I distilled it all into what is now known as the Sure-Fire Staff Selection System, a structured format that made practical sense within the operating realities of most foodservice operations. Here is how the process begins:

Start With Screening

Your guests pay for the value of the experience they receive, not just for the food. The better your staff, the more value they will add to the guest's experience. Hiring good staff is not a matter of luck when you have a way to identify terrific people before you hire them.

Imagine the possibilities if you could separate people who will actually add value from the ones who just need the money. The Screening Interview is one of the first steps in the staff selection process and can greatly improve the odds of selecting more service-oriented candidates. Here is what it will do for you:

It Identifies Characteristics Essential to Success in Foodservice

Observation of successful foodservice workers identified common traits that seem to lead to improved performance. The Screening Interview addresses those traits and suggests the extent to which the candidate may possess them.

It Saves Interview Time

It can help you quickly reduce a large influx of applicants to just those who are most likely to be successful. This is not an interview, merely a fast way to separate those who are likely to be successful from those who less apt to work out.

It Provides Documentation and Objectivity

The Screening Interview sheet is a written record of the applicant's pre-hire performance. The interview measures job-related factors and is equally (and consistently) administered to all candidates.

It provides a basis for staff selection decisions that is difficult for disgruntled candidates to successfully challenge because it gives you a way to prove you did, in fact, treat every applicant the same and made your decision of whom to interview based on validated job-related criteria rather than personal prejudice.

Success Characteristics

The Screening Interview measures four characteristics that describe every successful, productive foodservice staff member: extroverted, proud, responsible and energetic. Screening for these attributes will help you identify candidates who will make every effort to satisfy your guests and are appropriately sales- and results-oriented.

Extroversion

Extroverts are people-oriented individuals. Their behavior shows a sincere desire to be liked by others. This is particularly important for guest contact staff because these people need to be very outgoing and interact positively with people. Extroverts are generally very positive people with good social skills.

Pride

People with a high degree of pride view their work and other areas of their life as very important. They need to be a part of successful activities. They're particular about doing their job not only correctly, but in the best possible way. Proud people will make an emotional investment in your operation. They want you to be successful and be viewed as the best restaurant in your community.

Responsibility

A responsible individual follows through on commitments within a defined period. Responsible people feel accountable for producing a quality effort while they're on the clock. They're likely to provide a memorable dining experience and value-added service to every guest and in every job-related task they do.

Energy

Foodservice requires people with high energy levels and the ability to move quickly and appropriately under pressure. People with high energy levels often have varied interests and are involved in several outside activities. With proper direction and guidance, highly active people are likely to accomplish much more in shorter time frames and be more accurate in their work than inactive people.

All these qualities are important success factors for any foodservice position. You may choose to give different weight to certain factors for various positions. For example, an outgoing nature may be less critical in production positions where there is little guest contact (but what could it hurt?) Even allowing for minor differences, the Screening Interview has proven to be extremely effective and universally applicable across the full spectrum of foodservice positions.

Screening Interview

NAME:	POSITION:	

EXTROVERSION	**"YES" RESPONSE**	**"NO" RESPONSE**
Y N ? ☐ ☐ ☐ As a member of the staff, how would you help develop repeat business?	Specific answer that shows personal action or interaction; e.g. learn and use their names, make suggestions, make sure everything always looks great	Be friendly, give good service
☐ ☐ ☐ If I asked your best friend to describe you, what would he/she say?	People-oriented answers; e.g. outgoing, lots of fun, friendly, positive	Nice person, good worker
☐ ☐ ☐ If you saw someone you thought you recognized but weren't quite sure, what would you do?	Go up and ask, make an effort to talk to them	Just keep walking, wait until I was sure

PRIDE		
☐ ☐ ☐ What qualities do you need to be a great (position) in a restaurant?	Like people, work hard, do more than expected, smiling, flexible, patient, lots of stamina, good work habits, attention to detail, good communicator,	Be nice
☐ ☐ ☐ Is it difficult for you to carry on "small talk" with people?	No, not at all	Sometimes, depends on the situation
☐ ☐ ☐ What recent accomplishments do you take great pride in?	Specific advancement toward a goal; e.g. completed courses, finished a difficult project, job advancement, family success	Don't have any specific goals
☐ ☐ ☐ What are some reasons for your successes?	My personality, optimism, positive self-image, want to succeed	Just lucky, I don't know

RESPONSIBILITY		
☐ ☐ ☐ What would your previous employers say about your work?	Hard worker, dependable, valuable, ideal employee, would rehire	Did a good job
☐ ☐ ☐ What would you do to make a negative situation positive?	Find out what the problem is and fix it	Get a manager, stay calm
☐ ☐ ☐ What kinds of people irritate you?	Lazy, negative, complainers	I like everyone, I don't pay attention to them
☐ ☐ ☐ How do you decide what to do with your time off?	Make lists, organize, get right at things	Don't do it very well, go with the flow

ENERGY		
☐ ☐ ☐ What activities have you been involved in during the past two years?	Participative activities; e.g. aerobics, sports, volunteer work, charities	Not many, I just work
☐ ☐ ☐ What motivates you to get your job done?	Money, recognition, pride in my work	Making people happy, giving good service
☐ ☐ ☐ How do you feel about doing more than one activity at a time?	Like it, it's a challenge	Want to do one thing at a time, it doesn't bother me

Interviewed by:	Date:

I realize this form is difficult to read (and impossible to use) when it is this small. To make it easier, you can download a full-sized version at www.RestaurantDoctor.com/screening.pdf.

Let me relate a personal example to illustrate my first experience of using this resource to assemble a staff:

MY STAFF SELECTION BREAKTHROUGH

I was the Foodservice Director for the U.S. Olympic Training Center in Colorado Springs in 1986 when the World Cycling Championships, one of the world's largest annual sporting events, came to town.

It was the first time this event had ever been held in the United States so there were no precedents and no idea what to expect. The event organizers asked me to handle the concessions, catering and hospitality tents for the two weeks of competition. We would have a full house at the Training Center during the event, so I couldn't use any of my regular foodservice staff on the project.

My challenge was to create an organization of about 150 people from scratch, run it at full speed for two weeks, then disappear it! There would be just one opportunity to get the right people and there was no time to find replacements if someone didn't work out.

The town was excited and I expected about 250 people to respond to an ad for jobs but had no idea how to go about selecting the people it would take. As fortune would have it, I attended a conference two weeks before the event (yikes!) and found my answer.

A major restaurant group had noticed some of their staff members did a much higher sales than others. Because they hired everyone the same way, they expected more equal performance. In trying to uncover the reason, they learned the exceptional performers tended to answer questions differently from the more mediocre employees, even though everyone gave basically correct replies to the questions.

They researched this discovery and developed a list of 14 simple questions along with the desired type of answers. The score was all-or-nothing – an applicant received a point only when their response matched the "positive" answer expected from outstanding workers. They generously shared it with me. Understand at the time, I really didn't care if the system was accurate or not! I just wanted a way, any way, to make staff selections without spending days trying to do 250 interviews!

As expected, we had a huge response to our newspaper ad and held one employment seminar for the entire group. When I had presented all the relevant information, we had everyone fill out an application and talk with an interviewer who simply asked the 14 questions on the Screening Interview and noted the responses. I had six people asking the questions, three of whom I'd never met before that day! We screened 268 people in just over an hour – that's about as "quick and dirty" as you can get!

The Screening Interview was the full extent of our selection process for all positions. There were no traditional interviews because there was just no time for them. After totaling the individual scores, we started filling shifts. We started with those who scored highest and worked our way down the list until we completed our schedule. The last people assigned were still in the top third of the point scale. Once the staff was in place, we promptly forgot the scores and went to work!

The first week of racing started fast and got busier but my rookie crew handled it beautifully. Just two people failed to report for work. Everyone else did a tremendous job. They performed their tasks well, stayed flexible and kept a sense of humor in the middle of what was frequently an improvised situation. I couldn't have been more pleased! At the end of that first week, we had a few days off before the final races.

Since we didn't need as many staff for the rest of the events, we decided to give the extra hours to our best workers. My supervisors (friends from around the country I had coaxed into helping out) selected their "star performers" based on their demonstrated work performance and positive attitude. When I pulled their applications, I was shocked!

ALL our exceptional workers had scored 12, 13 or 14 on the Screening Interview scale!

54

Administering the
Screening Interview

Give the Screening Interview to ALL candidates who submit a complete application, no matter what position they seek or what your first impressions of them may be. That will keep any personal bias from figuring into the process and coming back to bite you later.

You or a member of your staff can ask the questions. The applicant should not see the Screening Interview sheet. The process is most effective when you ask the questions in a conversational tone without lengthy chitchat.

Greet the applicant, establish rapport and tell them that you have a few quick questions to help you get a better idea of how they view the foodservice industry. It will be less intimidating if you ask the questions in your own words. I also recommend you have the Screening Interview sheet on a clipboard rather than flat on the desk so the applicants cannot see it and become distracted.

As they respond to each question, casually tick off your opinion of how their answer meets the scoring criteria:

Yes (Y) = you clearly got the sort of answer you were looking for
No (N) = you clearly did *not* get what you were looking for
Maybe (?) = you're not sure

This allows the interviewer to concentrate on the applicant and not be distracted by making notes as the person speaks. You are only noting how the applicant's responses compare with the desired answers. Remember this is not an interrogation, merely a fast, friendly way to identify those candidates worthy of more detailed attention. The idea is to keep it quick and focused.

Do NOT review the questions with the candidate after the interview. Once the questions have been asked and answered, thank the candidate for their candor and tell them what to expect next.

The next step depends on how much of the Sure-Fire System you are using, but that program is only available to my Gold Group members (Page 269) and has more detail than I can address here. For a free outline of the essential elements *your* staff selection system should contain, go to www.RestaurantDoctor.com/gamble.html.

Scoring the Screening Interview

In initially working with the Screening Interview, I found I often got answers that didn't fit in the all-or-nothing criteria. For example, one of the questions asks how the applicant decides what to do with their time off. One woman replied, "I'm raising three kids by myself!" That wasn't one of the choices but certainly a valid response. So I changed the response scale to Yes, No and Maybe.

A Yes scores two points, Maybe is worth one point and no points are awarded for a No answer. The highest possible score on the Screening Interview is 28 points (14 questions at two points apiece). Scores of 22 or higher on the screening interview suggest prime (Yes) candidates, while scores of 16-21 suggest marginal (Maybe) applicants.

While different interviewers could give different scores to a particular answer, personal interpretation is unlikely to yield a score that will materially misrepresent a candidate's potential. In my experience, personal differences are not enough to make someone who is a good candidate for you score out as a marginal candidate for me.

All other things truly being equal (which they seldom are), candidates with the highest scores on the Screening Interview are more likely to be successful on the job. It is important to keep in mind that the actual test score is less important than what the answers reveal about an applicant's attitude and how they stack up against other applicants.

I don't recommend using this screening as your sole hiring criteria. Still, if you ever face a deadline and need to quickly fill a vacancy, the Screening Interview can stack the odds in your favor. If you did nothing else but interview only those who score in the top third, you'd be selecting from a more highly-qualified group of applicants.

Validating the Screening Interview

Can you look at your current crew and identify some who are clearly better performers than others? My guess is you probably can. I suggest that as a means of familiarizing yourself with the Screening Interview before actually using it with candidates, interview your current staff members. This will not only help you get familiar with the process but will give you some valuable support data as well.

I suspect your better performers will score higher than your not-so-good staff members. If so, you've just made yourself challenge-proof: you have a documented relationship between actual performance on the job and how someone scores on the Screening Interview.

You may even have one or two on your current staff who are just good enough not to get fired. If, when you conduct the Screening Interview with your present staff, the marginal workers score, say, 12 out of 28, you might make twelve your cutoff score.

3. Prepare the Dish Right

Left unattended, high quality ingredients will only produce high quality compost. How you deal with your raw ingredients (in this case, your people) will have a big impact on the final product.

Get a Good Start

It is perhaps the eternal cliché that you don't get a second chance for a first impression. That is precisely the role orientation plays in developing a top notch staff. Just as your professional success depends on meeting (and exceeding) your guests' expectations, success with your staff is built on their expectations as well.

Orientation is your chance to make a totally professional impression on your new staff members, share your values and vision and help them bond with the company and each other. Miss this opportunity at the beginning of your working relationship and you can never effectively regain it.

Orientation

The two essential elements of a good start on the job are a strong orientation and an effective adjustment period. Since orientation is the first step on the job, let's start there.

Why
The foodservice business can be hectic and it is often difficult to find time for all the little things. You also know that if you don't take care of the details you won't be in business long. Turnover carries a real price in terms of lost productivity, customer complaints and time ... not to mention dollars.

While it is certainly possible to do a better job of selecting higher-quality candidates the first time around, at best you get only a promissory note that the person chosen will be a future star. In the final analysis, effective workers are actually created – by you.

Remember how scary it feels to be a stranger in a strange place? That's how it feels to most workers the first day on the job. But the fear comes simply because there's a lot the new staffer doesn't know about the company. When you understand how insecurity can affect a person's thinking and behavior, you'll grasp the importance of a strong bridge over this initial period of uncertainty.

When

Orientation should be completed before a new worker ever steps onto the floor to start work or training. If you rush someone onto the job and promise you will handle their orientation later (when you have a chance), several things may happen:

First, you will never get around to the orientation because your life is already a series of crises and there are certain to be more.

Second, the new worker will be tossed to the sharks without the support needed to be successful. This increases the likelihood they will make mistakes, develop bad habits or feel like a failure, any of which can lower job satisfaction and trigger the worker's decision not to stay with your company.

To be fair, a third possibility is you may eventually get the orientation done, but you know the odds of that happening are slim.

Who

Because the first step is so important, orientation should be conducted by the most senior person possible. Many extremely successful operators take orientation so seriously they always have the program conducted by one of the company's owners.

Why? Because in their experience, when someone of lesser authority chairs the session, new workers don't get the same perspective of the culture and vision that are key to the company's success ... nor do they feel quite as important.

Larger organizations may already have a training manager who specializes in conducting new staff orientation. Like anything else, orientation skills are sharpened by repeated practice.

I suggest you will see more benefit from fewer experienced people conducting orientations more often than by just tossing the task to whoever is free at the moment or resorting to the "Follow Karen around and she'll fill you in" approach.

Where

Conduct orientation in a quiet. private area. The goal is to have an environment where the trainer and the new staff members can get to understand each other and where new workers can focus on the content and spirit of the orientation and comfortably ask questions.

This means the person conducting the orientation should not be pulled away in the middle of the program to take care of routine tasks like phone calls or other operational demands.

If you don't have a spot on premises that meets the criteria for a successful orientation, hold the session away from the property. Even if you must do it over coffee in a competitor's operation or pay for a meeting room, the inconvenience or expense is worth it. Orientation is an investment that will help you get maximum value from your most precious assets, your staff.

What

The following checklist was adapted from material developed by the National Restaurant Association and covers the essential elements in an effective staff orientation program. Topics can be addressed in your staff manual, presented in person or passed along by your staff ... but it is all important and should all be covered.

Use this list as a guide to be sure every important item is covered during the orientation so that each new member of your staff gets the right start. It will help you organize everything you and the new workers should talk about during their first few days.

Items marked with an asterisk (*) suggest there could be a state or federal law governing your policy in this area. If you are unsure, check with your legal advisor, the state restaurant association or call the National Restaurant Association for clarification.

Purpose of Orientation
❏ To introduce you to our establishment
❏ To get help you fit in and work well here
❏ To explain our policies and goals
❏ To answer all your questions
❏ To explain how you will be trained and what happens next

What We're All About
❏ History of the company
    ❏ How we came to be – when, where and why
    ❏ Our Purpose
    ❏ Who owns the company
    ❏ If a franchise or branch, a short history of the parent company
    ❏ What's special about us – stories, awards received, famous guests

Expectations
- ❏ What we expect from you
  - ❏ a day's work for a day's pay
  - ❏ your commitment to good service and fine food quality
  - ❏ concern for your co-workers and cooperation with our team
- ❏ What you can expect from us
  - ❏ proper training, so you know how to do your job
  - ❏ good working conditions
  - ❏ reasonable compensation for your efforts
  - ❏ recognition and reward for a job well done
  - ❏ respect and constant communication from management

Organizational Structure
- ❏ Chart of departments and supervisory levels
- ❏ Where you fit in the organization
- ❏ Who you report to
- ❏ Who reports to you

Payroll Policies
- ❏ How often you are paid (length of pay periods)
- ❏ When you can expect your first paycheck
- ❏ How you will get your check
- ❏ Who to see if you have questions about it
- ❏ Information needed for withholding: SSN, address, marital status, etc.
- ❏ *What deductions will be made
- ❏ *Eligibility for overtime and how it is calculated
- ❏ *Tip reporting requirements and procedures
- ❏ *Tip credit to be taken
- ❏ Policy on lost paychecks
- ❏ Policy on early issuance of paychecks
- ❏ Policy on advances or loans against pay
- ❏ Deductions made on tips (state and federal withholding, SS, etc.)

Work Schedules
- ❏ Hours of operation
- ❏ When and how your schedule is determined
- ❏ What your initial schedule will be
- ❏ How – and if – changes in the schedule can be made
- ❏ Who to see about changes
- ❏ *Timekeeping procedures (time clock, time cards, etc.)
- ❏ Policy on absenteeism
- ❏ Policy on reporting late
- ❏ How and when to report in if you are ill or expect to be late

Breaks and Meals
- ❏ *Scheduled break times
- ❏ *How many? how long?
- ❏ *How to record breaks
- ❏ *Paid or unpaid time?
- ❏ *How breaks are scheduled
- ❏ *Time allowed for meals

- ❏ *Can you leave the premises
- ❏ *Interrupting breaks or meals because of customer need
- ❏ *Where to take breaks/meals
- ❏ *How much meals are (% of cost? free?)
- ❏ *How to record them (on guest check? check on time card?)
- ❏ What may or may not be eaten
- ❏ Policy on coffee, soft drinks, etc.

Uniforms/Dress Code
- ❏ Grooming standards
- ❏ Hair clean, appropriate hairdo, proper covering
- ❏ *Length of hair
- ❏ *Facial hair rules
- ❏ Basic cleanliness, especially hand-washing
- ❏ Description of the uniform or dress required for your job
- ❏ Where to get the uniform
- ❏ *Who pays for it and how
- ❏ *If a deposit is required
- ❏ *How the uniform is to be maintained
- ❏ When you're expected to have your uniform
- ❏ What happens if you don't have it?
- ❏ What happens to the uniform when you leave (buy back?)
- ❏ Policy on types of shoes, sandals, etc.
- ❏ Policy on socks and hose
- ❏ Policy on make-up and jewelry
- ❏ Policy on tattoos and piercings

For Tipped Employees
- ❏ *Form or procedure for recording tips
- ❏ *How often tips will be reported
- ❏ How credit card charges are handled
- ❏ When tip reports must be turned in to assure paycheck

Salary and Performance Review
- ❏ If there is an adjustment period, how long it is and what is expected
- ❏ How often you will be reviewed
- ❏ When you will be reviewed
- ❏ Who will review you
- ❏ What the criteria for review are
- ❏ How you will be notified of raises
- ❏ When raises will become effective

Miscellaneous Whats and Wheres
- ❏ Layout of the establishment – where things are (walk-through)
- ❏ Where to enter and leave the building
- ❏ Where to park, where not to park
- ❏ Where to put your personal belongings (mgt's responsibility for them?)
- ❏ Location of restrooms for staff use

Grounds for Dismissal
- ❏ Number of warnings before termination
- ❏ Time allowed for corrections

- Conduct that can result in termination
  - continued violation of policies
  - insubordination
  - failure to maintain your schedule (tardiness and/or absenteeism)
  - lack of cooperation with co-workers
  - sexual harassment and bullying
  - improper respect for our guests
- "Hanging offenses" (immediate dismissal)
  - drunkenness
  - drug use
  - abusiveness toward guest or co-worker
  - theft

Quitting/Termination
- How to give notice if you are quitting
- How much notice is expected
- *When and how you will receive your final check
- If terminated, is there severance pay? under what conditions?

Policies (if any) About
- Conduct on the premises before and after work hours
- Moonlighting
- Hiring of relatives of employees
- Profanity
- Personal phone calls, texting and/or visitors

Promotions
- If management promotes from within, how you can apply
- What criteria other than job performance will be considered in promotion?
- If passed over, how you will be notified of why and what to do to improve?

Breakage and Errors
- *Responsibility for breakage, walk-outs or errors on guest checks
  - *conditions for determining whether you will be charged
  - *how much will be charged?
  - *how will staff pay (payroll deduction? cash transaction?)

Sanitation
- Importance of good sanitation
- How you will learn our standards
- Importance of frequent hand-washing
- *Policy on smoking

Emergency Procedures
- How and when to report accidents on the job
- What to do in case of fire
- What to do in case of power failure
- What to do in case of bad weather (storm, tornado, blizzard, hurricane, etc.)
- Where the first aid kit is and who has access to it
- Injured guest (911, Heimlich Maneuver, etc.)

Holidays
- Which holidays we are open and which ones we are closed

- ❏ How the work schedules are determined for those days
- ❏ If any special pay or consideration is given for working those days

Loss Prevention
- ❏ How you can help (portion control, waste, inventory control, etc.)
- ❏ Policy on theft
- ❏ Policy on surety bonding
- ❏ *Policy on polygraph tests

Vacations
- ❏ Who is eligible for vacation pay (FT? PT?)
- ❏ How long you must work here to be eligible
- ❏ Whether you must take vacation
- ❏ Can you get paid for unused vacation time? accumulate it? lose it?
- ❏ How much vacation pay you will get
- ❏ *How vacation pay is calculated for tipped workers
- ❏ How much in advance vacations must be scheduled
- ❏ Who gets first priority for dates or times of the year
- ❏ Who to see about scheduling vacation time

Sick Leave
- ❏ Who is eligible for sick leave
- ❏ How long you must work here to be eligible
- ❏ Whether you can accumulate it, or get extra pay for unused days
- ❏ How much sick leave, per month, per year, etc.
- ❏ Whether a doctor's statement is required after a prolonged illness

Insurance
- ❏ What kind of insurance is offered?
- ❏ When and how to become eligible
- ❏ Whether your family will be covered as well
- ❏ How much you and the company each pay
- ❏ How your share will be taken (payroll deduction? each month?)
- ❏ When and how you will receive more details about the program(s)

Other Benefits
- ❏ Other benefits we offer
  - ❏ pension or profit-sharing plan?
  - ❏ bonus system?
  - ❏ discounts for staff members' families or parties?
  - ❏ holiday bonus and/or party?
  - ❏ educational assistance?
  - ❏ credit union?
- ❏ What it takes to become eligible
- ❏ How each works and how much participants receive
- ❏ Who to see to get more information

What happens now?
- ❏ Description of the job
- ❏ How you will be trained
- ❏ Who will do the training
- ❏ How long it will take

This checklist is part of a total communication commitment to each new staff member. There are undoubtedly items you will want to add to the list (menu, operating policies and procedures, house rules and so forth) and there will be others on the list that won't apply to your situation. The important point is to give every new hire all the information they need to feel comfortable and succeed in their jobs. Fail to do that and your turnover rate will climb.

Orientation will be most effective when it is followed up by planned staff training and ongoing coaching consistent with the policies and procedures outlined in the orientation.

One of the most effective ways to break down barriers between operating areas is for new hires work in all other areas of the operation before they assume their regular duties. Angus Barn in Raleigh, NC has new hires work every position in the restaurant for a month before they're allowed to deal directly with a guest.

As you might imagine, being paid a training wage for a month can create issues for servers and other in positions where the primary income is tips. Owner Van Eure says, "Our on-the-job orientation period serves as an effective way to screen out those without a real desire to be part of the team. Besides, they more than make up for the reduced pay when they finally get on the floor."

The major benefit of a program like this is that it breaks down the "them and us" mentality between the front of the house (guest contact positions) and the back of the house (production positions). People are naturally more tolerant and understanding when they've walked in each other's shoes for a few days.

Probation

Everybody needs a little time to get comfortable with a new job and their new co-workers. Most typically, this takes the form of a 90-day probationary period. The idea is good, but I've always found the structure of it to be problematic. See if these points strike a chord:

It Doesn't Accomplish Much
Without a clear requirement for what must be accomplished during the period (other than not making mistakes too often), the average probation becomes little more than a limbo-like waiting period. Most likely, the reason new workers make mistakes is because they haven't been adequately trained ... and whose fault is that?

Decisions Are Often Made
Without Proper Consideration

Ninety days has a way of flying past. When the probation period is "suddenly" over, management is faced with a go/no-go decision with little real criteria for the choice other than whether or not they personally like the worker in question.

It Is Unfair

A straight 90-day probation for all workers means you don't have as much time to look at part-timers as you do to look at full-timers. Since the reality of probation periods is that they are primarily a chance to see whether the new worker has proficiency in the work to be done and has a good work ethic, the structure actually works against full-timers because they have more opportunity to slip up where part-timers can often slip through the cracks.

Probation Is a Law Enforcement Term

To make the leap from being a cop to being a coach, you must eliminate any terms that have an unwanted connotation. Probation doesn't exactly sound supportive and tends to reinforce the idea of a period of time when management is watching for you to screw up!

Confirmation Period

I wanted to come up with a better answer than the standard 90-day probation period. Consistent with the idea of never wasting time solving a problem you can eliminate, my answer to the problems described above was what I called a Confirmation Period.

I arrived at the term because rather than a time to catch mistakes, I wanted a period of time during which both the company and the new staff member could confirm they had made a good decision, there was a good fit and continued success on the job was likely.

On the next page I include the policy on the Confirmation Period from my Human Resources Manual. Feel free to adapt it in any way that serves your needs. Most of it is self-explanatory, but there are a few twists worth some clarification:

Fixed Duration

The Confirmation Period lasts a minimum of 160 hours but no longer than 320 hours, so a full-time worker could get on the regular staff in as little as four weeks.

If all requirements of the confirmation period have not been met after 320 hours on the job, the worker must be dismissed. This provision helps ensure that only those who apply themselves seriously to the company's standards will become part of the regular staff.

CONFIRMATION PERIOD POLICY

A newly hired staff member will have a period of adjustment to their job, the restaurant and the company's policies and procedures. This confirmation period will extend for at least 160 hours worked but not more than 320 hours worked. During the confirmation period they will be known as contingent staff. There will be continuing communication between the new hire and the coaching staff about training activities and performance expectations throughout the confirmation period.

CONTINGENT WAGE
Contingent staff will receive the contingency wage for their position. Upon acceptance as regular staff, their wage will change to the minimum of the salary range for their position although the Head Coach can authorize a higher starting rate when the individual has shown exceptional performance during the confirmation period. A starting wage above the first percentile of the salary range must be approved by the Managing Director.

CHANGE OF STATUS
Anytime after 160 hours worked, the company may accept a contingent staff member on the regular staff, provided the individual has accomplished the following:
1. Successfully passed tests on sanitation practices, safety procedures, dish machine operation and general cleaning (including restrooms)
2. Received the recommendation of their coaches
3. Received a vote of confidence from their co-workers
4. Received a satisfactory performance appraisal
5. Has no unexcused absences or disciplinary actions in the preceding 160 hours

DISMISSAL
The company may, at will, dismiss contingent staff at any time during the confirmation period without prior notice. If any of the above conditions have not been met after 320 hours worked (or cannot be met within 320 hours worked), the individual must be immediately discharged.

Equal Treatment

The confirmation period is based on solely on hours worked, so the company has the same amount of time to look at full-timers and part-timers. It also means that both full-time and part-time staff have the same amount of time to decide if they want to make a commitment to your organization.

Contingency Wage

The contingency wage is essentially a training wage. Since most workers expect a raise when the are accepted onto the regular staff, I built it into the system.

Upon successfully completing the confirmation period, the new worker will receive a raise to bring them up to at least the starting wage for their position (or perhaps a higher rate if their performance during training was exceptional).

Demonstrated Knowledge

To successfully complete the confirmation period, the new worker must show proficiency in the areas of safety, sanitation, dish machine operation and cleaning. The idea is to de-mystify these tasks, underscore their importance to the success of the restaurant and give everyone on the team – managers and hourly workers alike – a basic proficiency.

Endorsements

Successful completion of the confirmation period requires that both the coaches (managers) and co-workers agree they support bringing the new worker into the company.

I would avoid relying on anyone's "gut feeling" on this – even yours – because it is non-duplicable. Before I'd sign off on a new staffer, I want them to have demonstrated knowledge of the menu as well as the policies and procedures of the restaurant.

I want them to demonstrate they know how to clean the restroom and operate the dish machine. I also want a thumbs-up on their attendance, appearance, attitude, professional curiosity and demonstrated commitment to the overall success of the restaurant.

OK, perhaps the commitment idea is a bit of a gut feeling, but by the time they have worked at least 160 hours, you should have a sense of whether they are there to help you build your cathedral or just going through the motions.

As for a vote of confidence from the staff, you can use the criteria in the peer appraisal or just ask for a simple thumbs up or down from everyone ... and I do mean everyone.

Nobody should become part of the team unless they have at least met (and hopefully connected with) the other players on the team. The impact of this requirement on team-building is obvious.

Appropriate Incentives

The new worker has control over the length of time the contingency period lasts. In effect, they can give themselves a raise and start to accrue benefits in half the maximum time by applying themselves and quickly meeting the requirements of the confirmation period.

Habit Development

An interesting condition of my confirmation period is that there be no unexcused absences or disciplinary action in the 160 hours immediately preceding confirmation. So every time the new worker makes an error in judgment, they must put in at least another 160 "clean" hours before they are eligible for regular staff status.

This also means that if the new worker makes a serious error in judgment after 160 hours on the job, they must be dismissed because they won't be able to fulfill this requirement of confirmation before reaching their 320-hour maximum.

What constitutes a behavior issue depends on how rigorous you want to be, but in my organization that means anything I would normally want to write up: tardiness, failure to honor standards, not acting in the best interests of the guest or the company.

Of course if they commit a non-negotiable hanging offense (theft, drug use, drinking or using drugs on the job, endangering the health or well-being of staff or guests, etc.) they would be immediately discharged anyway, no matter what their status.

Drop Dead Date

If the requirements of the confirmation period have not (or cannot) be met within 320 hours, the worker must be discharged. This puts teeth in the process, creates a sense of urgency and requires all regular staff members to show the same professional competence and take an active interest in their own success.

The confirmation period is an opportunity for both the company and the new staff member to clearly demonstrate their commitment to making the relationship successful.

Every new worker is ultimately responsible for their own success, of course, but the actions of the coaches should demonstrate their belief in the competence of the new hire and their sincere desire to help them succeed in their new position.

Toward this end, some companies assign every new worker a buddy or a mentor. The mentor's job is to help the new worker adjust, answer questions, interpret events and in general be a resource to help assure the new person's success with the company.

Ideally, the mentor would be a peer of the newly hired worker rather than a supervisor or a person who would evaluate the person's performance during the Confirmation Period.

Training

Who's going to come to your circus if the animals aren't even trained?

Here's where the best raw ingredients start to turn bad. Recognizing that newbies don't know much about the company or its practices, most operators do a fair job of training new workers ... provided that training involves something more organized than "Follow Betsy around and she'll show you what to do."

The system usually falls down on the continued training of the more experienced staff. Take a waitress who has been with you for two years: what does she know this week that she didn't know last week? What can a cook make today that he couldn't make last month?

To keep your good people engaged, they need to be continually growing professionally. [Hint: if they don't want to keep growing professionally, they're not really your good people!]

Just as there's a difference between service and hospitality, there is a difference between training (teaching specific skills) and personal development (helping the whole person grow).

When you make personal development one of your competitive advantages, over time you will tend to develop (and attract) a more professional group of workers, enjoy lower turnover and be able to deliver a much higher guest experience no matter what the concept of your restaurant.

Here are a few thoughts on how to improve your effectiveness:

Have a System
Every activity you engage in should have a structure that is supportive of the Purpose you see for your business. This means training activities are planned out and scheduled in advance, not made up on the spot or put on the calendar "when there's time."

Learning/Memorization
Knowledge is more powerful than ignorance. Every member of the staff must know the menu forward and back, not only the items and what's in them but how they are prepared and some background information on the source of the recipe and its key ingredients.

Understanding is more powerful than knowledge ... but you only have knowledge as long as you remember it. In contrast, once you understand something, you have it forever. Memorizing the menu is only a necessary start. If the service staff can watch an item being prepared, perhaps even help in the process and taste the final result, they will understand the dish and be more effective at the table.

Training Games

Foodservice people are naturally competitive, so well-conceived games will engage them more than dry lecture. Divide the group into teams and have them compete against each other, whether it be performing a specific task in a relay fashion or a quiz show-like test of their knowledge. Doing it in teams builds camaraderie and keeps losing from becoming a personal failure.

Role-Playing

Everybody hates role-playing exercises. They don't want to fail or look silly in front of their peers. You can take that risk away by focusing on the things they do right, generalizing that as a lesson to the group and allowing people to develop at their own pace.

Drill, Baby, Drill

The military continually runs training exercises ... not because the troops don't know what to do or how to do it, but to keep everyone's muscle memory sharp so when life is on the line, they can react without having to think about the mechanics of the task. The same is true for world class athletes, dancers, firefighters, law enforcement officers and many other professions that involve physical activity.

Muscle memory is why fire drills and evacuation exercises are so effective at saving lives in a real crisis. It explains how you can be an excellent driver (after a few years) without the need to think about every little action involved when you are behind the wheel.

> ### HOT DOG HEAVEN
>
> Years ago I developed a quick service concept for a client. When we started training, I told the new crew we were going to drill the procedures until they could do them in their sleep – not because I didn't want them to think but because when they had to think about how to do their jobs, their focus was on their own issues, not on the guests.
>
> When they could handle the mechanics with a clear head, they just had to stay positive and be there for the guests. I assured them once they could do that, they would be awed by the quality of humanity that walked through our doors. The fact that someone crossed the street in the hot sun to get a hot dog from us could move them to tears ... and it did!
>
> That sounds a little dramatic, but almost from the day we opened, you could get a higher level of personal service at our little hot dog stand in rural Northern California than you could find in most upscale restaurants in San Francisco.

Develop Certified Trainers

It is unreasonable – even unwise – for management to be the only ones conducting training activities. Develop a group of certified trainers to share that responsibility.

Certified trainers are experienced staff members who have earned their certification, not from time on the job, but by demonstrating accurate product knowledge, personal proficiency in the tasks they will be training, patience, and a natural inclination to teach, along with positive feedback from management, guests and co-workers.

Aside from the advantages that come from getting your key staff more personally engaged in the success of the restaurant, front line workers are much closer to the realities of the job than their managers.

This helps keep the training real so your trainees won't feel they are wasting their time. (It doesn't matter how many years you washed dishes back in the day. Whoever is doing that job today knows more about what's going on in the dishroom than you do.)

To be certified to teach specific skills, policies or procedures, your trainers should be subject matter experts and be on the same page as management. To keep their skills sharp, re-test them every six months on the skills they're training the other staff members on. It's only right that a bonus accompany their successful renewal.

The idea is to maintain the rigor and not let things slide into "they say to do it this way but here's how most of us really do it." If that happens, you are effectively giving your staff – both new and old – permission to make it up as they go and you will never be able to achieve consistency.

How About You?

Are YOU an effective trainer? Have you had any training in how to train ... or do you just model your behavior after old teachers in school or those who trained you in the past?

Since your thinking will color the way training is done in your organization, a little attitude check might be enlightening at this point. Just for fun, rate yourself as a trainer on the next page. The answers follow ... but no peeking!

71

Test Yourself as a Trainer

To evaluate your qualities as a trainer, mark the following questions True or False based on your personal understanding of training and how it works.

T F

1. The restaurant has an obligation to provide its staff with the skills necessary to do their jobs.
2. Staff turnover is often related to training, or the lack of it.
3. Learning on-the-job is not the only way to provide necessary learning for new employees.
4. Training low-skilled workers may be just as important as training highly skilled people.
5. Prior to training, explain company rules and regulations to the new worker.
6. Prior to training, answer the unspoken question in every trainee's mind: "What's in it for me?"
7. Popular workers usually make good trainers.
8. Before actual training begins, explain the position as it relates to the total operation of the restaurant.
9. A person who performs well on the job is qualified to teach others the skills needed for the job.
10. To a large extent, the ability to train can be developed.
11. A trainer should spend at least as much time getting things ready for training as in actual instruction.
12. The trainer should know the desired results before beginning to teach and should list the key points around which the instruction will be built.
13. The trainer should learn what the student already knows about the subject before starting to train.
14. The trainer should have an organized plan and know the amount of learning expected day-by-day.
15. In setting instructional goals, give trainees more work than they can easily accomplish to demonstrate your high standards.
16. When a trainee performs correctly, reward the person with praise, something like "That's good," or "You're doing fine."
17. A trainer must never admit past or present errors or not knowing an answer to a question.
18. The best way to handle a cocky trainee is to put them down in front of others.
19. In training new workers, concentrate upon speed rather than form.
20. Surprise quizzes and examinations are good ways to ensure high level performance.
21. Expect that there will be periods during the training when no observable progress is made.
22. Expect some people to learn two or three times as fast as others.
23. Both tell and show the trainee how to perform the skill you are training.
24. When a trainee performs incorrectly say, "No, not that way."
25. After a task has been learned, ask trainees for suggestions as to how to improve the task.

Source: Donald E. Lundberg, *The Restaurant from Concept to Operation*, ©1985 by John Wiley & Sons, Inc., adapted with permission.

(answers on Page 74)

72

4. Observe Proper Sanitation

Health Department inspections verify your restaurant is meeting basic sanitation standards. They operate on the assumption that while most operators pretty much know *what* they should do, not all of them do it, at least not all the time.

The same general principle applies to the way you structure your steps of service. Unless you keep it clean (enforce your standards and insist on the desired results), people can get sloppy ... except instead of making people sick, they'll send them out the door with a ho-hum experience and you'll never see them again.

Keep Things Clean

The best health inspectors think of themselves more as educators than enforcers. They don't have a "Gotcha!" mentality. They understand they'll get a better end result (a safer restaurant) by dealing with any lapses in proper sanitation practices as signs the staff either doesn't know or doesn't understand the proper procedures. They are firm about compliance, but they are caring about how they achieve that.

As the leader of your organization, you have a similar role when it comes to service. You've outlined what you want and trained the staff how to deliver it. Now you must keep them on track. This makes your ongoing job one of continual coaching and counseling. Like the health inspector, you observe how the staff perform their work and when you see gaps and lapses, you take the appropriate corrective action.

The important thing is RIGOR
If you have standards but occasionally compromise them, you don't have standards

Deal With Non-Compliance

Let's say that you want a member of your staff to achieve a certain result and it's just not happening. The old management model calls for several counseling sessions (all properly documented, of course) followed by termination if the person was unable to deliver the necessary results. While termination may sometimes be an appropriate course of action, are there other possibilities that might explain a lack of performance and help you salvage the situation?

73

Test Answers

1. T One of the best summaries of the importance of training comes from Hap Gray, owner of the Watermark Restaurant in Cleveland. He says "My training program is what makes this *my* restaurant. If I didn't train my staff, I would only be a caretaker for the bank."

2. T Untrained people never understand what they are expected to do or how to do it. This leads to mistakes and negative feedback from management, both major factors in turnover.

3. T While learning on the job is certainly part of most workers skill development, it is not the only form of training,

4. T The only way low-skilled workers even get to *be* highly skilled is through training!

5. T To create learner interest, explain the benefits that accrue to the person. Set the record straight by explaining the company's rules and regulations. All benefits and requirements should be explained before skill training is started.

6. T People do what they do for their own reasons. Helping them see how training will benefit them personally gives them a vested interested in its success.

7. F Popularity does not necessarily correlate with being a good trainer.

8. F It is important to see each particular job as a part of the whole.

9. F The ability to teach is a skill distinctly separate from professional performance.

10. F Unfortunately, not everyone has the personality to be an effective trainer. While it's certainly possible for trainers to improve their effectiveness, qualities like desire, caring, patience and empathy – important qualities of an effective trainer – are not typically talents that can be trained.

11. T It is important for the instructor to be properly prepared. Inadequate preparation is unprofessional and makes the trainees less secure about what they are learning.

12. T Knowing this information gives trainees a context for what will follow and aids in their learning.

13. T To maintain interest, the level of the training should be compatible with the knowledge and skills of the trainee. Without this knowledge, it's easy to talk over the head of those with no knowledge or bore more advanced students. In either case, very little effective transfer of information occurs.

14. T This helps keep the training on track and increases the trainees' confidence in the process.

15. F Training is an occasion when success at every step is important. Standards should be set which are achievable and avoid the experience of failure.

16. T Positive reinforcement validates the trainee and encourages continued learning.

17. F No one expects a perfect trainer (except perhaps an *imperfect* trainer!)

18. F Even though a trainee is out of line, it does no good to embarrass the person. Rather, talk to the person privately.

19. F Form comes first, speed comes later.

20. F Surprises are not considered good in training.

21. T   There are times when consolidation of skills takes place and no observable progress is made.

22. T   There is a vast range of individual differences found in the general population.

23. T   Different people learn in different ways. Covering all the bases helps assure your training will "stick."

24. F   This is a negative way of teaching. Far better to emphasize the positive.

25. T   Every task can be improved by new techniques, new methods, new equipment, new skills. Or it may be completely eliminated as unnecessary.

Here are several potential explanations for a lapse in performance. I suggest you explore them – in the order listed – before you make the hard decision to cut a marginal team member loose:

They Don't Understand What You Want

Just because you know the results you're trying to achieve doesn't automatically mean your staff does. The first step is to be very certain they know exactly what you're after. This isn't always as easy as it sounds.

Lee Cockrell, VP of Walt Disney World once told me that people cannot deliver a higher level of service than they have personally experienced. If what he says is true (and I believe it is), does it make any sense to fire a person for delivering poor service if they really have no clear idea what that good service even *is*?

So start by determining whether or not the staff member has a true understanding of what you're asking for and be open to the possibility that you could be expecting something that is beyond their personal experience, even if – especially if – the task seems obvious to you.

They Don't Grasp Why It's Important

If, after really listening to the person, you are certain that they know what you want, the next possibility is that they don't understand why it is important. Sanitation practices can easily fall into this category.

Based on experience, I'd say that most restaurant workers have no understanding of the value of a repeat customer. Whose fault is that? If you don't tell them, how are they supposed to know?

So the next step in resolving performance issues is to educate the staff member on the importance of what you are requesting. Often, once they "get it" they will modify their behavior voluntarily and the situation will be resolved without a confrontation.

They Don't Understand How to Do It

If you have a tendency to yell at someone when they make a mistake, your staff will never tell you they don't know how to do something you ask, particularly when there are language issues between you. Nobody likes to be yelled at. They will just smile, nod their heads and hope you'll go away.

The lesson in the example below is that just because *you* know how to do something doesn't mean everybody else does. You'd do well to ascertain the facts before taking more radical action.

THE MYSTERY OF THE MOP

At age 14, I was hired by a small restaurant on Cape Cod for my first job: washing dishes (by hand!) during the summer tourist season.

My staff selection was one question: "Do you know how to wash dishes?" The training for my frightening new responsibilities was a single sentence: "Then get back there and do it!" And I had one sentence of counseling: "If you screw up, you're out of here!"

Welcome to the wonderful world of work!

Like most teenagers in the days before automatic dishwashers, I had lots of dishwashing experience, so that part of the job was pretty easy. But I still remember my terror the first time I was pointed in the general direction of the cleaning gear and told to mop the floor.

Talk about panic! I'd never seen a string mop in my life! We certainly didn't use one at home so I had no idea what it was or how to use it.

My boss had me so terrified of making a mistake that I didn't dare reveal my ignorance by asking him to show me what to do. I knew if I screwed up, I'd be fired!

Fortunately, Manny, one of the breakfast cooks, saw the terror in my eyes and took me under his wing. He realized I was clueless, taught me how to use the mop and patiently worked with me until I had mastered it.

In addition to being my mentor, he also became my inspector, making me re-do anything that didn't meet his standards while making sure I understood why it was important to do it a certain way. Almost single-handedly, Manny helped this frightened rookie survive his first big adventure in employment.

Thinking back, it's interesting to realize that I still remember Manny, but the names of the boss and the restaurant have long since slipped from my memory.

They Have a Better Way to Do It

If the task needs to be done and the what, why and how are covered, the next possibility is they are not doing it your way because they have a better way to do it! The way to avoid this trap is to focus on results rather than activities. If you are getting the results you want and no laws are being broken, who cares if one of your workers does it differently than the way you would?

When you define results rather than activities, you allow people to interpret their jobs in a way that works for them ... and that will always improve both retention and productivity.

They Can't Do It

The next possibility is that they just can't do what you want – physically or mentally it is simply beyond their capabilities. This doesn't make them incompetent, it just means they are miscast.

If you put a "numbers person" in a customer contact position or place a "people person" in a job where they have no interaction with others, you're likely to see performance problems. Everyone is really good at *something*. Just because they're ineffective in the job they're in doesn't mean they couldn't excel in another.

They Won't Do It

If you are comfortable that all the possibilities above have been considered, and you are still not getting the performance you need, the only other explanation is that the person just will not do what you need done. In that case, do yourself and the employee a favor and "free up their future" to pursue another line of work!

Given how difficult it is to find and retain quality staff, termination should be the option of last choice. Don't give up on anyone until you have exhausted all the possibilities and given the person every opportunity to succeed.

Keep It Fresh

To deliver personal service, it is important that the interactions with your guests be as fresh as possible. This is why scripts always sound so uncaring. Unfortunately, even the most clever spontaneous lines can start to sound flat if you repeat them 100 times a night. Think of your response to the typical brain-dead server who arrives at the table with, "Hi. My name is ___ and I'll be your server tonight."

Be a coach. Listen for patterns or staleness, call it to the attention of the staffer involved and challenge them to find another way to say the same things. If you start to notice issues in this area, you might bring it up in a staff meeting.

Explain the point you want to freshen up and make a game out of it. Go around the room and ask each person in turn how they might convey it to the guest. The ground rule: nobody can repeat what someone else has said.

Someone can stay in the game as long as they can keep coming up with yet a different way to achieve the end result than has already been mentioned. Repeat a phrase or come up blank and you're out. The winner gets a cool prize.

Try to catch people doing things right on the job. Notice, celebrate and reward originality. When you trust them to do the right things, your staff will amaze you with their creativity.

The service sequences suggest how the servers *might* proceed through the meal but don't get overly rigid about it.

There are different strokes for different folks and as long as every guest has a great time and nobody breaks any laws, why get overly anal about exactly how it happens? Yes, everyone must respect your standards and they must achieve the same end results, but within those parameters, leave the staff free to improvise.

DIFFERENT STROKES

When I opened my first restaurant, I told my service staff I wanted them to make sure every guest had a great time. I didn't get much more specific than that at the time because, frankly, I didn't know how to!

I was going through the dining room one night as one of my waiters sat down at the table to take the order. Now, we were a casual place, but it still scared me to watch this happening. When the party left, though, they were raving.

"We had such a great time," they gushed, "and our waiter, Sam, was crazy. He even sat down with us when he took our order!" I just rolled my eyes and blurted, "I'm glad you had a good time. Please come back."

That was Sam's style. He didn't do it with every table and he never did it when it didn't work, but his guests always raved about his service. I was at least bright enough not to say to my whole crew, "Okay, we're all going to sit down at the table to take the orders."

You might joke around, I may be more formal, but if the guests have a great time, what difference does it make?

5. Give It Some WOW

Even tasty, well-prepared dishes will have more impact if you create a spectacular plate presentation ... and the same can be said for service. Strictly speaking, placing plates on the table is service, but when you do something that adds a delightful surprise, it makes your service memorable. This is another way to exceed the guests' expectations ... and make it more fun go to work.

Here are a few examples of how a few creative operators in the US and Europe put some WOW into their service:

78

Lambert's Café is a casual country-themed joint in Sikeston, MO known for large portions of homestyle food and 5" rolls they bake fresh all day. The owner liked to personally hand them out hot from the oven, but one night they were slammed and he was way behind. Somebody yelled, "Just toss me one" ... and he did. Then another guest said, "Throw me one, too" and a phenomenon was born. Now Lambert's proudly bills themselves as "The Home of Throwed Rolls." This distinctive service technique has brought them press coverage from literally all over the world ... and keeps the place packed!

The Family Buggy Restaurant in Livonia, MI wanted to make the experience more of an attraction for children, so they bought a big stuffed bear and brought it to the table to "dine" with the kids. They started with one and immediately had to buy more because children went nuts if they couldn't have their special dinner guest. To adapt an idea like this, you probably won't even have to buy the bears. Go to a local retailer and make a deal. They loan you a bear and you refer people to the store if they want to purchase one.

The Herb Farm outside Seattle does so many things well. On our initial visit, rather than some cute young thing hiding behind a desk, the first thing we saw when we came through the door was a smiling man in a crisp white shirt who welcomed us by name (how did he know?) and said, "Our dinner service will start at 7:00. Can I offer you a cup of hot spiced cider while you wait?" We've been back to the Herb Farm several times since (the menu changes completely every few weeks) and there's always a free welcoming drink in keeping with the evening's menu theme.

Here's another WOW from **The Herb Farm**. When we were shown to our table on that first visit, there was a little silver heart-shaped frame with a message in calligraphy: "15 happy anniversary wishes to the Marvins from your friends at The Herb Farm." It is still on display in our living room.

At **Restaurant de L'Auxois** near Chateauneuf in France, we ordered the cheese selection as a dessert course. We were blown away with what they brought! I'm not sure a health department in the US would let you get away with a presenting a common tray of cheese like this but it was definitely a WOW for us when we saw it!

Ristorante Re de Macchia in Montalcino, Italy showed me how to elevate a Crema Cotta con Zuccharo Caramellato (creme brulee with caramelized sugar) from a common dessert into a WOW experience. It just took about half an ounce of Sambucca and a match!

Serve Hot Food Hot

Everyone says (positive) word-of-mouth is the best advertising, but there's no word-of-mouth without something to talk about. This is where the line between service and marketing starts to blur.

For example, in my San Francisco restaurant, I challenged my kitchen crew to come up with a plate presentation that would elicit a spontaneous, positive comment when the plate was presented to the guest. I told them I didn't care how they got it, just get it.

Their response was inventive fruit garnishes – quite common now but a rarity in the mid-70s. When we presented the plate, we usually heard a WOW from the guests, at which point, the server might say, "Isn't it nice to see a plate come out of a restaurant kitchen that isn't all covered with parsley!" Everyone would smile, nod their heads in agreement and chuckle.

When these same people went to one of my competitors and the plate invariably arrived covered with parsley, they would snicker and the following sort of exchange might occur with their table mates:

A: *"What's the laugh about?"*
B: *"Oh, it's just the parsley. They don't do that at Crisis Hopkins."*
A: *"Crisis Hopkins? What's that?"*
B: *"It's this great new restaurant over in Embarcadero Center ..."*

They would proceed to give a commercial for me because they had something to talk about. We had created a point of difference and educated our guests about it so that they had a story to tell. At the least, they would at think of us whenever they saw parsley on a plate.

Service Is Not Just For Guests

Our discussion of service has focused primarily on the interactions between the service staff and the guests, but this not the only place where service is important in a successful restaurant.

Service is also the way the kitchen staff and the servers interact with each other and the nature of management's relationship with staff, vendors and investors. Imagine what it would be like on the job if everyone dealt with their co-workers with an attitude of "How can I be of help?"

Instead of "giving service," see your work as "being in service"
It will make a big difference

5
Service Stumbles

Service Stumbles

The Devil in the Details

This section is taken from my book, *Restaurant Basics Revisited: Why Guests Don't Come Back and What You Can Do About It,* a look at the monumental minutia that negatively impacts the guests' experience. For the most part, people come to restaurants expecting to have a good time and if we don't blow it, they probably will. There are close to 150 items on this list (out of about 1000 in the book) that can lower the mood for your guests ... and those are just the ones about service!

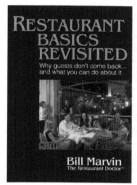

As unusual as some of these notions may sound, everything on this list has actually happened, either to me or someone I know. Not all details are issues for every guest, of course, and many of them won't apply to your operation. Still, each has the potential to weigh down someone's good mood and you will pay a huge price any time that happens.

You may even find yourself at odds with some of these ideas, but be careful. I don't suggest this material is any sort of gospel. It is, however, consistently oriented from the guest's perspective. Ignore it at your peril.

Any time you place your own convenience ahead of the interests of your guests, you're working against yourself. Beware of dismissing any ideas too quickly. Items that look like they'll take too much work, cost too much money or require too much training to correct are most likely to be in your blind spots (and likely issues for you already!)

You can't avoid every potential problem, but you can try. There are items on this list you won't do anything to correct, but you could. There are even items that will annoy you just by being on the list at all. (Those are usually the ones that hit too close to home!) Think about the risk before you decide a particular point is unreasonable or that you can't afford to solve it. What could it hurt to be guest-friendly?

Your service staff takes the largest responsibility for guest gratification since they are the principal point of contact. They orchestrate the dining experience. Their attitude, presence and skills will highlight or destroy the efforts of the rest of your crew.

It's easy to lay the blame for service problems at the feet of the service staff, but their behavior is only a reflection of the attitudes they see in their managers. Operators who deny this relationship are the ones with high staff turnover and perpetual guest relations problems, the ones who believe it's impossible to find qualified workers even as other operators in the same market have a waiting list for jobs.

It's not easy to acknowledge your own role in problems. Still, by taking responsibility for staff attitudes, you can change your level of guest service. We call this phenomenon "the shadow of the leader."

The good news is that you can change yourself – in fact you are the *only* person you can change. When your outlook changes, the outlook of your staff follows suit, something we talk about more in the next part of the book. I mention it here only to give you something to think about as we explore the many well-intentioned actions that can innocently destroy the guest service experience!

Remember your primary job is to give your guests a good time. Unless guests enjoy themselves inside your four walls, nothing else matters.

Annoying Attitudes

Attitudes are mindsets. A "bad attitude" is just a belief that your needs and convenience are more important than the needs and convenience of others. It's a contagious disease. Here are a few signs that tell you if this virus has started to infect your organization:

Needing to Be the Center of Attention
The need to be the focal point of everything suggests an individual with an ego problem. It implies that what is happening for them is more important than what is happening for anyone else.

These people cannot make your guests feel important until their priorities shift. Fortunately, their attitude can turn around if they adopt a guest-oriented stance to their jobs ... and that change can happen for them as soon as it happens for you (and not before!)

An "I'm Doing You a Favor" Attitude

It's easy to find arrogance and indifference in the world. People don't need to come to your restaurant to experience it. Besides, guests are doing you a favor by patronizing your place. They have many other choices ... and they *will* make other choices if you don't earn – and show them you appreciate — their business.

Socializing with Some Guests While Ignoring Others

Good service is fair and equal. Human nature being what it is, you will insult the slighted guests and they are unlikely to return. The solution is eyeballs in the dining room, compassionate coaching, continual training, and constant support to help your staff become more sensitive to the needs of *all* their guests, all the time.

Being Too Familiar or Excessively Chatty

Guests come to the restaurant for their own reasons. When a staff member personally interjects themselves into the guest's world without permission, they are an intruder. Undue familiarity creates withdrawal and resentment, while the staff member probably thinks they are just being friendly. Remember that good service is always defined from the guest's viewpoint, so know when to open your mouth ... and when to shut it!

Making a Fuss about a Dropped Dish

Accidents happen and nobody likes to be embarrassed. If you call attention to a guest's mishap, you'll drop their level of well-being immediately. This usually guarantees their outlook will be negative for the rest of the meal.

The most effective way to handle a spill is to treat it as the everyday occurrence it is. If you must say anything, a passing comment like "Don't worry about it. It happens all the time," takes the pressure off and helps salvage the evening for everybody.

No Sense of Humor

There are many unexpected events in the restaurant business and a sense of humor is often the lubricant that makes an evening flow smoothly. That's why it is important to at least have guest contact staff who can take a joke.

Mike Hurst, late owner of Fort Lauderdale's 15th Street Fisheries always asked job applicants, "What's the funniest thing that's ever happened to you?" He asked the question with a straight face and watched their reaction. Their answer is not important. He wanted to see a laugh and an animated response, figuring that people who can laugh at themselves were the "sparklers" he wanted to hire.

Visible Reaction to the Amount of the Tip

Nonverbal statements are often the most devastating because every guest in the room can read them, so it's appropriate to coach servers not to display a reactions to the amount of a tip.

A better question is why their first action would be to look at the tip? Be sensitive to the possibility they may be under some financial stress or feel underappreciated on the job. In any case, there is always more going on than you know about.

Making Light of a Guest's Complaint

How a restaurant handles complaints says more about its service orientation than almost anything else. Giving guests what they want is important to your success. Take all complaints seriously (the guest does!) Service staff who fail to treat every complaint as a significant opportunity to assure guest satisfaction will discourage the very feedback essential to their success.

Refusing to Take Payment to the Cashier

This attitude reflects an organization (or an individual) where guest service is an imposition. The fault most likely lies with the attitude of management. Precede any staff discipline actions with serious self-examination ... but address the attitude as soon as it appears.

Protecting the House

This usually happens when the guest has a legitimate complaint that goes against a house policy. The staff person ignores the well-being of the guest and defends the policy, probably because there are more rewards for following the rules than for pleasing the guests.

While you have every right to set restrictive policies for your own business, you must also be prepared to pay the price such arrogance may bring. Not only can it cost you your guests, but you could lose your service-oriented staff members as well.

Rushing Guests Off the Table or Out of the Restaurant

If you hurry a party out just so you can get an additional seating at the table, you may never see them again. What's even worse, their negative word-of-mouth will offset the good comments of five other parties. The implications of the math aren't difficult to grasp.

Repeat as necessary:
This restaurant is run for the enjoyment and pleasure of our guests, not for the convenience of the staff or the owners.

Expecting Guests to Know the Restaurant's Procedures

It's easy to get irritated when a guest asks about something that, to you, is obvious. We assume what is basic knowledge to us must be equally evident to everyone. It isn't. The safest attitude is to treat every guest like a first-timer and take delight in telling them details they didn't know about your restaurant.

Giving a Disgusted Look Following an Exchange with a Guest

This is an insult to the guests that everyone in the dining room can see. Remember that guests always have good (to them) reasons for their comments and questions. Mocking them only shows your ignorance, insensitivity and immaturity.

Calling the Guest by Their First Name

Using a guest's first name can sometimes be a plus, provided you know them personally and they've asked you to use their first name. However, the practice is offensive when there is no prior personal relationship and the staff member gets the guest's first name from a credit card.

For example, my legal first name is William but I don't use it and I don't know anyone who does. Those who know me call me Bill. Call me William and instead of coming across as friendly, you'll impress me as arrogant. When you get a guest's name from their credit card, use only their last name and be safe.

Refusing a Request to Change Tables

Does this suggest a control issue? If guest gratification is truly Job One in the restaurant, this sort of problem is unlikely to surface. If it does come up, you know where to point the finger first.

Ignoring Obvious Attempts For Attention

It is insulting to the guest and suggests a servers who feels *they* are the ones in charge of the dining experience, not the guest. They will not tolerate anyone telling them what to do. It is impossible for these individuals to give responsive service unless they can find humility. Help them straighten out their priorities.

Presuming the Tip

Always bring the change back to the table. Never assume a tip. A tip is a voluntary transaction between the guest and the service staff. If you take away the voluntary aspect, you may not only lose the tip, but probably lose the guest as well. Servers who engage in this practice may be insecure about their abilities and afraid they won't get a tip any other way. Straighten them out or cut them loose.

Using a Condescending Tone of Voice

The message you deliver is always in your tone of voice. Elderly guests, the handicapped and minorities are particularly sensitive to a condescending tone. Just because someone is different doesn't mean they are broke, stupid or undeserving of excellent service. These groups often receive poor treatment and will appreciate your responsiveness and respect.

Different Treatment for Different People

Beware of prejudice in all its forms. Do not draw conclusions just because a guest is young, arrived with a bus tour, isn't dressed well or has a coupon. There are no second-class guests in a legendary restaurant ... and becoming a legend is a worthy goal.

System Slip-ups

Many problems point to breakdowns in the restaurant's systems. The only effective way to solve these problems is to identify weaknesses and fix the systems. If you try to solve problems by fixing the people involved, you will never receive another suggestion from anyone on your staff. No one will dare point out a problem if it they think they might be blamed for it.

Wet Plates or Trays

If plates or trays are not air drying properly, it may mean your dish machine's final rinse is not hot enough. If there is no temperature problem, the dish crew may be stacking the pieces too quickly after they come out of the machine, either because of inadequate training or lack of adequate clean dish landing space. Whatever the cause, wet serviceware gets the meal off to a bad start.

Running Out of a Menu Item

First, you need effective forecasting and inventory control to reduce the problem of outages. On the other hand, never being out of stock may signal excessive inventory levels. The solution is attention to inventory management ... and the right choice of words.

When you *run* out of something, guests think you don't know how to run your business. If you *sell* out of something, guests think you have highly desirable items. If you cannot provide what the guest orders, always suggest alternative choices.

Bringing Food the Guest Did Not Order

People love surprises. Bringing them an unexpected extra at no cost is a good way to gain points ... but bringing them something by mistake only shows how haphazard your systems are.

Running out of China, Silver or Glassware

You can't talk your way around this situation! Small inventories can be false economy. The immediate problem is inconvenience to the guest and the potential loss of future business. When you finally buy the additional stock, if you can find it, it probably will cost more.

Also, having enough china, glasses and silver saves costly labor hours. If you don't have to wash dishes during the meal, you can "sandbag" soiled utensils, allowing the dishwasher to help in the kitchen and catch up on warewashing after the rush is over.

Orders That Arrive Incomplete

You have to get it right the first time or you will throw off the timing of the entire meal. In fast-paced operations, an expediter can be invaluable in assembling and checking orders. Incomplete orders cost you points with your guests and create additional work for your service staff.

Sitting at the Table Without Being Acknowledged

Most guests don't expect the immediate availability of the server. Guests just feel more comfortable when they know the server is aware they are waiting. Even if you're busy, it is important to at least let waiting guests know you noted their presence.

Approach the table within one minute of the guests' arrival, STOP, focus your attention, give a short welcome and let them know you will be right back. Talking to the table while on the move without stopping will only irritate the guests. Be sure your system allows enough time for this important first step of good service.

Not Serving Guests Promptly

Hot food must be hot. If you do not serve all guests at the table at once, some guests will sit with their food cooling while they wait for you to serve their companions – a socially uncomfortable experience that will not enhance your guests' enjoyment of their meal.

Not Providing Service in Order of Arrival

People expect to be served before parties that arrived or were seated after them. It is not an unreasonable expectation. Your greeter can help smooth out potential point loss by properly rotating parties between stations to keep the workload balanced. This assures a server will not get two or three new parties at the same time.

If for some reason you cannot avoid double seating, have a means of communication that will help the service staff be clear on which parties arrived first.

Not Receiving Coffee Before the Dessert

Many desserts taste much better with a cup of coffee. Delivering coffee before dessert maintains the flow of service between clearing the main course and serving the desserts. It also assures your guests will gain the most enjoyment from the efforts of your pastry chef. Since it takes longer to drink a cup of hot coffee than to eat most desserts, you also may turn the table a little sooner.

Meal Service Too Fast or Too Slow

Appropriate pacing varies with the type of restaurant and the meal period. In quick service operations, speed is always the most important factor. In table service, rapid service is usually more of an issue at breakfast and lunch than in the evening.

The higher the check average, the more time your guests expect to spend at the table. A possible exception is guests who are enjoying a pre-theater meal. They will be watching the clock closely. The more you know about the motives of your guests, the easier it will be to adjust the pace of service to be responsive.

No Place for Meal Debris

Give some thought to what the guest is going to need to get through the meal comfortably and be sure they have it. For example, where are they going to put clam shells, bones, cracker wrappers, etc.? Always have a spare plate or bowl for bones and shells.

To solve the problem of cracker wrapper clutter, just place the full cracker basket inside an empty one. When bringing the crackers to the table, separate the two baskets. You'll create a receptacle for the trash ... and a pleasant point of difference from your competition.

Slow Service at Breakfast or Lunch

Guests are rushed in the morning and have limited time for lunch. If you cannot regularly get them through either meal in 25 minutes, feature two or three items you can prepare quickly, perhaps with a guarantee of timely service. Remember the critical timing is from the time your guests arrive until the time they are out the door. This is different from the length of time it takes to deliver their order.

Endless Waits in the Drive-up Line

Fast food is supposed to be fast. Many operators have adopted cordless headsets to speed communication between the guest, the order-taker and the production line. The idea is helping. If slow service is a problem, involve your staff in identifying the lapses in the system and suggesting ways to improve your accuracy and speed. You may be surprised by their insights.

Food Sitting Visibly in the Pickup Window or On a Tray Stand

This has to be a frustrating experience for restaurant guests. I have even seen guests get up and serve the plates themselves! If your system cannot move hot food while it is still hot, consider a runner system. Under this structure, servers do not leave the dining room. The next available runner delivers hot food to the server as soon as it's up. If the sales person is busy, the runner can serve the entrees following the seat number codings on the guest check.

Waiting for Coffee to Brew

Everyone appreciates a fresh cup of coffee but nobody likes to wait for it. Particularly in fast-paced restaurants, you may want to assign someone to just brew coffee during the rush to be sure it will be made properly. The only thing worse than waiting for coffee when you need it is ending up with a bad cup of it!

Necessary Condiments That Don't Arrive Before the Food

Don't make guests wait for a condiment while their food gets cold. An effective system always allows the necessary accompaniments to arrive at the table before the entree is served. This assures that hot food will not sit on the table while you fumble around the service stand looking for the steak sauce!

Guests Having to Get Their Own Coffee

Americans expect prompt coffee refills. When their frustration reaches a point where they get it themselves, you've lost points. Either have enough staff to keep up with the demand or consider insulated coffee carafes you can leave on the table.

Serving Food Ordered by Another Table

Getting the orders confused is embarrassing for everyone. The guest doesn't know whether to eat the food or not, the service staff shows its ineptitude and the guest who originally placed the order doesn't get served when they should.

The situation is further complicated by the problem of what to do when you realize the mistake. You can't pick food up off one table and serve it to another.

The proper solution, if there is one, is going to be costly. I suggest you first acknowledge the mistake to both parties and apologize for the error. Leave the incorrect item as a complimentary gift to the party who received it and bring a complimentary replacement to the person whose order you misdirected.

Trying to talk your way out of the error or failing to correct the mistake will only irritate both parties. The cost of an extra entree is far less than the cost of losing two groups of potential regulars.

Mis-Packed Take-out Orders
This is the big reason for dissatisfaction among quick service patrons. Statistics suggest that fast feeders improperly assemble one out of three orders. This is particularly irritating at the drive-up window since the guest won't discover the error until they are well away from the property.

Horrible Habits

A problem with hiring "experienced" servers is that you don't really know the exact content of that experience. Many experienced workers have only succeeded in learning someone else's bad habits and poor attitude. Fortunately, you can overcome bad habits through diligent coaching, provided you know what to watch for.

Lack of Eye Contact
One of my favorite pastimes, especially in coffee shops, is to see if a waitress can make it through the entire meal without making eye contact even once. It's discouraging to see how often it happens.

Coach your staff on the importance of smiling eye contact. The idea is simply to start the relationship with every new guest by looking them directly in the eye with a sincere smile. Nothing warms the heart like smiling eye contact. When it doesn't happen, guests can think you have something to hide. They trust you less, tip less and are more critical of both the restaurant and your service.

Different Service for Perceived Low Tippers
People will tip what they can, when they feel they have received service worth the gesture. Your job is to be sure every guest in the restaurant has a delightful experience. Often, single diners will appreciate your caring and be particularly generous.

Many teenagers work in restaurants and understand what it is like to work for tips. They can be surprisingly liberal in their tipping if you treat them well.

Some seniors may not have as much money as other diners, but they are more likely to develop a dining habit than most other groups. If you treat them well, they will give you most of their business. They appreciate good service and will reward your respectful efforts with their regular patronage even if their finances may occasionally cause a smaller tip.

Snatching Away Menus Too Quickly

If you have the story of your restaurant on the menu, give the guest a chance to read it if they want. The menu can provide information that helps make your operation unique in the market and offers an excellent way to tell guests of policies and priorities that are difficult to convey any other way.

Invariably, just as the guest is getting interested in the back story, a server snatches the menu away and leaves the guest empty-handed! If guests are reading the menus, leave it with them. Single diners will appreciate having something to read. The more familiar guests are with your menu, the more reasons they'll have to return.

Talking to the Order Pad

Coach your staff to look at the guests – not their pads – when taking the order! The habit is irritating because it makes your guests feel that understanding what they want is less important to you than the process of writing it down. This lack of focus on the guest works against the goal of creating personal connection.

Pointing at Each Guest with the Pen

Your guests are not at the table to perform for you. Unfortunately, this is the impression you give when you point at each guest with your pen when asking for their orders. The habit is annoying and makes the dining experience less personal.

Unlike verbal mistakes, pointing with the pen is an error others can detect from across the dining room. This also makes it easy for the managers to notice. Becoming aware that this unconscious habit can be irritating is an important first step toward breaking it.

Repeating Each Item as the Guest Orders

This is particularly annoying when you repeat the order as a question. Guest: *"I'd like the club sandwich, please."* Server: *"Club sandwich?"* Guest: *"... with a side of french fries."* Server: *"French fries?"* You sound like a broken record and it annoys your guests. If you're unsure what the guest said or meant, repeat the order back to them, but do it after they are finished ordering.

Naming Each Item as It's Served

No comment is necessary when you serve an item, but if you feel it appropriate to say something, pass along some information about the item or its preparation. Provided the statement is true, saying "The salmon came in fresh this morning and the dill in the sauce came from our own garden" can elevate a guest's mood and give everyone at the table a story to tell. Just saying "here's your salmon" gains you nothing.

Thumb on the Plate During Service

Serious lapses occur when you don't pay attention. A need for speed never justifies careless or unsanitary service. Many guests will not say anything about a thumb on the plate, but that doesn't mean they haven't noticed the error.

Rather than risk a confrontation with you, they'll talk about it to their friends. If the rest of the meal experience was marginal, a misplaced thumb could be the reason they start dining elsewhere. Hold plates with the side of the thumb, not the tip.

Addressing a Woman as "The Lady"

People are people, not objects ... so watch your words. Always talk to each guest individually and personally, regardless of gender or age. If the waiter says something like, "What would the lady like tonight?" it comes across as impersonal and contrived. Make eye contact and address her directly.

Loosening Caps on Condiment Bottles

I'm sure those who do this think the practice is a courtesy. Not so much. The problem comes when a guest instinctively gives the bottle a shake before using it. You won't pick up any points when Worcestershire splatters all over your dining room!

Scraping Dishes in Front of the Guests

Once you remove a plate from the table, whatever you scrape off it is automatically considered garbage. You wouldn't bring trash to the table at the beginning of the meal, so don't do it at the end. Handle your garbage in the kitchen and avoid creating a negative memory for your patrons.

Approaching a Table with Dirty Dishes in Hand

This is like shoving garbage in your guests' faces. How receptive do you think they will be to your skillful dessert dissertation if they are looking at the remains of someone else's lunch while you are talking? Never address a table unless your hands are clear and you are entirely focused on the guests.

Not Facing the Bills When Giving Change

This simply means all bills are face up and arranged in order of denomination. It is part of treating money with respect. A jumbled pile of currency makes the guest feel you are treating their money casually. Bear in mind that the change is *their* money until and unless they decide to leave some of it as a tip. Proper currency handling shows professionalism and people will feel more comfortable entrusting you with their cash.

Using Restaurant Jargon

Each restaurant has its own verbal shorthand. It means something to you but sounds like another language to others. You wouldn't address your English-speaking guests in Turkish, so why would speaking in jargon be any different?

For example, don't tell them you have a four-top by the window, just say you have a wonderful table with a view. If you say their Chick Sand is almost ready, they may think you are talking about women on the beach instead of a broiled chicken breast sandwich! You get the point. Using these phrases can be an unconscious habit until you become aware of your words.

Loud, Harsh or Grating Voices

Some diner concepts can get away with an abrasive style of service, but unless this is part of your operating identity, you'll lose points with your guests if the server's voice is not pleasant and well-modulated. The more relaxed the pace of the restaurant, the more refined the appropriate style of speech.

Holding Glasses by the Bowl or Rim

Never allow your crew handle a glass by the bowl or rim. It not only leaves fingerprints, but it's like sticking your fingers in the guest's mouth! Many diners will send back glasses if you handle them this way. You don't need the aggravation ... and neither do they. Train your staff to handle glassware only by the stem or the lower third.

Placing a Tray on the Table

If the tray is large, put it on a tray stand. Hold a cocktail tray in your hand. Remember the table is the guests' private domain. You have permission to enter with food and beverage, but they will resent your claiming a portion of their space by placing a tray on the table.

If the table is empty, it is still poor practice to place a tray down. Other guests may not feel the bottom of a tray is particularly clean and that placing it on the table dirties the table top. (It probably does!) Just use a tray stand and avoid the problem.

Entering Guests' Conversation Uninvited

If your guests want a buddy, they'll invite you over after work! If you overhear one person at the table say the Yankees won and you know that's wrong, resist the urge to correct them. If they want your opinion on something, they'll ask for it. By the way, knowing the game results can be an important plus if you have a sports-oriented clientele. Just don't offer information guests haven't requested.

Interrupting or Asking Questions
While the Guest's Mouth Is Full

This behavior is rude and can make your guests feel uncomfortable. If the restaurant is on fire, you have a duty to interrupt. Outside of that, there's nothing you have to say so important as to be worth potentially irritating your patrons.

When you approach a table actively engaged in conversation, it is far more respectful to stand there quietly until your guests stop talking and look at you. Then say what you need to say. If they ignore your presence, quietly move away and come back later.

Sweeping Crumbs Onto the Floor

If you only tell your staff to clear the table, this is what you may get. They must understand their responsibility to maintain the ambiance of the dining room. Crumbs on the floor will be a distraction to your guests for the rest of the evening and will lower their opinion of your restaurant. Eventually you must pick up the crumbs anyway.

Marvin's Law of Creative Laziness says to never do any more work than necessary to accomplish what you want. Why clean up the crumbs twice? If crumbs do get on the floor, use a carpet sweeper for a quick, quiet cleanup.

Leaning On or Over the Table

This habit may be seen as an invasion of privacy. You can safely reach slightly over the table to pick up a menu or serve a plate, provided you don't stay draped over the table. Leaning on the table at any time or for any reason is always a poor practice. Show your respect by not violating guests' airspace.

Placing a Bus Tub on the Table or Chair

The situation is similar to placing a tray on the table. Bus tubs full of soiled dishes and food scraps are not clean. Dining room guests may think placing a bus tub on the chair will make the chair dirty and they're probably right. Then they start to wonder about the chair *they* are sitting on. Avoid lowering your diners' security level. Keep bus tubs on a cart or tray stand.

Language That's Too Formal or Too Casual

Incongruence makes guests feel something is wrong, though they may not know what. We've discussed the value of consistency in the execution of a restaurant concept. Language is another element of that consistency. The language expectations are different in a burger joint than they are at a white tablecloth restaurant. The more formal the operation, the more formal the language expected.

Handling Silverware by the Eating Surface

All guests notice this bad habit. Improper silverware handling can put your guests in fear for their health. Whether there is a real basis for their concerns or not, they may just decide not to chance it and take their business elsewhere. Thoroughly coach your staff on correct (and safe) way to handle all serviceware.

Not Serving Everything from a Tray

People carry plates to the table in their hands at home. To make dining out a more distinct experience from eating at home, trays are a good place to start. The way it looks to your guests, trays are clean and professional while carrying plates by hand or stacked up the arm is unclean and amateurish.

Fingers Inside Glasses, Cups or Bowls

We've discussed the dangers of fingers on the plates when serving the table. Proper handling of cups, glasses and bowls is even more critical. Mishandling these items places the fingers on a surface the guest may put in their mouth. Proper handling is essential when setting (and clearing) the table.

You can remove glasses faster when you put your fingers inside them, but then what? Other guests don't know if you washed your hands before you picked up their clean serviceware. How realistic is it to think you'll wash your hands in the middle of every clear and reset cycle? Guests are far more sensitive to poor sanitation practices than you may realize.

Not Bringing Enough Change for the Tip

While it's poor form to assume a tip, it is also reasonable to be prepared for one. If a guest chooses to leave a cash tip, they will appreciate having the proper change to do it. It is embarrassing to have to ask for change for a $20 bill. It slows down the guest and requires an extra trip to the table for the service staff. When bringing change to a guest, consider what the guest is likely to need for a tip and structure the change that way.

Telling Guests How to Order

It is not the place of the server to dictate how the order will be taken, particularly if the guests have other wishes. When serving large parties, it is often helpful to ask permission to start at one end of the table and take the orders in sequence. The important point is to ask permission first and be open to alternatives. Dictating to your guests will only build resentment that can interfere with their enjoyment of your restaurant.

Asking a Man for the Woman's Order

Perhaps you could get away with this fifty years ago, but now this disrespect is sure to offend female diners. Treat all guests as equals, regardless of age, sex or physical condition. Anything less can just create more problems than you are ready to handle.

Moving Condiments Directly from One Table to Another

If a table wants ketchup, get it from the service stand, not from the next table. It may appear more responsive but your guests won't see it that way. The table that just "lost" their ketchup feels diminished (you've taken something away from them) and the table you give it to will feel uneasy to get a "used" product.

For whatever it says of human nature, guests feel items coming from the service stand are clean, safe and acceptable. They view items taken from another table with suspicion and are uneasy when it happens, perhaps because they don't have the same level of trust with the stranger in the next booth.

Taking Men's Orders First

Proper etiquette is to handle service in the following order: children first (since they won't wait), women, elders then gentlemen. If the guests want to give you their orders in a different sequence, don't argue about it. Serve the entrees in the same order if you can. Some guests may consider it rude to alter this sequence.

Fussing over a Single Diner

Single diners are people who just happen to be dining alone at the moment. They usually appreciate a little more personal attention from the service staff, but making a fuss only embarrasses them. Be sensitive to their signals. Give unaccompanied diners the care and respect they deserve and you can gain a loyal regular guest.

Frustrating Focus

Focus is another name for presence. Presence is simply the absence of distractions. High presence makes others feel well-served, but when you are distracted – when your mind is on something else – the people you are with become annoyed. It's as simple as that.

Have you ever had a conversation with someone who was doing something else while you were talking? Even though they may have heard everything you said, how did their lack of attention make you feel? My guess is that found the experience irritating.

It is no different in the restaurant. If the service staff is thinking of something else while the guest is talking to them, the guest feels ignored. They may not understand why, but their experience will be that the service was not good and they will be in no hurry to return.

When managers clutter their staff's minds with rules ("The 6¾ Steps of Good Service"), they sow the seeds of their own destruction. If a sales person is thinking about the "6¾ Steps," they cannot focus on the guest. Even if they followed all those steps" to the letter, the guest wouldn't experience good service ... and certainly not hospitality.

On the other hand, lack of distraction produces the feeling of being well-served in spite of the circumstances. When a staff member has high presence, the "6¾ Steps" are irrelevant. Here are some variations on this theme to help you better understand the point I'm making. The same distracted state of mind is behind all of these problems.

Not Having Total Focus When at the Table

When your mind is somewhere else, it's impossible to give good service. Distraction in the server creates irritation in the guest. It is the feeling of glib insincerity you get when a server is mouthing words and you know they're thinking about something that has nothing to do you and your needs.

When you are at the table talking with guests, there is nothing you can do about bringing coffee to Table 17, emptying the bus tub or making an appointment with the dentist. Don't allow these thoughts to be distractions. It will cost you dearly.

Too Hurried to Be Attentive

Guest satisfaction comes from the quality, not the duration, of the contact. You will find a good example of what I mean on Page 138. When you're distracted, others feel unheard and will continue to dog you until they feel you actually got what they were saying. On the other hand, if you slow down, clear your mind and give the other person your total attention, the result is amazing.

Not Really Listening When Spoken to

Talking to someone who is not listening will create rage in even the most reasonable person. Any time you are talking with a guest, drop all other thoughts from your mind. Hear what they are saying, but pay particular attention to how they are saying it. The real message is always in the tone of voice.

Not Establishing Rapport with the Guests

Rapport is that warm human feeling of connection that comes easily when you are in an undistracted state of mind. To help establish rapport with your guests, take a deep breath and pause as you approach the table. Drop whatever else is on your mind, focus on the guests and wait for them to look up at you.

When they make eye contact, smile. Let yourself be touched by the opportunity to "make their day." Say what you have to say, find out what you need to know, smile and go on your way. This takes no longer than the scattered approach you see every day. The results, however, are dramatically different.

Operating in this manner, you keep perspective and control of your station. You'll hardly notice events others would see as crises. You easily handle your job in a relaxed and professional manner.

Inconsistent Service

You may have noticed some restaurants seem to have "good days" and "bad days"... but did you ever wonder why? Good days happen when the staff has nothing much on their minds except delighting the guests. Bad days are most apt to happen when the staff is so distracted they don't connect with anyone or each other. Your place will always reflect the state of mind of the person at the top, so if your crew is starting to lose it, look in the mirror.

The Feeling of Being "Processed"

Guests get this feeling when you do all the mechanical steps correctly but fail to connect with your guests on a human level. Coach your staff about the difference between hospitality and service, focus on the results you want and give as much latitude as possible to allow people to achieve those results in their own way.

Appearing Stressed or Out of Control

Lack of focus causes the events of your life to look overwhelming and you easily find yourself "in the weeds." As we discussed earlier, feeling stressed or out-of-control is just a symptom of a busy mind. When you learn to drop distractions, you automatically start to take things more in stride. There are no skills to learn. Events will just look different to you. You will instinctively know what to do.

The first step toward dropping distraction is simply to become aware of your busy mind. When you find your mind cluttered with thoughts or you feel yourself getting stressed, recognize what is happening. Relax, take a deep breath clear your head and get on with your day. If you don't take your own thinking too seriously, you will be on your way to greater control of your life.

Not Informing Guests of Service Delays

Focus makes you more naturally empathetic. As such, you are more likely to be sensitive to your guests' experience. You're more likely to want your guests to know of any delays in preparation or service because you know it matters to them. The details that are important to your guests become important you.

Being Insensitive to Guests' Needs

Every guest has special needs. Some are more obvious than others. The handicapped or the elderly may need special care. Teenagers and families have their own problems and priorities. Business guests need a different style of service than romantic couples. Groups celebrating a special occasion want a festive experience.

There are so many possibilities that you may feel overwhelmed. Relax. If you're undistracted and empathetic, you will instinctively do what works. All it takes is a focus on pleasing your guests and a clear mind.

> **TRUTH IS STRANGER THAN FICTION**
>
> Awhile ago I got the craving for a really great hot turkey sandwich. A local diner prided itself on real mashed potatoes and I figured if I'd find a world class hot turkey sandwich anywhere in town, this would surely be the place.
>
> I could already taste the thick slabs of freshly sliced turkey breast as I ordered, but when the sandwich arrived, it was made with some sort of shredded turkey-like product covered in a pale gravy that was more like library paste!
>
> The waitress came back a few minutes later to inquire about my meal. I told her the sandwich was not at all what I expected and I was very disappointed.
>
> "Yeah," she said. "A lot of people tell us that," and just walked away!

Spacing Out a Guest's Request

Poor memory is a symptom of lack of focus. When your thinking is scattered, write it down. Otherwise you'll try to think of everything at once and end up forgetting it all. Give your mind a break. Efficiency comes from lack of distraction not from increased activity. If your goal is to assure your guests have an enjoyable experience, keep your head clear and you're less likely to get behind, making it easy to handle changes and snags as they come up.

Doing Your Work at the Table

Never do anything at the table not for the benefit of the guests. Add up checks in the service stand, not on the table. Do you expect your guests to stop their conversation and just watch quietly while you take care of other business? Your inconsiderate behavior will only make them think less of the meal, the service and the restaurant.

103

Poor Policies

Many service problems arise from well-intentioned but misguided company policies. It puts your staff in an awkward position when they have to defend policies that stand in the way of guest gratification. If they displease you, they could lose their jobs. If they displease their guests, they go against all their instincts.

The only way out of this dilemma is to make pleasing the guest the most important job in the restaurant. Period. Give your staff the authority to do what they need to do to assure your guests have a memorable dining experience. Making sure guests enjoy themselves is the most important job in the restaurant.

Not Bringing the Full One Before
Removing the Empty One

This is such a simple touch, yet so often overlooked. If you take the empty one away before you return with the full one, guests will feel deprived for a period. There's an empty spot where the item used to be. Reverse the order of the tasks. You'll do the same amount of work but show far more sensitivity to the guests, an awareness that creates another point of difference from your competition.

Failure to Promptly Resolve a Complaint
(In Favor of the Guest!)

If you are serious about guest gratification, there is no negotiation when if comes to a guest complaint. The only approach that will work is to apologize for the situation and fix it immediately. Don't ask the guest what they want you to do – it puts them on the spot and makes them uncomfortable.

When you understand the nature and source of the problem, propose an overly generous solution that will make the guest happy. Remember that you're not just solving a problem, you are making an investment in securing a regular patron.

Stacking Plates up the Arm
to Carry Them to the Table

Many diner-style concepts and coffee shops use this operating style. The look may be traditional, but when the bottom of a plate sits on top of the guest's food, the novelty quickly fades.

If you are going to use this approach, coach your service staff that sanitation considerations are as important as how many plates they can carry in one trip. It is preferable to make an additional trip than to alienate guests because they feel you have soiled their food.

"Do-It-Yourself" Doggie Bags

If you pack your guests' leftovers for them to take home, do it with the same care and attention you show to everything else in the restaurant. I've seen servers simply leave a container or bag on the table and expect guests to do it themselves. Some guests may ask for it that way, but absent a specific request, this a practice developed for the convenience of the staff instead of the convenience of the guest. Stamp out this short-sightedness before it puts you out of business. Don't ask your guests to handle their own leftovers.

Adding a Tip to the Credit Card Slip

A brewpub in Park City, Utah had the nerve to do this to me ... once. They will never get a second chance. If a guest signs the credit card receipt, does not indicate a tip and leaves the slip untotalled, that's the luck of the draw. If you add a tip yourself, you've put your hand in their wallet without permission and likely lost them forever.

Even if the cardholder intended to leave a tip and just forgot to do so (like me!), they will not forgive your arrogance. If you feel it was an honest oversight, have the house tip the server. It will cost you far less than alienating a potential regular guest.

Slow Morning Coffee Service

Most Americans need a cup of coffee or tea to start the day off right. If guests get their coffee promptly, they will wait for the rest of the meal service more patiently. How you address this need depends on your operating style.

If your sales staff cannot keep up with it, perhaps the bussers could fill coffee cups. You might place insulated carafes on the table to take the pressure off. Whatever you do, find a way to get a hot cup of coffee (or tea) to your breakfast guests right away. You will have happier guests.

Confusing Service Format

A team service format can be effective, provided you explain it to your guests at the beginning of the meal. Without a clear idea of what is happening, having several service staff at the table can be confusing and lead to lower tips.

In a team service restaurant I had three staff members ask me the same question. I gave the same answer to all three and none of them filled my request! I didn't know who to be upset with or who to tip. If you use a team service format, be sure your guests understand how it works and have one person to look to if there's a problem.

105

No Fresh Fork for Entree or Dessert

You don't set the table with dirty utensils, why would you hand a dirty fork back to a guest and ask them to reuse it? The easiest approach is to have enough forks in the place setting to begin with. You may prefer the look of presenting the fork with the dessert. In any event, don't ask the guest to reuse a soiled utensil. Some guests will ask for a fresh fork; others will just remember it wasn't a memorable meal and go elsewhere next time.

Failure to Honor Menu Prices

You must honor whatever it says on your menu. I don't agree with the practice, but some places charge less for an item at lunch than they do at dinner. If you give a guest the wrong menu by mistake, honor the prices. You can never win those arguments.

Not Advising the Guest of a Service Charge

If you impose a service charge instead of voluntary tipping, courtesy requires you to note this on your menu and on your guest check. I also recommend you have your service staff verbally inform your guests of the policy.

If a guest feels they were not properly notified, they may suspect a ploy to gain a double tip. It may work once, but when your guests find out what happened (and they will), they will feel cheated. You can't cheat a person and expect to keep their business.

Not Making a Fuss for Special Occasions

If you are going to help guests celebrate a birthday or anniversary, then celebrate it! Decorate the table. Have candles or sparklers on the [preferably complimentary] cake. Sing a special song instead of falling back on the stale standards. Make the celebration tasteful and appropriate to the mood of your dining room, but celebrate ... unless, of course, the guest wants to stay low key. (Ask first!)

Glass Coffee Pots in Upscale Restaurants

In coffee shops and casually-themed restaurants, guests expect coffee from the standard glass pots. As the check average climbs, though, a more formal presentation is appropriate. Make your coffee service a point of difference and you can give your guests another reason to think of you any time they dine elsewhere.

Three-Foot Peppermills

Perhaps oversized peppermills were unique in the 60's, but they're quaint today (and who wants to use something that arrived tucked into a waiter's sweaty armpit?). The idea of offering fresh ground pepper is still a nice touch but think about your presentation.

How about small salt and pepper mills on the tables? If you must bring the monster, perhaps it could contain white pepper or some other uncommon variety of the spice. Re-think this practice and see if you can give it a fresh twist (pun intended!)

Failure to Accommodate Special Requests

In his book *It's Not My Department*, author Peter Glen offers a simple approach to special requests. He suggests you find out what people want, find out how they want it ... then give it to them just that way! (Duh!) People with special needs will give their business to those restaurants who can meet them.

Refusing to Heat a Baby's Food or Bottle

If guest service is your most important job, then service your guests. Warming baby food or formula is a simple task. There is no reason to treat a parent's request for this service as an imposition. If there are very young children at the table, offer this accommodation to the parents before they ask. They will recognize your caring whether or not they need the service.

Coaching Concerns

While all the points in this chapter are legitimately management's responsibility and therefore coaching concerns, some are more clearly so than others. As a manager, your job could easily become finding and correcting faults. That makes you a cop. If you approach your job like a coach, the job becomes discovering and developing the strengths of your staff. The shift is subtle but it will make all the difference in helping your crew recognize and correct these annoyances.

Inability to Answer Basic Menu Questions

Guests want to know about your food and you must be able to tell them. Thoroughly train the service staff so they can knowledgeably discuss recipe ingredients and preparation methods. If they know some interesting story about the dish, even better.

This information has the most impact when it comes from personal experience rather than a memorized list. This means your servers must have actually tasted everything on the menu and watched how each is prepared.

Make it like staging a television cooking demonstration. Include managers, greeters, cocktail staff and bussers in the classes. You never know who a guest will ask. Money invested in these training meals for your staff will pay regular dividends.

No Alternatives to Sold-Out Items

When you've sold out of an item, the situation is already awkward. You only make it worse if you do not suggest alternatives. How is the guest supposed to know what else they can order? Make a suggestion and you won't place them in an uncomfortable position.

Not Removing Extra Place Settings

Don't have anything on the table the guest doesn't need, including extra place settings. If you don't remove extra settings, guests may wonder what is going to happen with the place setting after they leave. Will it just stay there for the next diner? If that worry enters their mind, they may start to wonder about their own silverware.

Clumsy Handling of Credit Cards

When you deal with a guest's credit card, you have your hand in their wallet, a position of trust requiring you take particular care to avoid making the guest uneasy. Be sure all staff knows and follows proper procedures for handling credit card purchases.

It is equally crucial to handle the card itself with respect. This means never leaving a credit card unattended or handling it casually. A credit card is essentially a blank check on your guest's account. Make sure your behavior shows patrons you take that responsibility – and their trust – seriously.

Not Serving Children or Elders First

Serve children first. They have not developed social graces and will not wait their turn. Serve women next starting with the eldest. Finally, serve the men, older gentlemen first and the host last. The arrangement of the table or the size of the party may dictate a different order of service, but come as close as you can.

"Canned" Communications

Scripted communication is worse than no communication at all. Guest enjoyment is created by the human dimension in service, not the mechanical content. You need to communicate certain points to the guest at various times during the meal, but the real message is always in your tone of voice and the warm human connection you can establish with them.

After some basic skill training, it is usually more effective to specify the desired ends and leave the specific means to the discretion of the service staff. This allows them to be themselves and respond more appropriately to what the guests want. Anything less is about as satisfying as making love through an interpreter!

Serving with the Elbow in the Guest's Face

Serving from the left and clearing from the right is the preferred standard, but if you serve from the left with your right hand or from the right with your left, it puts your elbow in the guest's face. For smoother service, just be sure to use your left hand when serving from the left and your right hand when serving from the right.

Pushy Sales Techniques

Skillful suggestions can help guests have a more enjoyable evening, but give an insensitive, memorized sales pitch and you'll sound like a huckster and irritate your diners. The goal is to make people eager to buy, not to attempt to forcefully sell them something. The less distracted you are while at the table, the more personal and effective your check-building efforts will be.

Clattering Dishes

A professional restaurant staff doesn't call attention to themselves or detract from the guests' enjoyment of the meal. Clattering dishes are usually a sign of an over-eager busser who doesn't understand their behavior forms a part of the overall dining experience. Reset tables as quickly as possible, but never at the expense of diner enjoyment. Show bussers what to do and coach them on why the way they do it makes a difference.

No Suggestions or Recommendations

Your mission is to help your guests have a good time. Part of that is informing them of the unique and exciting choices your restaurant offers. If you don't tell them, how are they going to know? Even the most well-written menu is a poor substitute for an enthusiastic and knowledgeable personal suggestion.

Always offer two alternatives when making a recommendation to avoid appearing like you are pushing an item. If the guest wants something other than what you suggest, they'll ask about it. The important point is that they feel comfortable during the process.

Filling a Doggie Bag or Box at the Table

Never scape food off a plate at the table ... it makes it seem like garbage. Take the plate to the kitchen, place the leftovers neatly in the bag and bring a tidy package back to the table. Respect your food and your guests will do the same.

Napkins or Plates with the Logo Askew

Always place a customized item with the restaurant's logo facing the guest. Haphazard placement only shows a lack of concentration and inattention to detail. Guests may not always notice when you do it properly, but they'll always notice when you are sloppy.

No Prices for Oral Specials

Just because you recite the daily specials does not mean the price information isn't important. If you find it awkward to mention prices, complete the presentation by handing guests a small menu with the day's specials and their prices. This also will help them remember what you said when they make their dinner choices.

Inconsistent Service Methods

People are creatures of habit, and feel more comfortable when they know what to expect. Toward this end, always approach the table from the same position and always serve and clear from the same sides. Whether that is the classic "serve from the left, clear from the right" or not is less important to smooth service than consistency.

Not Warning of Hot Plates or Beverages

Refilling the coffee cup is part of good service, but make sure the guest is aware you've done it. If not, you take the chance they will burn their mouth on a cup of coffee that is suddenly much hotter than expected.

Ask permission before refilling the coffee, too, particularly if the guest uses cream and sugar. It is annoying to alter the balance of the cup when your guest has it adjusted just the way they like it.

Hot plates are a different issue because in a great restaurant, hot plates are the rule. If you can hold a plate of hot food without a towel, the plate is not hot enough to keep the food at temperature. Serving hot food hot requires hot plates. Make sure you do it and make sure your guests know you are doing it.

Not Moving With the "Speed of the Room"

Good service is almost invisible. Guests should only notice what is going on at their table and not be distracted by other movements around them. If you are moving fast in a slow-paced dining room, you will be a distraction. The same is true if you are moving slowly in a fast-paced room.

The speed at which you move from place to place is different from the speed at which you do your job. You can still be very quick and efficient in a slower-moving dining room. Your movements just take on a different quality.

The process is like the martial arts master whose power comes from a state of focused relaxation. If you can move with the speed of the room, you can give responsive service and your guests will hardly notice you are there.

Serving a Bowl Without an Underliner

Bowls hold liquids and liquids often spill. The only question is whether the spill will fall on the underliner or on the table! If it falls on the underliner (after it has been served), no problem. If it falls on the table, it affects the guest's enjoyment of the meal and creates a cleaning problem. Give everyone a break and make underliners standard practice in your restaurant.

Dropping Plates vs. Presenting Them

You show your respect for the work of your kitchen staff by the way you handle their food. Train your staff to *present* the plates at the table. Place plates in front of the guest with respect, entrees closest to the diner. If there is a logo on the plate, be sure it faces the guest. If you distribute the plates like you are dealing a hand of cards, expect your guests to be less enthusiastic about their meals.

Not Knowing the Brands at the Bar

How often can you say "I don't know" before you feel stupid? Basic service staff training must include a thorough knowledge of the bar operation. This includes knowing the brands you carry and the ingredients of your specialty drinks. If you have signature drinks (and I recommend you do), be sure your staff has tasted them and can describe them in an appetizing and accurate way.

Not Warning about Potential Food Hazards

There may be some legal implications in this point but it is just common courtesy to advise your guests of potential hazards in your menu items. For example, "boneless" fish could still contain some bones. If there is a potential hazard, you are only being polite when you alert your guests to it.

Not Bringing All Necessary Serviceware

A bowl of soup without a soup spoon is useless. If you forget, the soup will be cooling while you find a spoon and return to the table. Meanwhile, all your guest can do is sit there staring at the bowl and feeling awkward. As with condiments, it can be helpful to bring the necessary serviceware before you serve the item. This way you can be sure guests can eat hot food while it is still hot.

Not Checking Back Within Two Bites

If there is a problem with the entree or if the guest needs anything, they may not know that when you first serve the item. So, asking if they need anything else at the time of service is not the end of it. After two bites, the guests will know what they think of the food and what they may need to go with it. Give them a minute and then return to ask if everything is prepared the way they expected.

111

Not Regularly Scanning Your Station

The situation on your station can change quickly. A rapid visual check will provide eye contact with any guest who is trying to get your attention and allow you to identify new parties that have been seated since you left. If a guest is trying to get your attention and feels ignored because you don't notice, they will become irritated. Irritated guests seldom tip well or become regular patrons.

Clearing Before All Guests Are Finished

Many people eat slowly. It is embarrassing to them, and the others at the table, when they are the only ones left with a plate in front of them. I'm sure there are well-intentioned motives to remove a guest's plate as soon as they finish but be aware the practice places more pressure on those who are still eating. If a guest wants their plate removed, they'll let you know. Otherwise, it is always more considerate to wait and clear the entire table at once.

Uncleared Tables

The most attractive decor in a dining room is butts on chairs, not dirty dishes on tables. The problem is more irritating if the staff is taking a break while the condition persists. The excuse I often hear is that the rush just ended. If so, why isn't the dining room staff busy clearing tables? When the rush is over, the amateurs take a break. Pros get the place reloaded for the next rush, *then* take a break.

Not Clearing One Course
Before Serving the Next

You can't serve a meal gracefully if you're trying to set a plate down with one hand while you slide another out of the way with the other. Besides, nobody wants to look at soiled plates and fresh food in the same glance.

Once the table finishes a course, remove everything from that course. If they need a particular item later in the meal service, bring it back at the appropriate time. A clean table makes guests feel more comfortable with the meal service and the restaurant itself.

Having to Ask for Basic Condiments

Have salt and pepper on the table before seating the guests because they are likely to want these items throughout the early stages of the meal and it is impolite to make them have to ask. In most cases you can remove salt and pepper when you clear the entrees.

During the breakfast period, you'll want to have sugar on the table. At lunch and dinner you can create a small point of difference by bringing cream and sugar just before you serve the coffee. Don't waste time asking, just do it.

Refilling Water or Coffee after Each Sip

This annoyance happens when you've only told bussers to keep the water or coffee full. If they are eager to please, they will do just what you told them and do it aggressively. They need to develop a sense of what makes a good dining experience and understand how their job functions fit into that.

Clearing Plates Without Permission

You are there to enhance the guest's experience, not intrude on it. It is only common respect not to take anything away from the guest without their permission, particularly something as personal as their dinner plate. And don't reach for the plate as you are asking the question. Your eagerness and lack of sensitivity will cost you points.

That said, nobody likes to linger over soiled plates once they are through eating. As the last diner finishes, pause a few beats, make eye contact with the host for the OK, then quickly clear the table. The pause is important to prevent guests from feeling rushed.

Vanishing Waiters

Why can't you ever find a waiter when you want one? Most restaurant guests have had this frustration. The best defense is a good offense. Make a visual check of each table at your station every time you re-enter the dining room. If you take a break while you still have occupied tables, be sure someone else watches your station.

Even if your shift is over and you must leave while you still have occupied tables, don't just walk out. Thank your guests for their patronage, introduce the person who will see to their needs and reassure them the quality of their evening is in good hands.

The problem of disappearing waiters is particularly acute when the guest is trying to settle the check and be on their way. If you need an incentive, recall that this is when guests are deciding how much of a tip to leave. Don't blow it at the end!

Not Servicing the Table
After Presenting the Check

The meal isn't over when you place the change on the table. Service doesn't end until guests have left the building. They may need more coffee. They may decide to order after-dinner drinks. Anything could happen and your job is to stay alert so you can be there to handle it smoothly.

Sometime between the check presentation and when the guest gets up to leave is when they decide how much of a tip to leave. If there are still guests at the table, you're still on stage. Stay in character.

All Dollar Bills as Change

If you appear to be angling for a tip, you may irritate your guests. Make it as easy as possible for them to leave a reasonable tip but don't overdo it. The exception to this rule is when you make change for a blind guest. In that case, return only singles to reassure them they have the proper change.

Watching the Guest Complete
the Credit Card Slip

The tip is a personal decision. If you give the impression you're looking over the guest's shoulder, you have invaded their privacy. The sensation of being spied upon is extremely uncomfortable and gives the impression you're trying to rush the guest or pressure them to leave you more money – not good thoughts to implant while they are deciding your tip.

Not Thanking Guests When They Leave

Gratitude is powerful. All things being equal, people go businesses that appreciate their patronage. Thanking guests as they leave is not just courtesy, it is an investment in their future loyalty. When guests feel you are sincerely grateful for their business, they feel better about giving it to you. Gratitude is so uncommon that your guests will remember your appreciation and return for more.

Professional Problems

The next few items relate to the skill and knowledge of your service staff. Physical skills develop only with practice. Do not allow staff to serve your guests until they have been thoroughly trained and have mastered the basic knowledge and skills of their trade.

Dribbling Wine on the Table When Pouring

Proper wine service is smooth and unobtrusive. Dribbling wine is both annoying and unnecessary. Train your staff to roll the bottle slightly at the end of the pour to cause that last drop to stay on the rim of the bottle, not the table top.

As a further note, skill in opening and pouring wine only comes with practice. Ask your wine supplier to help you find a supply of foil caps so your staff can practice foil cutting. An "Ah-So" wine opener will allow you to re-cork the bottles for re-tries.

Drill your crew until they are confident in their abilities to handle wine service smoothly. The more comfortable they are with the process, the more likely they are to suggest wine to your guests.

Touching a Wine Bottle to the Rim of the Glass

It is bad form to touch the wine glass with the bottle. The outside of the bottle is not necessarily clean and many guests are sensitive to what touches surfaces from which they eat or drink. This is a simple training problem that may be caused by the server being unaware of their actions or trying to avoid dripping wine on the table.

Asking Guests to Help with the Service

People don't come to your restaurant to serve themselves. If you need help, ask another staff member. Do whatever it takes to make the service as smooth as possible for your guests. After the shift, turn this into a learning opportunity. Sit down with the crew and discuss what led to the need for the guest to get involved. Then determine what action, if any, is needed to avoid future repetitions.

Incorrect Change

If you return the wrong amount of change, guests may think you're either incompetent or trying to cheat them. Neither conclusion will work to your benefit. To be safe, coach your staff on proper cash handling procedures. Be sure they are clear on how much money the guest gave them. Train them how to count the change when they take it out of the drawer.

If you have a cashier, be sure she counts the change again when she hands it to the guest. If counting back change at the table would be distracting, fan the bills slightly and place the change on top so the guest can quickly be see you've returned the correct change. You can't be too careful when handling your guests' money.

Little Knowledge of Community Attractions

Newcomers to the area want good "inside advice" about where to go and what to do. It is helpful when all your staff can respond knowledgeably to these questions. Contact your local Chamber of Commerce or Visitors Bureau for information on events, attractions and activities. Update your crew at your daily pre-shift meeting. Remember the longer a visitor stays in town, the more opportunities they will have to dine at your restaurant.

Spilling Food or Beverage

Sloppiness is the sign of a distracted server in a rush. Part of the job of management is to help the service staff maintain their composure. If a staff member is getting buried "in the weeds," give them a hand and take some pressure off. Spilling food or drink is unprofessional and you can usually avoid it. If an accident occurs, try to take it in stride. Apologize, quickly and quietly, clean up any mess and continue the meal service. Don't get dramatic about the incident.

If you spill something on a guest, immediately make it right. Give them more than enough cash to cover the cost of cleaning, and something extra (like a dessert or after-dinner drink) to make up for the inconvenience. I also recommend a gift certificate for the next time they visit the restaurant. It is a generous gesture and improves the odds they will return to give you another chance.

Wet, Stained or Mis-Added Checks

Be sure everything you place on the table reflects the care and professionalism you want guests to associate with your restaurant. Messy food checks are the mark of an uncaring amateur.

Not Knowing How to Handle
Advertised Specials or Coupons

Special promotions are an effective way to create excitement and generate new business for the restaurant, but if people respond to an advertised offer and nobody knows what they're talking about, it creates an unpleasant situation for everyone.

Since (hopefully) many people responding to your special offer will be first-timers, they won't know if you are incompetent or just confused. In either case, it's not a desirable first impression. Be sure to train your staff thoroughly on the content, goals and procedures of your promotions *before* you advertise them.

Losing or Damaging a Credit Card

When you handle a guest's credit card, you are toying with their money. If you damage the card, they won't have access to their funds until they can get a replacement card. That's hard enough for local residents, but if your guests are from out of the area, the problem even is more serious. Vacationers who lose the use of their credit card may not be able to continue their holiday.

You must make a management decision about how to handle this situation if it occurs. Work out your plan of action now, not in the emotion of the moment. You may offer to cash a check so they can continue their vacation until a new card arrives. Take responsibility for finding a solution that works for them.

Cafeteria Calamities

Just because an operation has a self service format doesn't eliminate the need to provide exceptional guest service. Remember that it *is* possible to be the restaurant of choice ... even if your patrons don't have another choice. All it takes is the same service orientation we have been discussing. Here are some details to avoid:

Inattentive Line Workers

All the attributes of good table service apply in a cafeteria; only the context changes. The game is still about personal connection. This means the staff must be mentally present and listen carefully to the guests be sure they understand and respect any special requests. It will also build business – and make the shift more enjoyable – when the staff can relate to those in line as individuals rather than simply the next to be served.

Awkward Replenishing of Buffets

I was at a Thanksgiving buffet at a major new hotel. Since I hate lines, I waited until the main surge had gone through the buffet line before going up for my meal.

I was the last person in line when an overzealous staff member cut in front of me to replenish and rearrange the buffet line. I asked if she could let me go through before she continued but she ignored me. I stood there with hot food on my plate for several minutes while this thoughtless individual finished her work and left. Unless someone decides to buy my meal, I won't be back.

Pouring Old Product on Top of New

This is another bad habit developed for the convenience of the staff. It is dangerous – and repulsive to informed guests – because it is blatant cross-contamination. If the older product is tainted, it will contaminate the fresh product. Avoid it.

Present items in small quantities. Attend your line constantly so you can *replace* containers at once when they get low. Your line will look better, your guests will be happier and your food will be safer.

Unsupervised Buffets or Salad Bars

The major complaint against salad bars is that they're unsanitary. Some of the people you serve are very sensitive to this issue and some are unconscious. Children are proven violators of salad bar etiquette. They will stick their fingers in the dressing to taste it or nibble at something then put it back. They will refill a dirty salad bowl and spread your salads all over the floor. (As you may have noticed, children come in all ages and sizes!)

Unless you supervise the salad bar closely, these practices will drive away many of your guests. You also run the risk of passing a food borne illness to the ones you don't scare off.

A successful salad bar has a knowledgeable staff member constantly supervising. Display items in small quantities and allow them to run down before changing. Wipe up spills promptly. A great salad bar has striking presentation and that doesn't happen accidentally.

Not Changing Utensils When
Changing Food Containers

Always bring clean serving utensils when replacing food containers. If you place a soiled spoon back into crock of fresh product, that's cross-contamination again. Your guests will appreciate the gesture.

It is also annoying to use a serving utensil that has food smeared on the handle from a previous patron. Replace soiled utensils with clean ones, don't just wipe them off. It is more professional and increases your guests' confidence in your operation.

What you thought was trivial turns out to be monumental in the minds of the guests who don't come back!

118

6

Become a Place Of Hospitality

Become a Place of Hospitality

> "Hospitality exists when you believe the other person is on your side. The converse is just as true. Hospitality is present when something happens FOR you. It is absent when something happens TO you. Those two simple prepositions — for and to — express it all."
>
> —Danny Meyer, CEO, Union Square Hospitality Group

Hospitality Is Doing What Is Unexpected ... and Uniquely Personal to that Guest in that Moment

Read the quotation above. Does Danny Meyer's notion of hospitality make a difference?

Consider this: in the annual Zagat diner survey, out of 18,000 restaurants in New York City (22,000 counting pizzerias), the five fine dining concepts owned by Union Square Hospitality Group are consistently in the top twenty.

Even more amazing is that their Union Square Café has been voted the Most Popular Restaurant in New York City every year since 1997 ... except for when the top spot went to the Gramercy Tavern, another of USHG's restaurants, and Union Square Café "slipped" to #2!

Danny is the first to point out that none of his operations have ever been voted Best Food or Best Service, but when people are asked to name their favorite restaurant, for sixteen years straight he has taken the top two spots ... in arguably the toughest and most demanding restaurant market in the country! Unbelievable!

The message here is a clear testament to the power of hospitality:

To be exceptionally successful, you don't have to be the best at everything you do

You just have to be the favorite restaurant of the people you do it for

121

What Is Hospitality?

People in the foodservice and lodging industries like to say they're in the hospitality business, but what exactly is hospitality? Look it up and you'll find definitions like these:

- *Generously providing care and kindness to whoever is in need.*
- *The reception and entertainment of guests, visitors or strangers with liberality and goodwill.*
- *Receiving and treating strangers and guests in a warm, friendly, generous manner.*

Technically accurate, but do any of these definitions make you feel warm and fuzzy? They speak to what a hospitable person might DO, but that's just service. These actions are certainly *indicative* of hospitality, but just performing the tasks will not provide the *experience* of hospitality.

By way of example, are you now or have you ever been in love? Quite probably. Could you describe love to another person in such a way that they would be in love when you finish? Probably not. You know the *feeling* of love, you can see it in others, yet it is impossible to put into words. But once you experience it for yourself, you know.

Hospitality is love applied in a different context

Because they are rigidly systematized, franchise operations deliver product with consistent efficiency but usually without the experience of hospitality. Perhaps that's all their patrons expect, but impersonal efficiency leaves guests with a flat feeling – they have been fed but not nurtured. It's like a relationship without love and passion.

Just as you can't fake love, you cannot pretend hospitality – everyone recognizes a lack of genuine caring. That's roughly equivalent to the problem you face if you simply tell your staff to be hospitable and expect that will be enough to make it happen.

In many ways, hospitality is out of control. It is a personal expression of the humanity of the provider, not a rigid set of actions. You recognize it when you experience it and yet you really can't define what it is any more than you can adequately define your love for your parents, your mate or your children. You can talk about what you do for them or how they make you *feel*, but that can't duplicate the feeling in another person.

Recognizing Hospitality

As we have said, you really can't define the feeling of hospitality, but it does have several recognizable characteristics:

Respect
Guests (and co-workers) are treated with esteem for their worth and excellence as people

Presence
The staff is AT the table when they are at the table; no distractions

Responsive
Complaints are quickly resolved in favor of the guest

Personal
Guests are addressed by name; their likes and dislikes are known and respected

Non-Judgmental
Guests are never made to feel wrong; they always receive the benefit of the doubt

Non-Intrusive
Just as good service is almost invisible, hospitality does not call attention to itself

Relaxed
There is no feeling of being rushed or processed; the staff never shows signs of stress

Personable
The staff is always smiling and friendly, even with unfriendly or irritable patrons

Perceptive
Guest needs are met before patrons even realize they had the need

Consistent
Guests leave feeling connected although the specific execution may differ each time

Appropriate
The service always perfectly fits the occasion

Uplifting
The experience makes guests feel more positive; they "pay it forward" to others

Surprising
The staff goes beyond basic job requirements to do something memorable for guests.

These are all positive points that may help you recognize the end result when you have it, but they're still not that end result. You can't just give this list to your staff and tell them to be this way.

So What Is Hospitality?

I'm sure you've patronized a restaurant where the feeling in the place just drew you in. Every team member genuinely and warmly welcomed you and naturally treated you in a warm and friendly manner. It was obvious that their great pleasure was to be in service to you. You *feel* it ... and it feels good.

These extraordinary spots make it possible to have a memorable dining experience. You are drawn to return and tell others. The difference is invisible and impossible to define, yet you know when you feel it and you know when you don't. That invisible "something," that spirit of hospitality, can be your compelling point of difference in an otherwise impersonal marketplace.

Perhaps the best way to describe hospitality is that it shows up as a *feeling* that is generated by the prevailing states of mind of the restaurant's leadership and staff. We call this the climate in the business. It is invisible. However, like the wind, you feel its effects.

The Bad News:
The spirit of hospitality is not something that can be taught in the same way you might teach a service sequence or job skills.

The Good News:
Tapping into that hospitality spirit is an innate capability of all human beings. You don't need to teach it, you only need to create and sustain a climate where it can naturally emerge and blossom.

STOP MARKETING, START CONNECTING

Nobody gets up in the morning with an insatiable urge to give you their money. When guests honor you with their patronage, it's because of what you do FOR them.

You provide food and drink, of course, but that is merely what they pay for ... what they rightfully expect. The WOW comes from what you do for them that they DON'T expect ... and the spirit with which you do it.

If you really want to grow your business and become known as a Place of Hospitality, look for ways you can *give* more. Do it with love and enthusiasm, just because it's fun to do.

When you give to others for the sheer joy of giving, they will happily reciprocate by giving you their loyalty and support.

While the ability to be hospitable is innate and unteachable, you *can* squash it! In fact, my work with clients is usually about showing them how to *not* get in the way of what they're trying to accomplish.

But the challenge remains. You know how to teach people what to DO. How can you teach them how to BE? For that, we have to look a little deeper into human behavior.

The Impact of Climate

People seem to think the source of their experience is in outside circumstances ("she made me happy" or "this business is tough.") In that way we're much like the magician's audience. When we watch the distracting hand, we experience the trick as magic. If we watch the other hand, we can often understand the trick and appreciate the skill of the misdirection.

The source of the feeling of hospitality will not be found in what you or your staff DO, but rather in the "tone" or "climate" in your business. Think of the climate as the level of mental health in the organization – the feeling on the job – generated from the way you and your team are thinking.

Climate Starts at the Top

The climate – and therefore the feeling of hospitality – always begins with the leader of the organization. To evolve the climate of your operation, genuine hospitality must originate within your own thinking. It simply becomes how you ARE. From there it can eventually shift the thinking of your entire staff. Anyone who has experienced hospitality knows that it MUST be genuine or it won't have real impact ... and it won't last.

Like it or not, your organization will always tend to reflect your own state of mind. When you are relaxed and smiling, the whole place seems to work more smoothly. When you have a bad day, *everybody* gets to have a bad day!

Understanding Climate

There's a relationship between climate and hospitality – or any behavior, for that matter. When you understand how they interrelate, it will make a major difference in your ability to influence the results you and your staff are able to deliver.

I will talk more about the idea of above the line and below the line behavior but understand there isn't really a line. Below the line is dysfunctional and inhospitable. Above the line is productive and welcoming.

You can think of climate as the mood in an organization because groups, like individuals, can cycle up and down depending on the collective thinking of the majority.

The model below shows the relationship between the climate in the organization, the feeling on the job and the behavior you tend to see at various levels. Evaluate this concept from your own experience and see if it matches behaviors you have observed yourself.

CLIMATE	FEELING ON THE JOB	ORGANIZATIONAL BEHAVIOR	
EXHILARATION	*Effortless*	Creativity Magic Hospitality	Intuition Self-Management Service-Oriented
INSPIRATION	*Alive*	Teamwork Initiative Clarity	Productivity Freshness Professional Curiosity
CONTENTMENT	*Hopeful*	Flexibility Cooperation Extra Effort	Confidence Humor Attention to Detail
TENSION	*Stressed*	Gossip Tardiness Distrust	Whining & Complaining Defensiveness Resistance to Change
UNHAPPINESS	*Upset*	Suspicion Accidents Turnover	No-Shows Cliques Disagreements
CHAOS	*Frightening*	Fights Sabotage Anger	Theft Arguments Walk-Outs

Below the Line Behavior

If a company has a very low climate – call it chaos – the feeling on the job is absolutely frightening. The behavior you tend to see in an organization at this level is fights, theft, anger and walkouts. It is a very scary place to be. If you've ever worked in an organization that was running in chaos, you know what I mean.

As it gets a little bit better, maybe you reach a level of unhappiness. The feeling on the job is upset and what you tend to see for behavior is turnover and cliques. In a corporate situation, you'll see people hoarding information and building empires. There's a feeling you can't get ahead unless you keep somebody else down. Turnover is high because people don't want to hang out in that environment. It's a little better than chaos, but it is still dysfunctional.

A lot of restaurants run in tension. The feeling on the job is stressed and you're likely to see gossip, distrust, whining, complaining and petty sniping. Again, organizational functioning has improved, but you're still below the line and less productive than you could be.

Above the Line Behavior

When the climate moves above the line, you'll start to see more productive thinking. Contentment and hope start to reappear. You observe spontaneous, positive humor (as opposed to negative jokes at someone's expense kind of humor.) In general, your whole team starts to lighten up.

As the climate improves, you reach a level we might call inspiration. The feeling in the company is alive. You start to see natural, internal motivation, return of the team feeling, reduced accidents and higher productivity. The endless string of problems you find below the line now just look like minor details that can be easily handled.

In a very high climate – call it exhilaration – there is a feeling of effortlessness excellence on the job. What you see in the organization is creativity, magic and people managing themselves. This is where the innate hospitality we are all capable of naturally shines forth. At this level you see exceptional guest service because the warm feeling is rather like being in love. You don't have to talk to somebody in love about taking care of people: people in love take good care of other people cause they just want to do it.

In a positive climate you will naturally get teamwork, caring and motivation; in a negative climate, good luck!

The key to understanding organizational behavior lies in grasping two principles:

Behavior is a predictable symptom of a person's level of thinking

To change work performance, change the work environment

127

What Changes the Level of Thinking?

Let's look briefly at the factors that have an impact on an individual's level of thinking (moods and behaviors), either for better or worse:

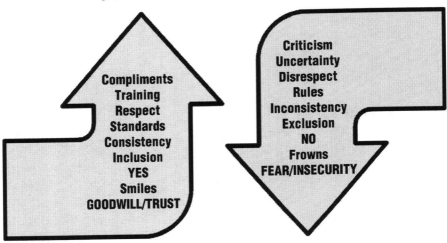

Compliments/Criticism

Compliments tend to bring the level up, criticism brings it down. (Don't you just *love* to be criticized?) Animal trainers know the way to shape behavior is to reward any small progress in the direction they want and ignore everything else ... but when will people typically get your attention? When they mess up, right? Cops look for problems, coaches build from strengths. Start to notice what catches your eye and accentuate the positive.

Training/Uncertainty

Apart from imparting job skills, the main benefit of training is that it increases people's level of certainty. If you throw someone into a situation they are unprepared for, they'll often panic, lock up on you, and go back to doing things the way they've always done them (because it's less threatening).

Respect/Disrespect

Not to listen is disrespectful. To discount someone's opinion because of age, gender, years of experience or the language they speak at home ... is disrespectful. To think there isn't something to learn from another person – whoever they are – is disrespectful ... and disrespect will drop the mood faster than anything I can think of. It comes from your own ego trying to run the show. Be aware.

Standards/Rules

There is a difference between standards and rules. Rules are hard and fast directives; standards are measures of performance you can coach toward. Let's say you want to orders out of the kitchen within 15 minutes of the time they're submitted. When you monitor your results, you discover it's taking 17 minutes.

If the 15-minute figure is a rule, what do you do? Fire somebody? But if it is a standard, you can be outside of it and still making progress toward it. What will it take to get it down to 16 minutes? Then can we get it to 15½? Do you see how that works?

Consistency/Inconsistency

If something is OK at some times and not OK at others ... or if it depends on the supervisor ... or the mood the boss is in ... it fosters the uncertainty that lowers the state of mind and negatively impacts the climate. The best interests of the restaurant (and your guests) are served when all your coaches are on the same page.

Inclusion/Exclusion

Several surveys have shown that the #2 thing people want from their jobs is to be *in* on things. They want to be part of those decisions that affect their lives. (Don't you?) Someone once asked me how they could make their staff feel part of things. I said, *"Make them part of things!"* I can't make you feel like you are if you aren't.

Yes/No

People love to hear Yes and hate to hear No. So say Yes to as much as you can say Yes to or tell them under what circumstances you could say Yes.

For example, if one of your dishwashers tells you he needs to make $30,000 a year, you might respond, "Terrific! Understand that what you're doing right now isn't worth that kind of money to me, so here's what you need to be able to do: [explain]. So let's get started. First we need to teach you how to do some prep work ..."

Smiles/Frowns

Your staff loves to see you smile. A frown makes them insecure, probably because they think you're displeased with something they did. This could be particularly true if you tend to micro-manage, be overly critical or stingy with praise.

If you're happy, notify your face! If you're not, it's best to realize you are a little off track at the moment. It's a good time to take a walk around the building or disappear into the office and do paperwork until you regain your balance.

Goodwill & Trust/Fear & Insecurity

This list could go on and on, but the simple truth is this: anything you do that contributes to goodwill and trust will tend to raise the level and you'll get the behaviors you see in a positive climate. Anything that contributes to fear and insecurity will lower the level and you'll see behaviors symptomatic of a low mood.

If you look at all this and wonder what it has to do with anything in the real world, let me share a vivid personal example:

THE DAY FROM HELL

In 1984, I was hired by the US Olympic Committee to run the foodservice at the U.S. Olympic Training Center (OTC) in Colorado Springs.

The OTC is a year-round operation whose dining program at the time was in desperate need of major surgery. In fact, foodservice had consistently been the leading source of complaints from the athletes about their training experience.

How Low Can You Go?
To underscore how bad things were, the day I arrived to take over the dining operations we had two knife fights in the kitchen!

Apparently, two of my workers got into an argument and were waving kitchen knives at each other with some degree of seriousness. Fortunately, no damage was done but everyone was nervous for awhile. This had all the signs of being a real "Day from Hell!"

I had received some excellent training up to that point in my professional career but nowhere had I received any instruction in how to deal with knife fights!

I hope you never encounter a predicament like this in your own operation but it could be an interesting case study. For a moment, put yourself in my position and imagine how you would approach a situation like this.

The Classic Approach
In the old "management expertise" (cop-based) mode I'd spent so many years refining, my first response to this predicament would likely have been to fire – or at least suspend or put on probation – the people involved. After all, it's important to deliver a clear message that we won't tolerate this sort of behavior, right?

After that, if I didn't already have one, I would have written a clear policy about knife fights. It would have specified that dangerous behavior was unacceptable conduct and could be considered grounds for immediate dismissal. I would have had everyone sign it and add it to their personnel files.

Then I would have held a special staff meeting to explain the policy. I would have made sure my staff understood how behavior of this sort worked against everything we were trying to accomplish. I would have talked about the importance of teamwork and cooperation, probably with some stirring Olympic analogies.

I would have shared my vision for the operation and tried to get my crew excited about what we could do together. It would have done my best to be inspirational and help my staff see that we were all in this together and we had to work together to succeed in providing memorable service to the athletes.

130

What's Wrong with this Picture?

I share this story in many of my seminars and when we reach this point in the discussion, I ask the group if this was roughly the way they'd handle it. The majority of managers generally agree they would take a similar approach. Wouldn't you?

My next question to them (and to you) is this:
"How effective do you think this strategy would be at eliminating knife fights forever and always in the organization?"

Somewhat sheepishly, the managers usually confess that while there might be some short term effect, they didn't really expect much would change.

The conversation usually sounds like this:
"Is this more or less the approach you would take?"
"Well ... yes."
"Would it work?"
"Well ... no."
"But it's still about the way you would handle it?"
"Well ... yes."

Do you see the problem?

Had I followed this scenario when the situation arose, this strategy wouldn't have worked either. Worse yet, when I didn't get the results I wanted, I would have looked at how to write a better memo or how to hold a more effective staff meeting!

I would worry that perhaps I didn't come down on them fast enough and hard enough. It would never have occurred to me that approaching the problem in this manner was a futile exercise from the very beginning.

This is what I mean about becoming better and better at doing things that don't work!

Applying a New Understanding

When the knife fights came up, however, I had come to a different understanding of the real cause of behavior. I had started to recognize behavior as just a symptom of a person's level of thinking as reflected in the climate of the organization.

Instead of seeing the knife fight as a statement about the people involved, I saw it as the indication of a low climate. The workers involved in the incident were simply in a state of mind where swinging knives at each other seemed like an appropriate way to settle a dispute. I understood the only way that behavior would change was when the level of thinking that created it changed.

In this case, I talked with the two combatants and suggested that carving up their co-workers was not a totally cool thing to do, but I never addressed the fight directly.

Instead, my conversation started something like this:
"Given what happened, it's obvious to me that something has you really frustrated. What's wrong with this chicken outfit? What's making your job tough?" Then I had the good sense to shut up.

My goal was to listen – not for hard facts, but for an insight into what was weighing on their minds. Whatever the preoccupation was, it was making their lives (and mine!) more difficult, affecting their thinking and leading to their unproductive behavior.

Here's the best part: To trigger those insights, all I had to do was quiet my mind and listen without judgement. I had come to understand the simple act of nonjudgmental listening was a major aid in helping other people return to a healthier state of mind.

I knew the behavior would change when their level of personal security and well-being increased. In a higher state of mind, the notion of attacking someone else would not even occur to them. The behavior itself was not the problem. It was just a symptom.

Learn from Your Staff
My discussions were revealing. I quickly discovered we had many more people on staff than we needed. Activity at the OTC was very seasonal at that point (November) and my predecessor had not trimmed the staff from its peak summer levels.

All he did was cut everyone's hours back. They didn't have enough hours so they weren't making enough money to pay their bills, but they couldn't afford to quit their jobs. Under these conditions, I would have been angry and frustrated, too!

This Is Not Management by Meditation
It became obvious that to eliminate the frustration I had to eliminate the problem of lack of hours. I held a series of one-on-one interviews to get to know my new workers as individuals and get a sense of where their heads were. Then I resolved the hours issue the only way I could: I fired half my crew, effectively doubling the pay of those I kept!

I placed on my termination list those I felt were the most negative or angry (in the lowest states of mind) but on a different day it well might have been a different group of people. Even if everyone had been in a great mood, I still would have let half of them go! As an interesting side note, the knife-fighters were among the people I kept on the team!

Then I said to the remaining crew, *"OK, you all have full hours now, that's not a problem anymore. What's the next thing we have to work on?"*

I admit "Black Wednesday" – the day I trimmed the staff – was nobody's idea of a good time, but when it was over, it was over. After the initial shock of the staff reduction passed, everyone immediately felt better. The whiners and complainers were gone and everyone who remained had a full schedule.

With the issue of adequate hours (and resulting lack of income) eliminated, the general work climate improved. In a more positive state of mind, people suggested other areas we could correct ... and every time we fixed an irritant (eliminated a distraction), the climate became more positive and behavior improved.

Some Interesting Things Happened
The next day, not only did knife fights stop, but the idea wouldn't even enter anyone's mind! In fact, we never talked about knife fights again and we never had a similar incident.

There were some other interesting benefits of this approach: Within about two months, foodservice had become the number one source of compliments from the athletes and coaches—all the more remarkable because this happened with the same workers who had once made us the number one source of complaints!

Over the next six months, dining room patronage nearly doubled. At the same time, our labor cost per meal dropped more than 20% and our food cost per meal declined nearly 25%. Staff turnover went from 300% to 25% without a change in wage rates!

Almost five years later when I left the OTC, the people involved in the knife fights were still on staff and were among our most productive workers ... and most people would have

Create a More Positive Climate

The notion that behavior in the organization is simply a reflection of the climate is so simple ... and yet revolutionary when compared it to the way we always thought things worked.

I know this idea can seem too simple, but the experience I describe above was typical of the effectiveness of these principles. The key is to create and nurture a positive climate on the job. Do that and most of your daily emergencies will seem to disappear as if by magic.

There are several management qualities that can improve the climate and bring out hospitality and self-motivation in the staff. Conversely, failure to observe them can plunge your place into constant conflict:

Listen

Listen with curiosity, listen with humility, listen for an insight. (Most people don't listen, they just wait their turn to talk. Some don't even wait!)

To make a major improvement in your operation, all you have to do is sit down with your crew one on one and ask, "What's making your job tough? If this were your place, what would you change about it?" Then shut up and listen.

You don't need to have an opinion about what they tell you. For example, if somebody said, "I want to eat my dog," you could entertain the idea and try to learn why that makes sense to them – without having to agree, disagree or express an opinion at all.

133

The perpetual question I regularly ask subscribers to my weekly e-letter is, "What did you learn from your staff today?" If you can't answer that question every day, you're not listening. If you're not listening, you're not learning ... and if you're not learning, you're going to be left behind.

Maintain the Benefit-of-the-Doubt

This may be just another way to listen, but assume the best until you have all the facts. There's always more information than you have.

Karen's been late three times and she's late again – it's easy to jump to a conclusion about Karen. But maybe this was the day her child got hit by a car and she's had other things on her mind.

I don't know ... but I know Karen would not have been late unless she had a reason that made sense to *her!* That doesn't mean I'll buy the story, but I want to consider it before I decide what to do.

When you assume the best, you will tend to get it. Certainly when I saw my staff as crooks who'd rob me blind if they could, I wasn't disappointed. When I saw some of the same people as intelligent adults who really wanted to make a contribution if they just had the opportunity, I wasn't disappointed either. *They* didn't change, *I did*!

Serve Your Staff

The manager's traditional job was to push past any obstacles that lay in his path. The new model recognizes all businesses have their own momentum and the manager's task is to guide it.

The analogy that comes to mind is the sport of curling, rather like shuffleboard on ice. One member of the team gives a heavy stone a push down the ice toward a target while two other team members move along ahead of the stone, sweeping the ice with brooms.

The sweepers have two jobs. The first is to make sure that the stone has a totally clean sheet of ice to run on. Then, depending on whether they sweep faster or slower, they make the ice a little faster or slower and that influences how far the stone will travel and how much it will curl, but momentum and direction are already established by somebody else.

Like the curling stone, your organization has a momentum – it is moving in a direction (roughly west, we hope!) As the manager, I'd rather be up in front with the broom, eliminating everything that might throw us off course, than to be in the back, trying to force the stone through a lot of debris.

The proper focus of management is to keep the company's energy flowing unimpeded, rather than trying to force the movement.

Value and Respect Your Staff

On one level, think of what would happen if everybody walked out in the middle the rush period.

But on a different level, when you allow yourself to connect with your staff as human beings, you will be moved by their innocence and heroism. Those may sound like odd words to describe your crew, so I'll explain:

I think it's heroic to be a single mother trying to raise three children alone. I think it's heroic to be sixteen: that's a lot harder job now than it was when we did it!

You have people on your crew who are up against some amazing challenges. They have family problems, money problems and many other struggles in their lives, but they show up every day and do the best they can. You've got to respect that.

When you allow yourself to experience this human connection, you start treating people well because you see them as worthy of the best care you can muster. When you deal with your staff from respect, 1) they will tend to treat your guests that way and 2) you will foster a more positive working environment.

Value a Free and Clear Mind

The most potent thing you bring to the job is your own mental health. Remember? The climate of the organization always starts at the top.

The reason you can't regularly work 70+ hours a week is that your mind gets scrambled, your own level of well-being drops and the productivity of the entire organization suffers. It's a radical concept called Have a Life! (Try it. You'll like it!)

You got where you are based on what you could *do*, but your future success will be based on what you can *get done* through the efforts of others. Someone on your staff is capable of doing – or eventually learning how to handle – virtually everything on your To Do list. Some of the same people who will be running your business in five years may breaking plates in your dishroom right now!

The only task you can't give away is the vision – your clarity about what "west" looks like for your company. That vision comes from a quiet mind, so be sure to give yourself quiet time. At this stage of your career it is highly productive activity.

If puttering in the garden or getting out on the golf course quiets your mind down, it is appropriate business activity and should be a regular item on your schedule.

Support Your Staff

In the long term, the only way your organization can succeed is if your staff succeeds. This sounds obvious, but somehow we got the idea we could be successful over the bodies of our crew.

Perhaps that came from those days when it seemed like we had disposable labor and we could treat people any way we wanted to. When they burned out or quit, we had a line of people waiting for their jobs. The labor market isn't like that anymore!

Adding people to your staff should represent a commitment on the part of the company (backed up by your words and deeds) to support their personal and professional development. If you aren't comfortable about making that level of commitment, don't bring them on board in the first place.

Respect the Power of the Climate

A compassionate leader understands staff members are always doing what makes sense to them in the moment, given their state of mind and their conditioned thinking. Negative attitudes and poor performance are just innocent conduct, not willful treachery.

Management becomes an easier, more enjoyable game to play when you respect the power of the climate. Instead of cluttering your head with new techniques, just understand what affects the working environment. Implement more things that foster goodwill and trust and eliminate practices that contribute to fear and insecurity.

Almost everything you want to happen will seemingly occur on its own in a positive climate: Teamwork and productivity happens. Exceptional service and hospitality happen. If that sounds too easy, then you're on the right track.

Like people, organizations have moods, too. When Id start to hear whining and complaining at the OTC (it would happen), it would just be a signal that I'd been spending too much time in the office.

So I'd make it a point to talk with my staff to find out what they needed. I'd hang out in the kitchen, notice what was working and commend them on their progress, no matter how small. The climate would immediately improve and the whining would disappear.

In a high climate, many of the problems you spend your time dealing with won't show up. Well, perhaps they will, but in a high climate, most problems just look like minor issues. If you had an "emergency" and it just looked like one more thing to handle, would your staff consider it a crisis or not?

Set a Personal Example

What *they* see is what *you* will get. You cannot kick butt, take names and then say "Go love the guests." You are the role model whether you want that job or not. The way *you* treat your staff is the way *they* will treat your guests.

Do you want your crew to show up on time? Show up on time. Want them to dress well? Dress well. Want them to listen? Listen. Want them to be open to new ideas? You get the drift.

When you lose it, the whole place loses it. When you let yourself become stressed, the whole place becomes stressed and guests feel uncomfortable. When the atmosphere in your business is calm and your staff is attentive and relaxed, your patrons want to return more often. That feeling also improves the climate and makes it a more enjoyable place to work.

The Power of Presence

The secret to creating impact with others is *presence*. Simply put, presence is a state of mind that is free from distraction. Your level of presence is the extent to which your mind is not occupied with thoughts unrelated to the project at hand.

Here are a two examples of what I mean:

Have you ever talked to someone who was listening to you ... and then suddenly they *weren't?* They may even have been looking at you and nodding their heads as you spoke, but didn't you know when their attention went elsewhere?

Or you're talking to someone on the phone. Can you tell when they have something else going on at the same time? Even though you can't see them, isn't it obvious when you don't have their full undivided attention?

These are both instances of a distracted state of mind which equates to low presence. Recall your experience of what it feels like to talk to someone who wasn't really listening. If you're like most people, you probably find such distracted behavior to be annoying at best ... and absolutely infuriating at worst.

We talk a lot about "reading the table" in our business, but your ability to read the table really comes down to presence. When you quiet your mind and simply allow yourself to connect with your guests as *people*, you'll almost always know what they need from you.

Distractions

A distracted state of mind creates irritation in others. You know how incredibly annoying it can be to talk with someone whose mind has wandered, yet the odds are that you regularly do the same thing to others. That's most likely because you've accepted the fallacy that the way to be efficient and get more done is multi-tasking – trying to juggle several tasks at the same time. Interesting in theory, but in truth, effectiveness comes from taking exactly the opposite approach.

Have you ever been on the phone, working on a staff schedule and trying to deal with a team member's issue all at the same time? My guess is that neither the person on the phone, the schedule, or your staff member got the undivided attention they really needed ... and the schedule was probably all screwed up, too!

In all likelihood you probably had to go back to one or all of these tasks for clarification, to correct mistakes or to make another try at resolving more "problems" that could easily have been avoided if you weren't so distracted by multi-tasking the first time around.

Presence and Productivity

You can really only focus your attention on one thing at a time anyway. When you are talking with another person, there is nothing you can do at that moment about finishing the schedule (or your budget, tending to your sick child or planning your vacation).

If your mind is preoccupied with extraneous thoughts, your attention is not fully with the person in front of you. Even if they don't call you on it, they will bug you again and again, trying to get through to you.

A LESSON FROM LIFE

Imagine a two-year old is looking for attention and you're in the middle of something. As they tug on your pants you say "Later, kid, I'm busy" without looking up from your work. Do they say, "Sure, Daddy, I understand?" Not a chance!

To take care of a two-year-old, drop what you're doing, get down eyeball to eyeball and give them five or ten seconds of your undivided attention. You'll buy yourself some time.

You may buy a few minutes and you may get an hour, but if a two-year-old doesn't get that degree of attention, they will pull on you for the rest of their natural lives! Am I right?

It's no different if they're twenty-two or sixty-two. People want to know that you "got it" – that what they had to say actually got through to you ... and this cannot happen if you are distracted.

The only difference between dealing with children and adults is that kids are more honest – they won't pretend they have your attention if they don't. Adults are usually more socially correct, but no less observant.

As with children, you can handle a situation in five seconds or five hours – the only difference is your level of presence when you do it.

The secret to productivity is to handle things exactly the way you would with a young child: drop distractions, focus your attention, handle one item at a time and move on to the next project. Presence (or lack of distraction) will enable you to more accurately assess the situations you face and deal with them more effectively.

Presence and Service

In my service seminars, I point out that the reason guests leave a tip of 10% or 30% depends in large measure on the level of personal connection servers create with their guests. **Presence increases the personal connection between people.** In fact, without presence, there can be no personal connection.

I watched one server increase his tips from 12% one night to over 30% the next night by, as he put it, "just trying to be *at* the table when I am at the table." I had a manager tell me half of his "people problems" seemed to disappear when he started becoming aware of – and releasing – his distracting thoughts.

When your guests have a complaint or when your staff members have questions, what they want most is to feel you really heard what they had to say. Most people don't expect you to resolve every concern on the spot, but they want to sense what they had to say was as important to you as it was to them.

Just as a distracted state of mind creates irritation, presence makes people feel more positive and better-served. You convey your caring and respect through your level of presence and people highly value the message they get when you are in the moment with them. In work with tipped workers (restaurant staff and hair stylists), we found that increased presence improved their tips by 250%!

If you have ever worked for someone who didn't listen, you know the feeling of being ignored. You can't tell someone who doesn't listen that they're not listening because, well, they don't listen! Interestingly, most people who don't listen really think they do, so your challenge is to be sure you're not guilty of the same sin when someone needs you to be there for them.

Presence and Enjoyment

There is a direct connection between your level of presence and the enjoyment you derive from what you are doing. Have you ever been so immersed in an activity that you totally lost track of time? If so, you had the experience of operating in a state of high presence (without distracting thoughts.)

If you find your job irritating, the only problem may be that you're distracted. Clear your head, focus, and watch how much fun things will become. Anything worth doing is worth doing fully present.

A Natural State

Presence is not something unnatural. We are all born with it. Little babies have amazingly high presence because their heads aren't yet cluttered with thoughts – they only know how to deal with what is right in front of them at the moment.

This sounds too simple, but think about what happens when you bring a newborn baby into a room. The baby immediately becomes the focus of attention, right? You start to smile and forget about your own issues for a few minutes. The baby's not doing anything – just being there – yet everyone around them feels a little better.

This demonstrates the power presence has to make others feel more positive. High presence is our birthright, but also something we can easily lose sight of as the pace of business speeds up, our lives become increasingly complex and we take on more "responsibilities."

Start to Notice

It is unrealistic to think you will always operate without distractions, but you *can* start to become aware of distracting thoughts when they clutter your mind. One way to tell this is happening is the people you are talking to will get restless or you will start to see a glazed look in their eyes. When your attention wanders, so will theirs.

The good news is that simply becoming aware of the fact that you are distracted will automatically start to put you back on track. When you notice, gently let go of stray thoughts and let your attention return to the task at hand. Your increased presence will make whoever you are talking to feel better-served and bring more impact to your message.

Hospitable Practices

While true hospitality comes from how you *are* rather than what you *do*, it is also true that the actions which make sense to you are a direct result of how you are thinking in the moment. Once you develop a hospitality mindset, everything you do will come across as hospitable.

Here are some practices that reflect that way of being in the world:

The Unexpected Extra

Everybody likes to get something for nothing. The unexpected extra is just some small gift to guests as a gesture of caring. In New Orleans culture, the word for this is *lagniappe* (it's pronounced like "LAN-yap") and means "something extra."

The unexpected extra can be anything. Some operators have institutionalized it: the donut holes for waiting male guests at Lou Mitchell's in Chicago (women get a small box of Milk Duds!) or the complimentary glass of Northwest sparkling wine to start the meal at Brix 25° in Gig Harbor, Washington, my home town. Others prefer to mix it up. At Gramercy Tavern in New York there is always a different take-home treat from the bakeshop when the check arrives.

The unexpected extra could be an offer to sample a new appetizer, a taste of new wine you just received or the recipe for your daily special. When I was a Navy foodservice officer in the Philippines, we had our cute female line attendants pass out hors d'oeuvres to the sailors waiting in line! The possibilities are endless.

The impact doesn't come from the gift, but from the gesture itself ... provided it is offered from a hospitality state of mind and not just another task. To set yourself apart from others, "Give 'em!"

Remember Likes and Dislikes

Everyone has personal preferences. For example, my wife has sensitive teeth. She prefers water with no ice. When we go to a new restaurant, though, they automatically fill the water glass with ice.

So we have to ask for a glass without ice. Servers often roll their eyes and walk away mumbling something about being picky. Eventually they bring it the way she wants it. Halfway through the meal they'll refill the glass ... with ice! Lately she's just stopped asking for no ice in a new restaurant. She just won't drink any water.

Places that know us bring it the way she likes it from the outset and it's *so* nice not to have to deal with that hassle!

Servers who are truly present will ask if her teeth are also sensitive to heat (they are). When they bring her coffee, they bring a dish of ice cubes on the side to help her cool it down. Brilliant!

Detroit's Rattlesnake Club kept a card on all their regular guests with everything they knew about them: family names, food and drink preferences, even trips they were planning.

When a regular made a reservation, the server got the card. Their challenge was to learn something new on each visit. By now I'm sure they've put that database on a computer, but it doesn't matter *how* they keep the data. The important thing is they want to know more about their guests ... and have a way to do it.

Remember Names

Do you have regular guests? Do you know their names? Probably. If I came to work for you, is there a *system* in place so I'd learn that information as well? Remember the theme song from the old TV show, Cheers? "Sometimes you want to go where everybody knows your name." It's true.

Personal connection is the key to building a following and nothing is more personal to someone than the sound of their own name. If you see the importance of this seemingly small point, you will develop a system to know not only the name of the host, but that of their mate, their kids, their dog and their boat! If it's important to them, it should be important to you. But for that to happen, you need an actual system, whether that be captioned photos on a bulletin board or continual coaching.

WHOSE JOB IS IT?

I had a favorite dry cleaner in Colorado Springs. They did good work at a fair price, but so did others. I patronized them because they always remembered how I wanted my shirts done.

I was usually in a rush and liked that I could just drop my cleaning and run. They'd take care of everything else ... except when there was a newly-hired counter person on the job.

When that happened, my normal dash for the door was abruptly halted when the new staffer demanded to know who I was and what I wanted them to do with this pile of clothes.

I understand why that might happen, but it's not my job to train their staff. If they were really serious about my business, *they* would have found a way to educate new workers about their regular patrons' expectations.

To get on the regular staff at Shari's, a Northwest coffee shop chain, you must know the names of fifty regulars. If you can't learn fifty names, you don't work there. After that, for every hundred names you learn, you'll get your name on a plaque on the wall. There are some servers in this coffee shop who allegedly know 1400 names ... because they have a system that's part of their culture.

Community Support

Communities support those who support the community, but many businesses – certainly many small independent eateries – seem more focused on how to pry as many dollars as possible from their market areas. This is where a giving nature and an impersonal Purpose will help set you apart from the rest of the herd.

The more you involve yourself in activities that benefit the community in general and your immediate neighborhood in particular, the more you will be seen as one of the good guys ... and that can only bring good things.

Steve Butcher (remember him from Page 9?) considers his support of the community to be a critical part of the success he has had at the Nutcracker. He said, "Being involved and generous is critical. It is also something you simply can't fake. Do it because you want to and if its genuine, it will repay you over and over!" It seems counterintuitive but it's true: the more you give, the more you get. That's the power of hospitality!

Be visible in important local events, host fund-raisers for worthy causes, sponsor a ball team or a Scout troop. Keep your name out there in a context other than being one more business with its hand out. Being an event co-sponsor is a good thing but the best long term bang for your buck will be to create your own unique annual events.

Once you get the logistics of a major event down, it tends to get bigger and easier to run every year. Case in point is Kitty Hoynes Irish Pub in Syracuse, NY, the first restaurant to be certified as A Place of Hospitality. Since 2004 they have sponsored a St. Baldrick's Day event to raise funds for pediatric cancer research.

Owner David Hoyne reports that the first year they brought in less than $100,000. The most recent event raised close to $450,000! As evidenced by the money raised and the 550 or so who showed up to have their heads shaved this year, this has become a major event in downtown Syracuse and keeps Kitty Hoynes in the minds of the community in a very positive manner.

In Punxsutawney, PA, Scott Anthony of Fox's Pizza Den has run an annual fundraiser for the local fire department since 2001 called Pizza & Prevention. He stages it on 9/11 and last year sold over 5000 of his Big Daddy pizzas and pizza coupons for $9.11 each.

Most of the work of making and delivering the pizzas is done by the firefighters themselves. Local businesses sign on as co-sponsors and 100% of the sales (and all the tips) go to purchase new equipment for the fire department. In 2012 that totaled close to $50,000.

As a result, everyone in the county now knows Scott's pizza and his company is regarded as a vital part of the community. The 1500 or so pizzas he actually delivers on the day of the event cost him around $4000 with the rest of the coupons trickling in (or not) over the following months.

Scott calls it the cheapest and most effective advertising he does all year... and he meets a real need in his community at the same time.

Staff Recognition

Do you have - or ever had - an Employee of the Month program? Is it an outstanding success? As well-intentioned as they are, I have seen few of these programs endure for very long or truly accomplish the purpose for which they are intended. The difficulty lies in how to fairly decide who is, in fact, the Employee of the Month.

If you were truly honest, the honor would rotate among a few staff members. When you attempt to broaden the basis for award, it starts going to people who are obviously less deserving and that will ultimately undermine the integrity and meaning of the award.

When I started a "Star of the Month" program at the Olympic Training Center, the first selections were obvious, but then it got tougher. In a futile effort to broaden the responsibility (and perhaps get myself off the hot seat), I got my crew involved in the process.

It was a good theory but it quickly became a political nightmare. The death knell came when the group said, "Let's give it to Tony. We know he's marginal but we all like him and he's never won anything." I was stuck. Tony didn't really deserve it, but I thought I'd do more harm if I overruled the will of the group. (Bad call.)

The program collapsed after that. Its demise was clearly my fault for the way I had structured it but I'm willing to bet many operators have found themselves in similar situations and made similar mistakes with similar good intentions. Let's go back to basics:

Why would you even *have* an Employee of the Month program? "Well, to recognize excellence," you say. OK, but excellence at what? If Job One is making the guest happy (it is!), I suggest you reward anyone who goes beyond the routine expectations of their job in the interests of exemplary guest service. In other words, a Hero! The idea of looking at your crew as heros may be a tricky concept to grasp, so here are three (true) examples of what I'm suggesting:

EVERYDAY HEROS

Situation:

It was an evening in early June, the night of the Senior Prom. Two lovely young women sat in a restaurant waiting for their dates. Eventually it became obvious the dates were not coming. Just another teenage tragedy, right? In most cases, probably so. But Beth Sayers, manager at Clinkerdagger's Restaurant in Spokane was touched by their plight.

She asked the girls if they would mind being escorted to the prom by two of her waiters she recruited to be Prince Charmings. She obtained the requisite approvals from the girls' parents and even asked for an OK from one waiter's wife, who was thrilled that her Australian-born husband would have a chance to see a slice of typical Americana!

The restaurant not only supplied the dates, but paid for the appetizers the girls had eaten while they waited. Sayers even gave the waiters money for pictures and other prom expenses. The story made the front page, second section of the Seattle Sunday paper.

Commenting to the media, Sayers said "Sure it was a nice thing, but what the girls did was far more courageous. We had the easy part. What's important is that in the face of embarrassment and humiliation, these girls went to their prom." Beth Sayers is a Hero.

Situation:

A guest's four year-old daughter is upset. The little girl wants a peanut butter sandwich but there isn't one on the menu. Instead of simply turning down the request, the waitress asks the kitchen what they can do.

The chef comes out in his whites to talk with the child. They put their heads together and have a serious discussion about various brands of peanut butter, the merits of chunky vs. creamy and the best kinds of jelly to put on a peanut butter sandwich.

Armed with the proper inside information, the chef sends someone to the grocery store on the corner for the needed items. The little girl is thrilled, the parents are grateful (and stunned!) The chef, the waitress and the runner are all Heroes.

These are the acts that raise the service awareness of other staff members. They'll start looking for opportunities to "make someone's day" with an unexpected act of kindness and a natural, healthy competition can develop to see who can go the farthest to make the guests happy. Instead of an Employee of the Month, look for a Hero of the Month and watch what starts to happen!

Behavior that gets noticed, rewarded and celebrated tends to be repeated

Guest Appreciation

Is your business all take and no give? In addition to the Unexpected Extra, some operators go even farther to give back to their guests. One who did it best was David Duthie in Lambertville, NJ.

David retired in 2000 to pursue his dream of sailing around the world, but for its 22 years of operation, his restaurant was known for its fine food and wine, full moon parties, teen disco, and its unwavering support of worthwhile causes in their market area.

Every year he held a complimentary Guest Appreciation Dinner, an over-the-top banquet to acknowledge his regulars for their many contributions during the year. Among the awards he gave out were his "Being There" awards for those who volunteered to help with events like the Muscular Dystrophy Walkathon. The big honor of the night was naming his Patron of the Year who received a bronze plaque on the wall and a host of special perks.

Joint Ventures

Many independent business owners operate from a sense of lack. They feel there's not enough to go around, grab every dollar they can and hang on tightly. They remind me of a nest of baby birds with their mouths open screeching, "Feed me, feed me." Surely there must be a better way to do business. (There is!)

Regardless of your type of restaurant, there are other reputable businesses in your market area – hairdressers, dry cleaners, auto dealers and such – establishments your patrons should know about. I also suspect these businesses have the sort of customers who should know about what you have to offer.

What do you think might happen if you approached these owners in the spirit of giving and offered to promote them to your guests, no strings attached? It might be an endorsement in your newsletter, a coupon for a special offer or an invitation to an open house.

Human nature being what it is, my guess is they'll ask what they can do for you in return. Reciprocity can't be a condition of your offer to help, of course, or you'll just look self-serving and shallow, but we are all hard-wired to return favors. It only backs up the notion that the more you give, the more you get.

Joint ventures can be an effective way to reach out to others from a sense of giving and grow your own business at the same time. They help create a more positive feeling in the community and separate you from all those other chirping mouths.

Never Say Never

When people hear you say No, it can drop their mood (along with the check average and your tip!) Always tell a guest what you *can* do for them, never what you *can't* ... particularly if they seem to be in a touchy mood.

For example, if they want a brand of Scotch you don't carry, tell them what you *do* have to choose from. Keep it positive.

If they order your Sea Bass special and it's gone (you always *sell out*, never *run out!*), you could say something like, "I'm so sorry, we've sold out of that already. We only make a limited number of orders and tonight it seems like everybody wanted it. If you really like Sea Bass, leave me your phone number. The next time we have it on the menu, I'll give a call and reserve some for you. In the meantime, let me suggest ..."

Handling things this way is more considerate of your guests' sense of well-being, increases personal connection, and it makes the shift a lot more fun for you as well!

Go the Extra Mile

Going the extra mile means doing more than the guest asks for ... or even expects. It is being in the moment with others (presence) and recognizing those moments when you could do something that would really WOW them. It's what Danny Meyer calls writing a great last chapter. These opportunities appear out of nowhere (and disappear just as quickly), so there are no guidelines on what to do or how to do it.

But if your head is clear and your heart is in the right place when you recognize a moment like this, you will instinctively know what to do ... and it will work. But you must grasp the opportunity of a lifetime during the lifetime of the opportunity!

Hospitality is a State of Mind

We've already discussed the idea that your actions are determined by how you think. When hospitality becomes who you *are*, everything you do will be an expression of that. For example, clean restrooms are not, strictly speaking, hospitality. But you take extra care to have sparkling restrooms because it would be inhospitable not to. (You clean the bathroom before company comes to your home, right?)

Similarly, it would be inhospitable to have trash in the parking lot, dirty windows or burned-out light bulbs. It would be inhospitable not to offer newly-arrived guests something to drink or be unable to answer their questions about the menu. It would be inhospitable not to offer diners a second glass of wine or fail to entice them with an exquisite dessert. It would be inhospitable not to perform the basic functions of your job in a competent manner.

Because hospitality is how you are in the world, you notice all those details. They take on more importance to you and you handle them because that's just the right thing to do. When you live your life in the spirit of giving, it would be out of character if you let them slide.

And hospitality isn't just how you are with your guests. It is the way you relate to co-workers, your family, and strangers you meet on the street. It is about how you are behind the wheel of a car. It is ultimately what defines the way you live your life.

The Hospitality Edge
... and Why You Need It

The bad news was announced in February of 2012: Restaurant visits had fallen since the recession and the bulk of those lost customers – 87% in fact – abandoned independent eateries. According to research company the NPD Group, Americans ate out 60.6 billion times in 2011, down from 62.7 billion in 2008. Of the 2.1 billion visits lost, two billion were at the expense of independent restaurants. Is that bad enough for you yet? There's more ...

The report went on to say that consumers were patronizing larger restaurant chains, which had added 4,511 units since 2009. But since the fall of 2008, more than 7,000 independent eateries had closed.

The previous alone, they reported visits to chain restaurants were up 1% while meals at standalone businesses slumped 4%. Small restaurant operations were down to 27% of the US restaurant industry after steadily losing market share to chains.

The NPD analyst said the reason for the decline was that independent restaurant operators had neither the money nor resources of the chains. She said they lacked the marketing power to drive traffic and the monetary buffer to get through the difficult times during the prior several years.

Overall, I agree with her conclusions ... but therein lies a seed of good news. You see, while independents likely do not have the financial depth and marketing muscle of a chain, they do have – or can have – a very real competitive advantage in the market, one that the chains are ill-equipped to counter.

For the independent operator trying to hold their own against the onslaught of national chains, the competitive edge is the experience of hospitality

National chain restaurants are focused on process and profitability over creativity and truly personalized service. As a result, industry experts note the overall dining experience in the country is becoming increasingly impersonal and unremarkable. Chains equate hospitality with service, not personal connection.

In fact, because the individualized nature of the hospitality experience does not lend itself to top down, numbers-driven controls, chains don't know how to deal with it, let alone foster it ... and that is ultimately their Achilles heel when going head-to-head with a savvy independent.

The proof of this edge can be seen in the restaurants who have become certified Places of Hospitality – all independents. Every one reported 2011 was their best sales year ever! Now *that* is really good news!

What is Killing Hospitality?

Independent operators like to blame their struggle on the spread of national restaurant chains but, other than perhaps in access to capital, the independent really has the advantage in the marketplace.

A good independent can be closer to the market, more adaptable and generally more focused on creating personal connection with their patrons. Entrepreneurs might also be surprised at just how much a restaurant's success hinges on an owner's ability to keep the pressures of work from affecting life at home.

A study by a professor at Ohio State University found that one of the most critical factors contributing to a restaurant's success – more important even than "location, location, location" – was actually how well an owner juggled the demands of the business with family life.

He determined that, "beyond muddled concepts, failure seemed to stem in large part from an inability or unwillingness to give the business sufficient attention, whether due to lack of time, passion or knowledge."

Most of the failed restaurant owners he interviewed attributed their downfall at least partly to competing family demands, including divorce, ill health, and retirement. Some owners voluntarily closed when the family sacrifices became too much, like one owner who said she didn't want to miss seeing her children grow up.

So if the competitive edge in the hospitality business comes from the ability to run an efficient business and actually deliver the experience of hospitality as Danny Meyer's group demonstrates. If the owner is in a constantly scrambled state of mind due to lack of time, conflicting interests, poor organization and lack of understanding, its no wonder so many restaurants fail to gain the traction necessary to grow.

Just as love cannot flourish in a climate of indifference, the spirit of hospitality cannot exist in a climate of fear ... and many independent operators are running scared.

In a book called *Waiter Rant*, the author – a working waiter – pointed out why the true hospitality experience may be so rare in an industry that espouses it. Here is an excerpt from his writing:

"Over the years I've come to realize that [the owner's] anger and anxiety stem from his fear of losing everything that he's worked so hard to create. [He] is no stranger to failure. He flunked out of a dozen jobs before finding success as a chef.

"He also has a strained relationship with his ex-wife and children back in Italy. Now, at forty-six, he has a new wife, a new son, and a robust business. [He's] got a second shot at happiness and he doesn't want anything to mess that up, but I worry his anxiety will destroy the very thing he wants to protect.

"[His] worrying has turned him into a jumpy, irritable, and angry man. Like a soldier just home from war, his eyes are always scanning the horizon for threats. This anxiety hurts him in social settings. Because thoughts are banging around the inside of his head like electrons colliding inside a particle accelerator, his attention span can be measured in nano-seconds.

"While [he] has the capacity to be very charming and considerate, he's usually on his best behavior only when dealing with people who have something he wants. [He] doesn't have the energy or inclination to be nice to people he perceives as beneath him ... and if you work for [him], he thinks you're beneath him."

Not all restaurant owners are quite this stressed, of course, but to one degree or another, these feelings are common in many independent operators. This leads to a high burn-out rate among single unit owners, dissatisfaction and cynicism among restaurant staff and a resulting general absence of true hospitality for restaurant patrons.

Add to this a typical chain's focus on process and profitability vs. creativity and personal service and it's easy to see how the overall dining experience in the country became increasingly impersonal and unremarkable. Finding a workable answer to this dilemma is critical.

The National Restaurant Association estimates the industry's share of the food dollar increased from 25% in 1955 to around 48% in 2012. Over half of adults say restaurants are an essential part of their lifestyle. A vibrant (and viable) restaurant industry is critical to the well-being of the country.

Perhaps independent restaurants themselves are not be an endangered species, but the spirit of hospitality – the true lifeblood of the industry – may well be. It might even be true in your restaurant. What to do?

Getting There From Here

Knowing where you want to go is one thing, but actually getting there is another. How many good ideas have failed to gain traction because you didn't quite know where to start or what to do?

I'd hate to see ideas as powerful as the ones we have discussed meet the same fate but in all likelihood, you will grasp these principles intellectually well before they rock your world and really "stick." It's when things shift at that deeper level that everything suddenly looks different: fresh, simple and filled with promise ... but it helps to know how to at least start down that path.

The good news and the bad news here are the same: there's nothing you can or must do. The shift comes from the inside out and happens in an unexpected moment of personal insight. It is permanent, painless and is likely to hit you when you least expect it, most likely when your mind quiets down enough for you to recognize it.

The most elusive part of what I am trying to pass along is its elegant simplicity, but since what you need to understand can't be adequately conveyed in words, perhaps you can relate to this example:

> Your two-year-old has been driving you crazy all day and you're about ready to throttle the little bugger! You finally get the child in bed but you're still wound up from all the frustration they put you through today.
>
> Then you look in on them when they're asleep and your heart is touched by their innocence. You feel a flood of warm feelings sweep over you and in that instant, everything changes. Suddenly there's no way you can possibly think anything ill of this marvelous little creature. You have had a change of heart.

That's the way it seems to happen: a "blinding flash of the obvious" when suddenly you see everything in a completely fresh way.

While the change can only come from inside each individual, there is a proven process that will help you and your organization steadily move in the right direction, elevating the level of the experience you provide to your guests as you go. It will always be a work in progress but it is rooted in proven principles.

I brought the best minds in the business together to re-think how restaurants operate ... to imagine how they could be ... not waiting for change but becoming the catalyst for it.

Rather than trying to figure out how to make present operating formats work better, we focused on larger questions: "Is this the way the business should be run in the first place?" and "How can we re-invent restaurants to be true places of hospitality, making full use of the technology, tools, and understanding available today?"

We were committed to discovering a solution that met the following four criteria:

- To trigger a contagious resurgence of hospitality in the world by delivering the experience of heart-felt caring to every patron of every independent restaurant, every time.

- To be an elegantly simple system that could provide the logic, methodology and support structure that would enable every foodservice venue to operate with effortless excellence.

- To provide restaurant owners and staff with a fulfilling sense of purpose and the joyful experience of enriching the lives of the people they serve.

- To be so irresistible and easily affordable that hospitality could truly become the competitive point of difference for every independent restaurant in the world.

The result of "reverse engineering" the industry this way is called A Place of Hospitality™, a breakthrough business model that offers a totally fresh step-by-step approach to deliver what has always led to success in the restaurant business but which seldom happens because operators "don't have the time" – hospitality itself.

A Place of Hospitality is a certification and support program to recognize restaurants that have not only made a commitment to exceptional personal hospitality ... but who have succeeded at it! The certification cannot be purchased and a restaurant cannot pay to keep it. They must continue to earn it every day or lose it.

A Place of Hospitality is based on the knowledge that operators can prosper if they make hospitality their competitive point of difference, learn how to interact with their staff and guests in more productive ways and have access to effective systems to tend to the details of the business so they become free to nurture a positive work environment, assure memorable guest experiences, and have a life themselves!

If the way operators were currently approaching their businesses was going to give them effortless lives, they would already have effortless lives! The simple truth is that for a business to expand, the owner's thinking has to expand first. You cannot be successful in the future using the thought processes and management models of the past.

The competitive climate (and guests' expectations) have changed. Not too long ago, it was enough to just get the job done properly ... but today's dining public wants more.

The competitive advantage for independent operators is hospitality and true hospitality comes from a state of mind, not a checklist. The key to success in this new era lies in reaching a deeper understanding of people and how they work together to create a climate where the guest feels well-served, the staff and managers are happy and the needs of the company are also satisfied.

Hospitality is clearly a "people business," yet few operators ever receive any real education about what makes people tick. In fact, there *was* no such training in our industry ... and no support system to give context to its implementation ... until now.

Over the years, franchise groups and a few exceptional individuals developed approaches that produce consistent results for their own operations, but until now, no one has dared take on the "impossible" challenge to revolutionize the way independent restaurants of all types and at all levels operate in the real world.

If you would like access to the tools and systems usually reserved for franchise operators and a structured way to implement the ideas discussed in this book, you really should give A Place of Hospitality a serious look. You've got a lot to gain and nothing to lose but your struggle! You'll find information on how to get involved on Page 269.

The Ripple Effect

A restaurant can do more for the well-being of a community in one day than all the mental health professionals in town will do in a year because the restaurant will touch more people.

Human beings tend to treat others the way they are treated and it has to start somewhere. Who better to trigger a resurgence of hospitality in the world than the hospitality industry itself? What better place for that ripple to start than inside your four walls?

When guests feel well- and personally-served, they leave feeling better about themselves and life in general. As a result, they are naturally more considerate of the people they deal with. In this way, hospitality has a way of paying itself forward.

When you are focused on nurturing relationships with your guests rather than simply trying to pry every dollar you can from their clutching fingers, your patrons will have more trust in you, return more often and happily pay full price.

They will recommend you to their friends and become fiercely loyal fans. They will stick with you through tough times and patronize you because they WANT to! You become their Restaurant of Choice.

The result is higher sales, lower marketing costs ... and a happier service staff making better tips. It is truly a win-win-win situation.

Better yet, once the dining public has experienced the warmth of true hospitality, they will be less willing to tolerate the indifference and callous attitudes found in many corporate eateries and most inept independents. In ever larger numbers, they will favor – and be drawn back to – a true place of hospitality.

The ripple effect from more and more restaurants delivering the experience of heartfelt caring can trigger a contagious resurgence of hospitality and consideration for others that will spread, transform the communities they serve and make life more pleasant for everyone.

In the words of that great American philosopher, Rodney King: "Why can't we all just get along?"

Yes, courtesy begets courtesy. It is indeed contagious ... and very, very compelling. Hospitality is noble work.

Hospitality Is about Giving
The More You Give, the More You Get!

7
Recover Gracefully

Recover Gracefully

Try as you will to make it perfect, from time to time things will go wrong. Some will be caused by the actions (or inactions) of the staff and some will be due to circumstances beyond your direct control. But *regardless of the cause of the glitch, it is your responsibility to make things right.* A hospitality professional simply will not allow guests to have less than a memorably positive experience.

Recovering gracefully when the wheels come off is an integral part of providing memorable service and legendary hospitality

Foodservice problems come in all shapes and sizes, from fires in the kitchen, medical emergencies, power failures and mice running across a table to errors with the food, service stumbles, trashed restrooms and spilled food. Guests are often the cause of their own sticky situations. Just ask a group of operators about problems and they can go on for hours on end!

In this chapter we'll look at some of the common issues you may face in the normal course of business and what you can do to recover. As a start, perhaps we should look at why you should care what happens at all. [Hint: this is a good discussion to have with your crew!]

What Is a Guest Worth?

Why should you be concerned about making it right every time? I mean, nobody's perfect and if you win more than you lose you'll come out all right ... won't you? Customers are so demanding they'll surely tell you about every little thing that is wrong ... won't they? The answer to both questions is a resounding No!

Unless you consistently have more business than you can handle, I suggest you can't afford to let *anyone* get away! More to the point, you can't count on seeing every problem yourself or rely on your guests to tell you any time something isn't right. You may understand this on an intellectual level but it might be interesting to explore the economic impact of repeat patronage.

159

As a start, let's calculate what losing a moderately enthusiastic, loyal guest is worth to you over five years. I use five years because I think people have an attention span with restaurants. Some guests will leave town next week and some will be around twenty years from now. However, if you never change anything in your place, within five years most guests will get bored and take their business elsewhere.

To err on the side of conservatism, let's ignore the cost of securing the guest in the first place and look at the value of a patron who comes in twice a year and spends just $25 each time. That is $50 a year in sales ... and that's nothing. Over five years, this person will spend $250 with you. Acceptable, but nothing to get excited about, right? Well, the true cost is a little higher than the modest $250 figure might suggest.

Doing the Math

Let's figure it out. First of all, pre-Internet statistics indicate that a satisfied guest will tell five others what a great place you have, and that has a major impact upon the equation.

Here are the assumptions:

1. A happy guest (Patron A) spending $50 a year with you tells five others a year.
2. Those five (Patron B's) become regulars.
3. Each tells five others (Patron C's) within a year,
4. The Patron C's each tell five others (Patron D's) and so on.

Here's what the progression looks like:

	Patron A	Patron B	Patron C	Patron D	Patron E	TOTAL
# Patrons	1	5	25	125	625	
Year 1	$50					$50
Year 2	$50	$250				$300
Year 3	$50	$250	$1,250			$1,550
Year 4	$50	$250	$1,250	$6,250		$7,800
Year 5	$50	$250	$1,250	$6,250	$31,250	$39,050
TOTAL	$250	$1,000	$3,750	$12,500	$31,250	$48,750

The mathematically-inclined will carry this projection out several more years, come up with a gazillion dollars in sales and write off the entire exercise as wishful thinking. You never reach the huge number because the progression never moves ahead forever – guests move or die, they get bored, you lose patrons through inattention or inconsistency, competition and a variety of similar factors.

Still, failure to create and keep a happy guest will cost you not only their future business but the loss of business represented by referrals you never got. This is bad enough but there's an additional price to pay when you lose a guest.

The Cost of an Unhappy Guest

It is easy to think people would tell you when something isn't right but you can't count on it. Have you ever visited a business – maybe a restaurant, maybe something else – had less than an exciting time, never said anything and just never returned? It happens all the time ... and it's happening to you every day.

Statistically speaking, a typical business only hears from 4% of its dissatisfied guests. One in twenty-five will actually tell you when things are not right. The other 96% just quietly go away and 91% of those will never come back.

As if this wasn't damage enough, you've surely heard the statistic that typical dissatisfied patrons will tell 8-10 people about their problem. One in five will tell twenty ... and that was before Yelp, TripAdvisor and Urban Spoon!

Of the people who hear the story from someone else, 10% will pass the story along to others ... and this doesn't include those who will post it on the Internet and perhaps tell millions! In general, the worse you botch it up, the better the story and the more people will learn of it. You could even end up with a YouTube video going viral. Yikes!

The Numbers Add Up

All these statistics can get quite dry so let's consider what happens if you blow it with that $50-a-year guest. If they become dissatisfied, they probably won't tell you ... but they will tell their friends. If this disgruntled guest tells another 10 people with similar spending habits not to patronize you, that will cost you another $2500 in future sales (10 people x $50/year x 5 years).

So when you look at the real cost of losing a moderately enthusiastic, regular guest, the total loss comes in two ways: positive word-of-mouth lost and negative word-of-mouth gained.

In this case, the incident really cost you $48,750 in lost sales as a result of lost positive referrals and another $2,500 in lost sales resulting from negative word-of-mouth – a total potential loss of $51,250 ... merely because you were careless with a $50-a-year guest!

Worse yet, if one person at the table has a bad time, *everybody* at the table will have a bad time! If our disgruntled diner was in a party of four, you must take the loss times four. This makes a four-top of $50-a-year guests worth more than $200,000 ... and you debate about whether you ought to buy a potentially dissatisfied table a round of drinks or comp a dessert! Really?

Two hundred thousand bucks! The problem is that this isn't money you lost – if you lost 200 grand you would be *excited!* This is money you never *got!* It is already factored into your volume because not everyone you serve has a good time and most of them won't volunteer that information so you can fix it.

How much money do you spend on advertising in an attempt to generate just a fraction of $200,000 in sales? What might happen if you invested some (or most) of that ad money into giving your current guests a more memorable experience?

The Service Staff Loses, Too

Just as the operator may at first consider the cost of a dissatisfied table as only the loss of their check that night, the servers who handled the party (and didn't understand the cost of a lost guest) may only think they're out a ten-buck tip!

When you take the long view, the loss for the service staff is even more frightening. If you figure a 15% tip, the loss of $200,000 in sales also means $30,000 that's not on the tip tray anymore ... and that's just one table of four $50-a-year guests!

Implications

Do you find this discussion on the cost of losing a guest at all scary? You should. What this example suggests is that, over five years,

every patron is potentially worth 1000 times what they would spend with you in a year!

Might there be some implications here with regard to the importance of thorough training before turning a server loose on your patrons? There are. Can you afford "warm body" hiring and haphazard training when you have that kind of money riding on the outcome? My suggestion is that you absolutely cannot.

Good News

If guests have a bad time it doesn't necessarily mean you'll never see them again or that they will say terrible things about you. However, I think it's reasonable to expect that, at the least, you will see them less frequently and they'll be less inclined to recommend you to their friends. In either case it costs you money ... and it represents sales you didn't have to lose!

Bad News

These figures were based on a guest who comes in twice a year and spends $50 during that time. Most of your guests – certainly your regulars – come much more often and spend far more every year.

Should you get serious about making sure every guest has a wonderful experience every time they dine with you? How much business are you prepared to give away?

Regulars

Oh yes, one more thing: do you have regulars – loyal guests you see over and over again? Of course, you do. All these calculations go out the window when you talk about frequent guests.

Let's look at Bob and Nancy, a couple who normally comes into your café twice a month and spend about $25.00 each time. Over the course of a year, they will contribute $600 in gross sales. Using the formula we calculated earlier, this potentially makes them worth $600,000 to you over five years.

It's easy to take your regulars for granted. ("Bob and Nancy are like family. They'll understand if they have to wait while we take care of something else first.") It doesn't work like that.

Bob and Nancy understand they are regular patrons and are apt to believe because they're more loyal than the average diner, they are entitled to preferential treatment ... and they are correct to think that. You'd do well to recognize and accommodate their mindset.

> *"I like to think of our staff members not as servers, but as surfers. Surfing is an arduous sport and no one pursues it involuntarily. No one forces you to become a surfer, but if you choose to do it, there's no point in wasting energy trying to tame the ocean of its waves.*
>
> *"Waves are like mistakes. You can count on there always being another wave, so your choice is to get back on the surfboard and anticipate it. The degree to which you ride it with better form than the next guy is how you improve and distinguish yourself."*
>
> **– Danny Meyer in *Setting the Table***

The more people patronize you, the more they expect!

You must do *more* for your regulars than you do for occasional guests ... and you should! You could certainly do worse than seeing Bob and Nancy as a $600,000 investment. I guarantee they see themselves as that valuable, even though they've never made the calculation.

In reality, alienating Bob and Nancy will cost you more just because they *are* regulars. If you give regulars a bad time, it is a personal affront, not just a normal service lapse. If they feel personally put out, they're likely to tell far more than ten – or even twenty – others!

When It's Not Your Fault ...

Many of the sticky situations arising in the normal course of business will not be your fault ... but they are always part of your guests' experience of patronizing your business. You're going to take the rap anyway, so you might as well accept responsibility for, as Danny Meyer would put it, "writing a great last chapter."

This means no matter the mistake may be and no matter who or what may have caused it, you must find a way to turn the experience into a positive story for the guests to tell their friends.

Perhaps the easiest way to give you an idea of what I'm talking about is to share three real-life examples:

#1: A patron was in for a late afternoon snack at a McGuffey's Restaurant in North Carolina. When he was done, he headed out the door but came racing right back in. "I'm in trouble," he said. "I locked my keys in the car."

"No problem," said the manager. "I'll call AAA and have them send somebody right over to open your car."

"You don't understand," said the now frantic man. "I have to pick up my son at day care and I'm already running late. If I don't get there in the next ten minutes, it's going to get really complicated."

The manager reached into his pocket, handed the man the keys to the brand-new car he'd just picked up that morning and said, "Go get your son. By the time you get back, we'll have your car open."

#2: A friend put together a ski trip in the Sierra Nevada Mountains with a group of executives. One night they went to the Dragon Fly restaurant in Truckee, California. Originally there were four in the party but the last of the group made it through the snow storm early and joined the rest for dinner, so they suddenly became a table of five.

The restaurant was busy, of course and their reserved table was too small for the five of them. What to do? The restaurant's manager explained the situation to a party of four who were already seated at a six-top and asked if they would change tables with the group. They agreed.

With good humor, several servers quickly carried all the dishes and drinks between the two tables. The manager comped the displaced party's desserts for making the switch and comped bowls of soup for the new party as well. The rest of the evening flowed flawlessly.

The owner called the next day and asked about the service. Of course my friend gushed about what had happened and thanked him profusely. The owner's classy comment was "I like calling new customers because my team seems to regularly get applause for their service."

Not only did his group have great service but the food was fantastic and the hospitality was memorable. Will he go back? You bet! Will he tell his friends? You bet! (... and look, here I am sharing the story with you!)

#3: A guest and his wife were enjoying an anniversary dinner at Eleven Madison Park in New York. Over a glass of complimentary champagne, they asked the maitre d' a technical question. "We have a very special bottle of champagne at home to celebrate with after dinner. But the bottle was warm, so before we came here tonight I put it in the freezer. Is it going to explode?"

"Yes, I'm afraid it will explode," the maitre d' said. The man stood up in a panic and said to his wife, "Oh my God, honey, I've got to go home and deal with this before that bottle blows up."

The maitre d' saw a great last chapter taking shape. "Listen," he said, "you're here for your anniversary and we want you to have a great night. If you'll give me your address, I'll gladly go to your apartment and take the champagne out of the freezer."

"All right, you're on," the man said. He called to alert the doormen and the maitre d' took a cab to their address where he transferred the champagne from the freezer to the refrigerator. Next to the bottle, he set some dessert chocolates from the restaurant and a small tin of caviar along with a note that read, "Happy Anniversary from Eleven Madison Park." These folks became dedicated regulars.

I have hundreds of similar stories of proactive solutions to potential problems, none of which were issues *created* by the restaurant ... but all of which were potential evening-killers that were averted when the restaurant took responsibility to go the extra mile.

This is what I mean when I say hospitality is doing what is unexpected ... and uniquely personal to that guest in that moment. Actions like these create the personal connection that causes people to happily return again and again (at full price!)

What sort of stories are people telling about YOU?

Cashing In On Complaints

Complaints, on the other hand, are usually in response to something you did ... or didn't do ... or that failed to meet the guests' expectations for one reason or another. Nobody likes to get complaints but if you know how to mine it, there's gold in those gripes. I even wrote a book about how to do just that!

Unpleasant as they often are, complaints are pure feedback from your guests, telling you where your system broke down which, in turn, can show you where and how to improve your operation.

The operator who can respond positively to a complaint, who understands how to effectively deal with the disgruntled guest, who truly sees the grievance as good news rather than a personal affront, is in the best position to profit from the disappointed diner and tap this rich source of information to increase future sales.

Try as you will, you won't win them all. But here's an interesting fact:

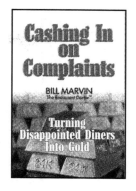

A guest whose complaint is handled well can actually be more loyal to you than a guest who never had a problem at all!

I'm not suggesting you should screw it up just so you can fix it; enough things will fall through the cracks on their own. But there is a long term financial benefit when you (and your staff) learn how to deal with complaints effectively.

Most people handle complaints poorly because they've never learned what to do (and not do) when confronted with a disgruntled diner. They react defensively and lose twice – once because they forfeit the guest's patronage forever and again because they fail to learn the lessons that the complaint could have taught them.

The Importance of Complaints

As a young operator, I always hated complaints because they seemed like a personal affront. I tried very hard to make it right for my guests and when they complained, it felt like a knife in the heart. I always wanted to sit them down and set them straight about what it really takes to run a restaurant! (Yeah, *that* would have worked well!)

Complaints disrupted the daily routine. When a complaint came in, it meant I was going to lose productive time to investigate, ask questions and write letters. If it was a complaint someone was making in person, I'd have to drop everything else to deal with them. Since I was already pushed to my limit, I saw complaints as intrusions.

Complaints always seemed to throw me off track, sometimes for days. I would be depressed when we dropped the ball in an area where we should have known better.

Often I would start questioning whether or not I knew what I was doing. I started looking at my staff with suspicion. I know I was far more critical for awhile, both of my staff and myself. The service lapses hurt ... and those were only the ones I found out about!

Undiscovered Complaints are Expensive

According to a survey by the National Retail Merchants Association, 14% of the people who stop patronizing a business did so because they had a complaint that wasn't handled well. That's a lot of business to give away because of lack of skill and understanding of how to deal with guest complaints.

If people would tell you when things aren't right, that would make it a lot easier, but as I've mentioned, statistics suggest every complaining guest could represent two dozen others who had a similar problem and chose not to tell you about it.

Statistically speaking, we said a complaining guest will tell 8-10 people about their problem. One in five will tell twenty. (One in a hundred will probably tell thousands, but that's life in the Internet age) and we've already calculated the cost of losing a single $50-a-year guest could exceed $50,000 over five years.

If you grasp the significance of these numbers, you can see the potential income you have at risk if complaints are not properly handled and appreciate the need to identify and solve any potential difficulties before your guests even become aware of them.

Handling Complaints

Eery manager should have the following posted prominently in both the office and staff areas:

**Stamp out inconveniences
before they become irritations.**

**Stamp out irritations
before they become complaints.**

**Stamp out complaints
before they become problems.**

**Stamp out problems
before they become crises.**

Unlike fine wine, complaints do not improve and mellow with age. Left unaddressed, a minor inconvenience can become a full-blown crisis, at least in the mind of the guest.

The most common mistake is getting defensive and wanting to explain It never helps and almost always makes things worse. Handling a complaint well is not about determining who is right and wrong – it's about saving a disappointed guest and retaining the business you would lose by alienating them.

Another stat of interest: 70% of complaining guests will come back again if you resolve a complaint *in their favor*. I suggestion there is NO way to resolve a complaint other than in favor of the guest.

Resolve a complaint on the spot and 95% of complaining guests will return. The only people on the spot are your service staff. If you need a case to give your crew the authority to do what they have to do at the table at the time, this is the case – 95% vs. 70% retention.

Goals When Handling Complaints

It helps to remember there are only two goals when dealing with a complaining guest:

1. Calm Them Down So They Won't Bad-Mouth You to Others

90% of your loss comes from the people that a disgruntled guest influences. For example, of the $50,000+ we calculated it cost when you lost a guest, all but $250 of that came from people other than the person involved.

2. Get Them Back as a Patron If You Can

If you can't get them back, you at least want to make sure they don't go out and do you any damage.

That's it! These are your only two concerns. Don't get confused by thinking there can somehow be a winner and a loser. When you're handling complaints, there is only win-win or lose-lose. If you resolve the problem successfully, the guest will come back and you'll both win. If the problem is not handled well, the guest will never come back and you'll both lose.

The Energy Equation

Escalating an incident adds energy. If you escalate by getting angry, frustrated or raising your voice, you've just added negative energy to the interaction. If you escalate with a calm demeanor, soothing tone and encouraging words, you've just added positive energy.

Once the energy is added, it has to go somewhere. Often, the person you're engaging throws it right back, or even increases it. A talented, mature person might take your negative energy and de-escalate it, or even swallow it and permit the conversation to calm down or end.

But don't count on it. Sure, you can "win" an argument if you can overwhelm your opponents with more energy than they can handle. Of course, they're not your opponents ... and you don't really win.

Staying aware of the energy you add or remove from interactions is a sophisticated technique that radically changes the outcomes of the conversations that fill your day. Add the good stuff, absorb the bad stuff and focus on the outcomes, not the bravado.

Dealing with Difficult People

Did you ever run into a difficult person? If you've been in the hospitality business for more than a day, you probably have. The question is, "Why would anyone *want* to be difficult?"

Do *you* want to be difficult? *Are* you difficult occasionally? When you're being a jerk, don't you pretty much know that you're being a jerk? You just-can't-quite-stop-being-a-jerk right now! Right?

People are difficult because they just can't help it at the moment. They're just stuck in that weird place and they can't stop it at that moment any more than you can when you are in the same situation. I'll grant you some people may spend their whole lives stuck in that mood, but they wouldn't live like that if they could see any other way.

The secret to dealing with a difficult person is recognizing their upset state of mind

If you understand that people are basically good (have you met any evil babies lately?), then when someone is being difficult, you tend to see them as a normally nice person who's just a little off track at the moment. You notice their thinking more than their behavior. When you see the situation like that, you tend not to over-react to what they do or take them to task for what they are doing.

If you don't take a person's aberrant behavior too seriously, it's easier for them to pop out of their distressed mood naturally. But if you back someone into a corner when they're off track, they'll defend it to the death! (Don't you?)

The more you understand human behavior, the more you see poor behavior as merely a symptom of someone's thinking and the less impact their bad moods will have on you

It's nothing personal. Another person's upset is not a personal attack. It has nothing to do with you, even if they use your name – that's just the way people behave when they're a little off track.

If you have a child, has he or she ever screamed, "I hate you, I hate you?" Probably. Do you check yourself into therapy as a failed parent? Probably not. You just see it as a three-year-old throwing a tantrum. While you may not like it, you don't take the behavior too seriously because you see it only for what it is.

Somehow we think it should be different when people become adults, but it isn't. Twenty-year-olds throw tantrums. Fifty-year-olds throw tantrums. We still do many of the same things we did when we were kids, we're just a little more sophisticated about it.

What do *you* do when you're being difficult? Have you ever been mad and said things you didn't really mean or exaggerated the "facts" to make your case look better when you were upset? Don't take it too seriously when someone else does the same thing.

Fatal Mistakes

There are five things I suggest you NEVER do when dealing with an irate guest:

Don't let your attention wander

You know how annoying it is to talk to someone who's not really listening to you. The irritation is directly proportional to how emotionally involved you are with what you're saying. (An irate guest is *very* attached to what they're saying!)

Remember the cost of losing a guest. If one of your patrons has a problem, I promise there's nothing else you can be doing at that moment that is more valuable than what it will cost you to lose their loyalty forever. Focus.

171

Don't raise your voice

We tend to raise our voices when facing someone who is a bit out of control. This may happen because either we're frustrated ourselves or because we are trying to be heard above the ranting of the guest. Whatever the real cause may be, increasing volume can only escalate the confrontation. Modulate.

Don't take it personally

The situation has nothing to do with you, even if they use your name and blame you for the problem. That's just what you should expect from people who are a bit out to lunch! If you get caught up in someone else's drama, the only thing that happens is that both of you get lost in drama. Don't go there.

Don't touch them

When a person is upset, touching them can seem like a personal attack and they will react, sometimes violently. It's always best to maintain your composure, keep your arms down and watch that you don't clench your fists (or your jaw). Breathe.

Don't take everything they say literally

Did you ever get angry and exaggerated your case or said something you really didn't mean? Most of us have. It helps to remember that what you're seeing and hearing is natural behavior for someone who is a little off track at the moment, nothing more. Relax.

Calming Language

As skillful as you may be, occasionally you'll have a guest blow up in your face. When you can see them as otherwise nice people who are just a little lost at the moment, it's easier to keep from reacting.

Fortunately, there are a few things you can say to an irate guest that will help both of you defuse the confrontation. Understand that you are dealing with a dynamic human situation and that it takes more than just the words to calm a guest down.

You must be present (nothing else on your mind except the well-being of the guests), you must stay calm and you must make eye contact. The operable attitude is still, *"It matters to me what happens to you."* With those conditions met, the phrases below can help you make the best of a bad situation:

In most cases, all an irate guest really wants is someone to show they care and will address the problem. Often someone will raise their voice as they get angrier and angrier. The louder they get, the more likely you are to tune them out (because you don't need that noise in your life, right?) The problem is that the more you tune them out, the louder they'll get because they're still trying to get your attention!

To make a clear personal commitment that you will handle the situation, start your statement with: **"I will ..."** "I will take care of that right away." "I will replace that for you immediately." It's a personal commitment and helps people see their business is important to you.

As the guest is blowing off steam, try interjecting one or more of these phrases. You will be surprised at how effective they can be at getting people's attention and calming them down:

"This is important."
"This isn't at all the kind of service I want to give you."
"Your business is important to me."
"I apologize."

It's amazing what phases like these will do to defuse the anger so the other person can hear you.

Powerful Language Habits

Sometimes you'll have a guest who's right on the edge – it could go either way for them. For example, my first restaurant was in the financial district of San Francisco. That part of the City was populated by attorneys, stockbrokers and other lesser life forms, many of whom worked under extreme pressure all day.

We were the gathering place of choice after working hours and we saw them all. When they came into the restaurant, they could be wound up tighter than a clock. It seemed one wrong word and they might explode!

We could often defuse a potential explosion with a line like this: "Wow, it looks like it's been one of those days! But you have come to the right place. Let me find you a spot and get you a drink." You could almost hear the pressure escaping as they breathed a sigh of relief!

Here are a few simple phrases that can help you deal more effectively with guests on the edge:

"I will..."

This is a personal commitment on your part to handle whatever it is that the guest needs. Since hospitality is a business of personal connection, this position is very powerful. When you let your guests know their needs are important to you they will be less defensive and more reasonable.

"You can..." vs. "We can't..."

Tell them what they *can* do instead of what you *cannot* do. (Remember? We talked about this on Page 147.) Let's say a guest comes in and asks for a poached egg. If you say, "We don't do poached eggs," you're asking for an angry diner. Instead, say, "We can scramble them, we can fry them or I can make you a terrific omelette," and reduce your chances of setting the guest off.

"Will you?" vs. "You have to"/"You should have"/ "You made a mistake"/"I need"/"Why didn't you?"

Be careful that your tone of voice or choice of words doesn't come across like an irate schoolteacher lecturing an errant 8-year-old. Your guests are completely untrained ... and they don't *want* to be trained or ordered around. Irritation, harsh tone or inappropriate words when speaking to your guests is disrespectful ... and dangerous.

Give the Reason First

If you have to tell guests they can't do something, take a hint from the airlines and give the reason first: "For your own comfort and safety, please stay seated with your seat belt fastened until we reach a complete stop at the gate."

If someone is headed for the door with a drink in hand, you might say, "To comply with state liquor laws, we ask that you keep open containers inside the building." In a deli, it could be, "To be sure we can serve everyone in the order of arrival, please take a number."

When you provide the reason first, it gives your message a context so the guest can more easily understand why you are making the request. When they understand the reasons, they are less likely to react negatively, particularly if they are already touchy.

Handling Complaints in Person

Here's my approach for dealing with complaints received in person. Written complaints call for a slightly different approach. (Find details on that and much more in my book, *Cashing In on Complaints*).

I devised this approach as a bit of a formula to give myself a track to run on since I knew if I took a complaint personally I'd mess things up ... and I didn't trust myself not to get defensive.

Because these situations play out in real time, you must think on your feet. With that in mind, having a plan (and a little practice) is a good idea. Here's the plan that has always worked well for me:

Recognize the Gift

A complaining guest represents 24 others who chose not to speak up. That is truly a gift and you should thank them for caring enough to give it you, even if you don't like the way the gift is wrapped.

Listen Without Distractions

We've talked about how a distracted state of mind creates irritation in others. Don't throw gasoline on the fire. When someone is complaining to you, do not let your attention wander – it could escalate the problem and cost you that guest's business.

Calming Language

If the guest is being difficult or unreasonable, the calming language ideas we discussed can let the guest know you are listening and help to get them off the defensive.

Apologize

When the guest is calm, you have to use one of two words – either "sorry" or "apologize". You're not going to say, "Gee, I'm sorry I poisoned your whole family." In fact, a complaint with potential liability must be handled very differently. You don't have to confess to anything. All it takes is a sincere apology like, "I'm so sorry that you're upset." People just want to know that it matters to you what happens to them.

Offer No Defense or Excuses

Remember that getting defensive and wanting to explain is the biggest mistake you can make when handling a complaint. It's not about right and wrong. It is about saving that $50,000 guest.

Remove the Offending Element

If it is a food-related complaint, get the problem item out of there! If a guest complains about a bug in the salad, don't let them watch that critter crawl around the radicchio while you discuss it. The salad is gone ... right now!

Suggest a Generous Replacement or Solution

You know what's right. Most people won't try the problem item again, so offer to replace the item with an alternative that can be dished up quickly. Remember the others at the table already have their meals and it is an awkward situation. While the kitchen is replacing the problem dish, bring a quick (complimentary) item so they can be eating something with their companions.

Don't Negotiate

Don't say, "What would it take to make this right for you?" This is very awkward for many guests. I've had managers tell me that when they ask guests to suggest a solution, they usually come up with something less than the manager was willing to give. That is OK as far as it goes, but I wonder if the guests ever came back!

Make it Right

If you're going to comp something in the end anyway, tell them right now that you're going to comp it. Don't leave them sitting around wondering what you're going to do. The longer they stew, the lower their mood gets, the bigger the problem will seem and the larger the solution it will take to make them happy.

Allow for the Hassle Factor

Replace plus one. Make it better than it was. "Of course there's no charge for the soup and dessert's on me tonight." The idea is to compensate the guest for the inconvenience caused by the fact that things weren't 100% right the first time.

Give a Reason to Return

As ever, you must replace the experience of "it went wrong and they fixed it" with the experience of "it was perfect" ... and the only way to do that is to get them back.

> In my opinion, everything to this point can be done – and should be done – by the server at the table at the time. If you can see the advantage in shortening the time between the problem and the resolution, you can see the case for giving your staff the authority to handle most guest complaints on the spot.

Manager Follow-up

After the guest is satisfied, the staff member should let the manager know about the situation and how it was handled so that it can be noted and avoided in the future. This also allows the manager to follow up with the guests, if it seems appropriate, to backstop the staffer and be sure the guests are happy.

Complaints With Potential Liability

Complaints that may carry some possible liability, such as incidents of suspected food borne illness, cannot be handled like typical garden variety gripes. The overall goal is the same – to calm the guest down and get them back if possible – but you must be a lot more cautious, tactful and deliberate.

A complaint like this will usually come in the form of a phone call from an upset guest who has come down with symptoms they assume are the result of a meal in your restaurant. The caller is apt to be angry, scared and unreasonable. (These calls are a trying experience for the person receiving them as well.)

On the next page is a form developed by the National Restaurant Association to help gather the information needed to determine cause and identify responsibility for a food-related problem. This is another form that's difficult to read when it's this small, but you can download a full-sized version at www.restaurantdoctor.com/liability.pdf.

I suggest you devise a similar form (or use this one), drill *everyone* on your staff on how to use it and have blank copies near every phone where you might answer a call from a complaining guest.

You don't want to ask an upset guest to wait while you hunt up a form, or trust your memory to make sure you get all the information you will need. You also don't want to ask them to phone someone else or hold while you look for a manager. They are upset and actions like these can seem like stalling or lack of concern. If that happens, it will only make the caller more anxious and upset.

Here are the steps I suggest when you receive a complaint that could carry potential liability for the restaurant:

Get the Facts

The first thing is to learn the facts of the matter so you'll be able to determine what actually happened. The safest attitude is to assume the complainant has a valid claim. If it turns out the problem does lie with the restaurant, you'll need every possible scrap of information to locate and eliminate the cause.

At this point you won't know if this is an isolated case or the first of many calls, so be careful that your tone of voice doesn't convey a defensive attitude.

177

Foodborne Illness/Complaint Report

Complainant: Name _____ Phone (Day)_____

Address: _____ Phone (Eve) _____

_____

Others in party? _____
(Get name, address and phone.
Use back of form if necessary.) _____

_____

Time and date of meal: _____ Unit location: _____

Staff member serving meal or otherwise involved: _____

Onset of symptoms: Date _____ Time _____ Symptoms: _____

_____

_____

_____

Medical treatment/Doctor _____

(Hospital) Name _____ Addre ss _____ Phone _____

Suspect meal: _____ Amount eaten _____

Identification (brand name, lot number): _____

Description of meal: _____

Did others in the party have the same food? _____ Who? _____

Leftovers: _____ (refrigerate, do not freeze)

Other foods or   Date   Time   Location   Description
beverages
consumed   _____
before or
after the   _____
suspect meal

_____

Other agencies notified? _____

Complainant's Attitude: _____

Remarks: _____

_____

Received by: _____ Date _____ Time _____

Apologize for Any Upset
the Guest May Be Experiencing

You must be precise when dealing with complaints of this sort, but you can still be compassionate. This is a human person who was a guest in your restaurant and who is now experiencing a major upset for which you may (or may not) bear some responsibility.

178

Do your best to stay neutral. Your safest path is to be neither an advocate for the complainant or the company. Simply saying, "I can hear that you're upset and I'm so sorry" is often enough.

Don't Argue or Admit Liability

You don't have to admit to anything in order to be empathetic. You are not trying to resolve the matter, only to collect the facts. Resist the urge to react to the complainant or the problem, particularly if they seem overly agitated, their statements sound irrational or their demands seem unreasonable.

Resist the temptation to admit that it was all your fault and throw yourself on the mercy of the caller. This posture can be tempting just because it will end the conflict, but remember you are a detective at this point, not a peacemaker.

Don't Offer to Pay Medical Bills

Unless you've been otherwise advised by counsel or your insurance agent, stay in the fact-finding mode. Anything you say can easily be misinterpreted. In the hands of an adversarial attorney, even innocent comments can be made to look like an admission of guilt. Stick to the facts and leave the solutions to others.

Let the Person Tell Their Own Story

You are looking for the grains of truth that will enable you – and any third parties who may become involved in the case – to determine what actually happened.

The best eye-witness you have may be the person on the phone so let them pick their own words and tap their own memories. Any attempt to "help" by putting words in their mouth will only muddy the waters and make it harder to sort out the truth. Trying to shut the caller up or hurry them off the phone will create resentment that can only make it harder to reach a resolution.

Don't Suggest Symptoms

Symptoms are the first clues to what really caused the problem. It is vital that the complainant deal from their own experience about what symptoms appeared and at what time.

People who are very upset can easily take any symptoms you suggest and think that they apply. If the person on the phone is trying to scam you, suggesting symptoms can make it easier for them to fake the problem. Be patient, ask good questions and just write down what they tell you.

Record the Type of Symptoms and the Time They Started

Many types of food borne illness have an incubation period. For example, the symptoms of salmonella poisoning don't appear for 2-6 hours after eating a contaminated product. It's not appropriate for you to make comments on, or have an opinion about, what the complainant is saying. Just record what they noticed and when they noticed it. The Health Department will determine what is relevant.

Try to Get a Food History

The problem may be food-related but have nothing to do with you, so ask what they ate or drank before and after their visit. Most food poisoning actually happens in the home but people who get sick assume it must be from a public restaurant. An accurate food history will enable the authorities to determine where the fault actually lies.

You not only want to know what was eaten but how much of it was consumed. Many food borne illnesses are dose-related, meaning the severity of the problem depends on the quantity of contaminated product ingested. Find out if anyone else in the party ate the same foods so someone can follow up with them.

Don't Offer Medical Advice

Even if you are a trained medical practitioner, it is inappropriate to offer medical advice. If the complainant is experiencing discomfort, you might inquire if they have consulted a doctor or if they plan to do so. Don't react to what they tell you, just write it down.

Find out What Actions They've Taken

You want to know if they have been to a hospital or seen a doctor. Ask if they have called the Health Department yet. A caller may threaten reporting you to the authorities in an attempt to extort a settlement, but in cases of potential food borne illness, the Health Department can actually be your best ally.

Let the caller know you plan to notify the Health Department as soon as you have all the facts. This lets them know you are not intimidated by the authorities and helps make sure the Health Department doesn't take your call as the report of a second incident.

Reassure the Complainant

Tell the complainant you will investigate and be back in touch as soon as possible. When you have all the information you need, set a time to get back to them and be sure you return the call at the agreed-upon time, even if you have nothing new to report. At this point, actions speak louder than words. You want to be sure the caller knows you are not taking their problem lightly.

Notify the Proper Authorities

Call the Health Department, let them know that you have had a complaint and are investigating. Fax or email a copy of the incident report and ask for their advice.

Notify your attorney and your insurance agent, fax or email them each a copy of your report and ask their advice. Your best course of action is to be proactive rather than reactive. Be actively involved in getting to the bottom of the situation rather than hiding out in the hope it will all blow over. (It won't!)

Be Smart

If a food item is called into question, take it off the menu and store samples in a secure location for later examination. If it starts to look like you have a major outbreak on your hands, consult your legal advisors, work closely with the Health Department and keep the press informed.

The Positive Side of Complaints

Many operators tend to think of complaints as bad news. While nobody likes to get a complaint, there is a lot that can be gained from them. Here are a few of the positive aspects:

Tough Guests Force You to Be Your Best

It is easy to get complacent and let down on your standards. Demanding guests keep you honest by telling you every time your attention wanders or your standards slip. They are always right (at least from their perspective). Nothing slips past them.

Admittedly, demanding guests can drive you crazy sometimes. But pleasing them is the only reason your restaurant exists and they are in the best position to tell you how you are doing at it! Your guests will always see things you will never notice. Rather than driving off demanding guests, use them like an in-house shopping service.

Every Complaint Is an Insight into How to Improve Your Business

Every problem has a gift for you in its hands. People go out to eat expecting to have a good time. They want it to be great.

Since you're in business to make sure your guests are happy, the comments and suggestions they give are invaluable research into how to do your primary job better. This is where the gold is. Even if a complaint is entirely off the wall, there is still a nugget of truth in there somewhere. If you can dig it out, you can profit from it.

181

Guests Are More Likely to Complain
If They Think You Care

If you look like you don't want to hear it, nobody will bother to tell you. The more interested you are in learning the hard truth of your guests' experience and the more receptive you are to suggestions on how you can do better, the greater the chances you will get the feedback. Some will delight you, some will distress you, but it's all valuable information that will help you improve and prosper.

I acknowledge that being this open requires a degree of vulnerability that many operators find uncomfortable, but if you have a problem and don't identify it quickly, it will cost you a lot of money. It could even cost you your restaurant! Now *that* is uncomfortable!

Resolving Complaints Satisfactorily
Increases Guest Loyalty

Statistics suggest if someone's complaint is handled well, they are more loyal than if they never had a complaint at all. Perhaps it is because handling a complaint well is a personal statement of caring that establishes more of a personal connection between the guest and the restaurant, but complaining guests can often become your most loyal patrons.

Most Complaining Guests Care About You

If people didn't care, they wouldn't take the time to speak up – they would just leave and never return. Most complaints, particularly written ones, are cries for help that are really saying:

"Say it ain't so, Joe!"
"My feelings have been hurt by an old friend."
"You probably didn't know about this, but ..."

Don't panic when you get a complaint. It means they care

The worst sort of feedback is none at all. It means they're indifferent

8
The Bottom Line

The Bottom Line

> *"All things being equal, the profit and loss of a business tells an owner how well (profit) or how poorly (loss) a business is meeting the wants and needs of individuals in society."*
> — Jonathan Mariano

Most independent operators are fixated on marketing, believing all they need to succeed is to get more people through the door. That is important, of course, but *people only come back because they want to ...* because you are becoming their restaurant of choice and an important part of their lives.

Operators talk about marketing, but what they really do is advertise: offers, coupons, specials, events that scream, "Buy something!" or "Feed me!" At best, it becomes boring and people turn it off. At worst, it causes them to see you as being just the same as every other place in town that's doing the same desperate things in the same way.

Building a Business

The traditional approach to building a restaurant business has been to focus on marketing (driving sales) and controlling costs, treating the process as a straight math exercise. More dollars in and fewer dollars out equals more profit ... or does it?

The math is accurate but the logic is flawed. Let me explain.

To maximize profitability it helps to keep a long term perspective. If there's a "get rich" secret in this business, it surely must be to get rich slowly. People ask me, "How can I maximize profitability?" My response? "Stay in business a long time!"

It's easy to think of profitability in the short run: "What were our sales tonight?" A much smarter approach is to give more, do it better and make a little less money for a lot longer.

Planet Hollywood did big numbers when they opened, but have they really maximized profitability? The once-hot chain is now found only in a few resort areas where tourists visit once out of curiosity and never again. The mediocre food, overpriced drinks and indifferent service don't provide any real incentive to return.

185

So don't try to pry every penny from your guests' wallets tonight. It's not the hospitable thing to do anyway. Leave them with a little change so they can patronize you tomorrow (and have the desire to do it!) Under-promise and over-deliver. Do more than you have to. Give them something for nothing. Make a friend. It's actually a lot more fun than endlessly grubbing for money.

Building Sales

Building a business involves building sales of course. However, that is only a short range plan. We are at the intersection of sales, service and hospitality here. I hope to show you how the three interact:

Sales-building really has two components: Trial and Repeat. You must first attract new guests, then you must make them want to return. Long term success requires that you consistently excel on both counts. There are two roads that will take you toward higher sales.

The Low Road: Marketing

Many people equate marketing with advertising – either in mass media (print, radio, TV, Facebook, etc.), through direct mail or by sending targeted offers to existing guests. Those may all be part of it, but I prefer to start by defining the term a bit more narrowly.

To my way of thinking ...

Marketing encompasses activities designed to encourage trial by newbies or give current guests a reason to return at a specific time for a specific reason.

That's all marketing is good for. Nothing more, nothing less. Marketing is a necessary activity and it has its place, but it can be expensive, difficult to measure and, if it is your sole means of driving sales, relentless.

When your business model is based just on building sales, you fixate on transactions. Your focus is short term. You grasp at any bright shiny object that looks like it will lead to a few more sales, but you live your life on a treadmill and there are lots of treadmills – Groupon, Facebook, Valpak, Entertainment Book and the like. The only thing that really changes is which treadmill you spend your time on.

186

Coupons Are the Cocaine
of the Clueless!

Sure, people will patronize you when you offer them a large enough discount, but when the coupons stop – or when a competitor offers a better deal, they'll be gone in a heartbeat. Don't get mad at them. These are "coupon people" and that's what coupon people do.

There is no real loyalty created by discounts. You can build sales this way, but you can't build a business, because once you start you can't stop. Discount coupons have a place in your marketing plans, but there are some potholes on this section of the low road:

Discount Coupons are Expensive
When you offer a dollars-off coupon, it costs you 100% of the face value in cash. Ten dollars off is ten bucks that won't be in the cash register at the end of the day, but all your expenses stay the same. The margins in the restaurant biz are enough anyway. Industry-wide, the median pretax profit is only about 5% of sales.

Discount Coupons are Common
Everybody has coupons. The pizza industry has educated the public not to buy a pizza unless they have a coupon ... and it's killing them! If everybody is doing it, the playing field is still even, it just sinks to a lower level and nobody stands out (or makes the money they could). To be memorable in the minds of the market, you can't do what everyone else is doing. Pay attention to what your competitors are up to, of course, but the idea is to zig when they zag.

Someone Will Always Sell for Less
You have to decide if you want to compete on price or on product. If you choose product, you're in a race to the top. If you choose price, some other clueless operator will always undercut you, not realizing he's actually losing money on the sale. Don't get in a race to the bottom. You might just win.

Either Regulars Feel Cheated ...
or You Give Away Sales
Current patrons will take advantage of your coupons, of course. Why pay more if you don't have to? You can't exclude them from a dollars-off deal you offer to the public without the risk of alienation, but in the absence of a discount, these guests would pay full price and not think a thing about it. Making a buck in foodservice is hard enough without giving away profits unnecessarily.

187

A recent survey by the NPD Consulting Group determined, "Some 42% of consumers return time and again to their favorite restaurants whether or not there are deals."

Everyone Will Hate You

- If a coupon deal causes an unexpected surge in business, your systems can break down, the experience will not be pleasant and the coupon people will hate you.

- Your kitchen will hate you because you created pandemonium in the back of the house and stressed them out.

- Your service staff will hate you because coupon people are notoriously cheap. If they tip at all, they only tip on what they paid, not on the retail value of what they received.

- Whether or not a coupon offer packs the place, your partners, your lenders and your accountant will hate you because you'll hardly make a profit in either case.

- Your family will hate you because you'll crawl back to the house exhausted, discouraged and grumpy.

Once Hooked, It's Hard to Kick the Habit

If you build your business on coupons as many pizzerias have, you can't stop couponing without tanking your sales. Essentially you have been buying transactions, although not very profitable ones. If you stop buying, coupon people will just go to the next place that buys their attention with another coupon or a deeper discount.

Discounts Compromise Price Integrity

If you'll run a $14.95 Prime Rib dinner special for the summer, how can you ask me to pay full price ($22.95) for the same meal in September? By discounting, you essentially tell people you can make an acceptable profit at the lower price. That probably isn't true, but when you raise the price back to where it should be, it seems to consumers like you're now trying to gouge them.

A NOTE FROM THE DOC:

The only safe way to offer a dollars-off deal is when it is for a very limited time and for a very specific reason. For example, there's no damage done if you celebrate your restaurant's 20th anniversary by dropping your prices to their 1994 levels for a week.

You could even offer a great price on crab (while your supply lasts) if your vendor was overstocked and gave you a deal. You need to explain all this when you make the offer, though. (Hint: An offer like this works best if you don't normally have crab on your menu)

Not All Coupons are Discounts

Most coupons are typically dollars-off discounts, but there is another type that carries less risk: the value-added deal. This type of offer basically says, "Buy one of these and I'll throw in one of those." A good example would a free dessert or a free glass of wine with dinner.

Full Price or Free

You won't harm your value proposition if you offer something either at full price or free because both items still retain their full value. That $8 glass of wine is still worth $8 after the offer expires. What makes this idea more attractive is that the $8 gift only costs you $2 to give.

Here's a summary of the relative cost and risks:

COUPON OPTIONS	Dollars Off	Value Added
Cost to you	100 cents on the dollar	product cost (25-35%
Attraction to responders	Price	Products
Average check/tips	Lower	Higher
Likelihood of patron's return	Only for a better price	No guarantee, but improved
Pricing structure integrity	Compromised	Intact

Give Guests a Reason to Return

There are many ways to encourage guests to return at a specific time for a specific reason, but to enumerate all of them would turn this into more of a marketing text than one on service and hospitality.

If you want marketing, I have several books on it in the Resources section. However, it is consistent to at least talk about one of the most common ways to do full price marketing that does have some service aspect to it: promotions and festivals.

Promotions and festivals provide a natural, logical reason to invite guests to return and gives them something to talk to their friends about. "Come back next week for our salmon festival" sounds much better than "Come back on Tuesday because it's a slow night and we really need the business!"

Festivals are special events highlighting a particular type of cuisine or a specific food product. They are a great way to break the monotony for staff and guests alike, plus they provide a way to experiment with new recipes or take advantage of seasonal products.

Special events can be run regularly on a specific night (such as a "Thursday is Pot Roast Night" program) or for a specific period of time, usually a week or two at most. Promotions that run longer than a month lose their special-ness and might create some confusion in the minds of the market as to what sort of a restaurant you actually are.

No matter what sort of festival you conduct, it must be appropriate for your restaurant. I have a hard time imagining a successful cherry festival in a pizzeria, for example, but an Italian restaurant could easily run a festival featuring shrimp.

Special events should be run often enough to break up the routine but not so frequently they lose their uniqueness, confuse the market or become a career in themselves. A two-week festival every other month is more realistic because it lets you take advantage of seasonal changes and won't overwhelm either the staff or the guests. Take it slowly and do a memorable job with each event. Build on a strong foundation.

Food festivals typically coincide with the height of the season for that particular product (a strawberry festival in July, for example) when supplies are at their peak, quality is high and prices are low. That being said, there might be some real talking power in an off-season event, like a fresh raspberry festival in February.

Protein products (like lobster) lend themselves to an array of appetizers, soups, salads and entrees featuring the product. Fruit or vegetable products can be worked into appetizers, soups, salads, side dishes, sauces and desserts.

The High Road: Connection

Here's where service, hospitality and the bottom line really come together. Marketing builds short term sales but personal connection is the way you build a sustainable business for the long term.

Connection is the personal relationship that causes guests to identify with your restaurant and prefer doing business with you over your competition

No matter what your business, you surely have a few loyal regulars. These are the people with whom you've developed a personal relationship. You know each other by name. You know what they like and don't like. You're their favorite restaurant. They patronize you – and gladly pay full price – because they WANT to. They recommend you to their friends and feel like unpaid members of your staff.

This is the group you must cultivate and grow to build a real (that means profitable and sustainable) business. Hospitality is the magic wand that creates the connection, connection creates steady sales and steady sales allow you to grow and prosper.

Create Community

What you're really out to do is create a community of people with shared interests. Initially that interest may centered around your food or ambience, but for patrons to feel a personal connection to your restaurant you must connect with them as people.

People are more loyal to other people than they are to places. Until and unless you can establish a person-to-person relationship, you will just be another place to eat.

The key to connection is Presence – being *with* the guests when you are with the guests as we discussed in Chapter 6. That should be a constant in your dealings with both guests and co-workers ... but what do you do after that?

Here are some simple suggestions:

Watch Faces

As you go through the dining room, you'll naturally look at the table tops to see where diners are in the service sequence and if they have everything they need. While that will tell you something about the service, their faces will tell you a lot more.

That's where you will be able to plug into their experience. When your head is clear, you'll instinctively know if they're annoyed, happy, confused, bored or if there is something on their minds.

If their focus is on each other, all is well and it's not an appropriate time to visit the table. When you see their eyes are not focused on their dining companions, it may be an opening to approach the table without intruding. In fact, it may be a welcome break for them.

191

If they have a problem, solve it. If they're confused, get things back on track. If they have a suggestion, listen to their idea and ask a few questions to be sure you understand their thinking. Sensing an unspoken need and responding to it is a nice thing to do for another human being. It opens a dialogue and plants a seed of connection.

Non Task-Related Conversation

If the only interactions between your staff and the guests are related to the mechanics of the meal (taking orders, checking back, etc.), that's the only relationship you will nurture. The goal is to sense any natural openings for a brief chat on a topic of personal interest.

That might be sports, current event, the weather, their children, favorite foods, even a sincere compliment on something they're wearing. The safest question may be just to introduce yourself and ask a new guest where they're from.

In the course of conversation you might learn you have a common interest, know some of the same people, lived in the same cities, enjoyed the same restaurants or traveled to the same countries.

I'm not suggesting you pry or try to get adopted(!) – it is certainly inappropriate to be overly chummy. The idea is to be personable yet professional. Keep the focus on the guest and their interests (rather than on you), don't push, and be sensitive to "vibes" from the table.

Learn More About Your Guests

Collect information, not just business cards. We talked about the value of knowing your guests' personal preferences and pet peeves ... and having a system for making that information available to the server before the guest arrives.

What do you know about them besides their names? Do you know where they live? ... their children's names, ages, schools and activities? ... the name and breed of their dog, cat, rabbit or fish?

Do you know where they work and what they do? ... where they go on vacation? ... what they like to do on weekends? ... what local activities and charitable causes are important to them?

The important thing here is to develop a relationship over time that makes the guest feel comfortable sharing information like this. Initiate the relationship whenever it seems natural and appropriate, but it can't become an interrogation – that would be uncomfortable and therefore, by definition, inhospitable.

192

Connect the Dots

In his book, *Setting the Table*, Danny Meyer puts it this way:

"Dots are information. The more information you collect, the more frequently you can make meaningful connections that can make other people feel good and give you an edge in business. Using whatever information I've collected to gather guests together in a spirit of shared experience is what I call connecting the dots."

"If I don't turn over the rocks, I won't see the dots. If I don't collect the dots, I can't connect the dots. If I don't know that someone works for, say, a magazine whose managing editor I happen to know, I've lost a chance to make a meaningful connection that could enhance our relationship with the guest and the guest's relationship with us. The information is there. You just have to choose to look."

Connecting the dots helps in another way: If you know that two of your guests are avid golfers, introduce them to each other. It may lead to a foursome – even develop into a larger golf group that has you and your restaurant in common. You may learn that one guest has a need or a talent that matches up with what another guest is seeking or has to offer.

Do this enough and the community of people who look at your restaurant as their home away from home will grow. You'll increasingly become their favorite restaurant, an integral part of their quality of life and the last little luxury they are willing to give up. You will be their Restaurant of Choice.

Create Perks

Human nature being what it is, people like to be able to do things other people can't do. You can make that possible by establishing a "club" with special privileges for "members," giving guests a sense of belonging and reason to come back more often.

You can make a club out of almost anything. All you need is a premise and a benefit. There are various types of clubs you can use to your advantage. Here are just a few:

If you sell draft beer, start a mug club. Members of your mug club buy a personalized beer mug that is kept for them behind the bar. Whenever they come in, they drink from their own mugs and receive a special deal. For example, if you sell a 12-oz draft for two dollars, the mugs for club members might be 14-16 ounces for the same price.

This idea isn't limited to beer. You could adapt the same idea to breakfast by offering a great-looking personalized coffee mug and a deal to make it interesting to members of your coffee club.

You could establish a wine club where members receive an oversized crystal wine glass with their initials etched on it, the better to (frequently) explore the finer wines from your cellar ... or just show off for their friends!

Regardless of their form, the premise behind mug clubs and their kind are similar:

1. The mug, glass or cup stays on display at the restaurant so the guests have to return to the property to use it.

2. The appearance of the vessel is distinctive, obvious to the other guests in the room when it is being used, making the user (member) feel privileged.

3. The container is personalized with the name of the member and the restaurant's logo to tie the two more closely together.

4. Club members receives a deal – usually either a lower price, more product at the same price, or access to entirely different products, like a special wine list only available to wine club members.

> **CASEY'S MUG CLUB**
>
> Jim Casey implemented a mug club at his Casey's East Restaurant in Troy, New York. It cost $5 to join the club (which paid for the mug and your first beer) after which members could get a refill for 25% less than a non-member would pay for an equal-sized pour.
>
> When he first started the idea, Jim figured that one or two dozen people might take him up on it. Mug club membership rose to over 100 in three months and kept growing.
>
> Jim said the camaraderie among the members helped keep his bar full and his regulars became a lot more regular when the program went into effect.

Marc's Restaurant outside Denver, Colorado instituted an Oyster Club. To be eligible for membership, guests had to order 200 oysters at full price from the oyster bar.

Once they qualified, their name was added to the Oyster Club membership plaque and they were entitled to happy hour prices on oysters at any time. Over 1000 diners took the challenge and joined Marc's Oyster Club.

Tell Me a Secret

People also like to know things other people don't know. To tap into this human tendency, tell guests something that isn't public knowledge. What secrets can you let people in on?

It's hardly a secret anymore, but drive-thru chain In-N-Out Burger has a "secret menu." Those in the know can order a "3x3" or ask for their burgers "animal style" – combos not found on the menu board.

I know of restaurants where the best-selling item on their menu is not on their menu at all ... and never has been. But if you know to order it, you can get it. Human nature being what it is, once you know the secret, you'll order the item simply because you can!

If you limit the number of portions you offer each night, it elevates the power of this idea even more. "Get there early and be sure to order the lamb shank. They always sell out early!"

It can be as simple as "leaking" the word that you have a wine special coming up before you announce it to the public. Or tell them you just received the last known case of 1997 Santa Cruz Pinot Noir on the planet. You won't be putting it on the wine list but you'll keep it aside for members of your Wine Club or those few insiders who know to ask for it.

Tell them about the things that fall into the "it's not on the menu but if you ask, we'll make it just for you" category. Sharing secrets is a great way to tie people more closely to your restaurant and give them things to talk about to their friends.

A word of caution, though: Secrets must remain relatively secret to spread by word-of-mouth. You can put out the word (once) in an email to your VIP members but don't promote it in a newspaper ad. Once a secret is public knowledge it loses most of its talking power.

Get Me Involved

Everyone says [positive] word-of-mouth is the best advertising. It is. People will talk when they know things that others don't know ... and they will talk when they get involved with your products.

If you have the best pot roast in town, you can create a loyal following of pot roast fanatics, particularly if they know how it is prepared, why you chose the cut of meat you use, where your recipe came from, why your pot roast is better or different and so forth.

People also talk when they get involved with themselves. This can happen when you help your guests feel like a pioneer by trying something new or unusual.

For example, when I was catering functions for the US Olympic Committee, one of my favorite items to include on a reception menu was rattlesnake chili – not because there was some pent-up demand for rattlesnake (I assure you there wasn't!) but because every guest would talk about it, often for a year or more, whether they had tried it or not! The same principle can be applied to your operation.

195

Before We Move On ...

Let's review the two business-building models we've discussed:

> **BUILD SALES WITH MARKETING COUPONS**
> - Buy Transactions
> - Blend Into the Crowd
> - Struggle Continually
> - Go Broke Slowly
>
> **BUILD BUSINESS VIA PERSONAL CONNECTION**
> - Make Friends
> - Stand Out From the Herd
> - Create Relationships
> - Get Rich Slowly

Any questions?

Hospitality and the Bottom Line

Becoming known for your hospitality is more than just a nicer way to run your business, it is also a smart business decision. Rather than having to buy traffic with discount coupons, you can create a steadily growing group of fiercely loyal regulars who will come back again and again because they *want to.*

Take care of your guests and the sales will take care of themselves

Make a friend and the sales will follow

Danny Meyer's incredible success certainly shows what good things happen when the entire company is focused on providing memorable hospitality, but spectacular results are not limited to upscale places. His Shake Shack concept is famous not only for its burgers and shakes but for long lines of patrons who wait patiently to get them.

For a wider sample, consider that the restaurants who have achieved actual certification as A Place of Hospitality – from fine dining Meccas to funky family eateries and pubs – report their best sales years *ever* since hospitality became their point of difference in the market. Some have seen sales increases of more than 20% from *any* previous high ... in the middle of a depressed economy!

Before you start to whine that the chains are stealing all your business, here's a bit of news that may help put your dilemma into perspective:

196

The Bad News:

The chains can probably outperform you. They have more money, better systems, more experience, superior talent and often more attractive locations.

The Good News:

Performance is no longer the differentiating factor. Just having good food and good service is the price of admission, not enough to make you stand out in the market.

The Great News:

You don't have to be the best, you just have to be their favorite! When people talk about their favorite restaurant, they are talking about what a place does FOR them ... and when people talk about what a place does FOR them, it means that hospitality is present.

When you become known for your hospitality, people will spend their money with you because they *want* to. They have other choices and they choose you. You are their Restaurant of Choice.

A Universal Truth

If you operate in a non-commercial environment, never think because you may have a captive audience, you don't have to make the effort. The principles that create connection and generate enthusiastic traffic in full service restaurants can be successfully applied to the unique needs of catering, institutional feeders, quick service, fast-casual, snack bars, or whatever your business looks like.

I believe the application of these principles is one of the big reasons the attitudes toward foodservice at the Olympic Training Center turned around so dramatically. My predecessor saw it as a 1960-era military mess hall whereas I saw it as a great self-service restaurant and approached everything we did as if we had to earn the business.

You can be the restaurant of choice ... even when they don't have a choice!

197

The Cost of Turnover

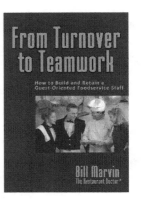

We said hospitality builds sales and is a natural result of an organization with a higher climate. Another predictable symptom of a high climate is a serious reduction in turnover ... and that puts money in your pocket, too. Let me explain:

For years I'd seen numbers tossed around about how many thousands of dollars turnover costs a typical restaurant and frankly, I had a problem accepting the figures.

I didn't doubt turnover had a high cost, but the numbers I'd seen were frightening and I'd never seen the calculations that supported them. So when I was working on my book, *From Turnover to Teamwork*, I wanted to do the math for myself. It was worse than I thought:

I came to understand that rather than just being a straight calculation, staff turnover has both direct and indirect components:

The direct costs are those expenses that arise solely because a worker quits or is terminated. They can be calculated on a per-person basis.

Indirect costs arise as a result of the impact the staff change has on the ongoing operation. These are harder to quantify because they show up as increased costs for the entire operation.

Let's look at those a little closer.

Direct Costs of Staff Turnover

On the next page, I lay out my take on the costs incurred when you lose an hourly worker. Take a look at the summary, check the assumptions and see if it helps put the costs of staff turnover into perspective. The expense categories in brackets are from *The Uniform System of Accounts for Restaurants* by the National Restaurant Association.

WyckWyre, a restaurant recruiting firm, put the median restaurant turnover rate in the US at 113% a year in 2012. This means a typical full service casual restaurant with 50 people on the payroll would turn over 57 people every twelve months – new crew members who must be recruited, hired and trained.

198

DIRECT COSTS OF TURNOVER

Recruiting Costs:
[Administrative & General Expense]
  ads, materials

$50 - 100

Staff Time (present staff):
[Payroll Expense/Employee Benefits]
  during interviews, orientation, training, counseling
  (20-80 hr x $12) plus 20% benefits

290 - 1150

  administrative paperwork, signing out old workers, signing in new workers
  (1-3 hr x $12) plus 20% benefits

15 - 45

Staff Time (new staff):
[Payroll Expense/Employee Benefits]
  during orientation, training, counseling
  (10-60 hr x $8) plus 20% benefits

95 - 575

Unemployment Claims of Departed Workers:
[Employee Benefits]
  increase in premiums

100 - 200

Administration fees for benefits sign-up
[Employee Benefits]

30 - 50

Overtime:
[Payroll Expense/Employee Benefits]
  allowance for additional hours to cover while the position is vacant
  (30-60 hr x $15) plus 20% benefits

540 - 1100

Other Turnover-related Costs:
[Direct Operating Expense]
  training materials, uniforms, uniform cleaning/renovation

200 - 400

Direct Cost per Person   **$1320 - 3620**

To keep the implications of this simple, let's split the difference and figure the cost for each of those 57 staff changes is $2500 per person. That's a whopping $142,500 a year ... and I haven't even included a calculation for salaried personnel, which most estimates place somewhere north of $10,000 per person!

$142,500! If that cost were a line item on your P&L, you'd be all over it. But it's a stealth number, factored in among all the other costs of operation so it doesn't pop out at you.

You can get part of this money back by creating a more positive climate and slowing the revolving door ... but there's still more to the equation:

Indirect Costs of Staff Turnover

Hidden in among the operating numbers are the indirect costs of turnover:

1. Increased turnover creates inconsistent (decreased) guest service which tends to lower your reputation in the market which increases negative word-of-mouth and reduces repeat patronage resulting in lower sales. **Estimated impact: sales are 5-15% lower**

2. Increased turnover means more lesser-trained workers which increases waste and translates into higher product and operating costs. **Estimated impact: operating expenses are 5-15% higher**

3. Increased turnover means the operation is staffed with generally less-productive workers, which contributes to a higher labor cost. **Estimated impact: labor cost is 10-20% higher**

4. Increased turnover leads to the loss of team cohesiveness which increases staff alienation fueling staff turnover and keeping the process going! **Estimated impact on sales and operating costs: escalation of the relationships previously outlined.**

By the same token, organizations with lower turnover can expect improvement in all categories (higher sales, lower costs) by about the same percentages.

Running the Numbers

To put the indirect costs into perspective, let's look at their potential impact on a full service restaurant doing $1 million in annual sales:

According to the annual *Restaurant Industry Operations Report* from the National Restaurant Association, a full service restaurant with typically has the following median operating results:

	AMOUNT	RATIO
Sales	$1,000,000	100.0%
Cost of Sales	332,000	33.2%
Payroll	294,000	29.4%
Staff Benefits	45,000	4.5%
Other Operating Expenses	171,000	17.1%
Operating Income	**$158,000**	**15.8%**

Then I projected the impact on the typical operation of a turnover rate 50% higher than the median (170% a year) and also ran the numbers for a rate 50% lower than the median (55% a year).

Here is the effect the rate of turnover would have on the sales and operating expenses of the operation:

CATEGORY	IMPACT	CHANGE TO MEDIAN FIGURES
Sales	± $100,000	± 10% of sales volume
Cost of Sales	± 3.3%	± 10% of cost of goods
Payroll Expense	± 4.4%	± 15% of payroll expense
Staff Benefits		same relationship to payroll expense
Other Operating Expenses	+ 1.7%	+ 10% of other operating costs (high turnover)
Other Operating Expenses	− 0.9%	− 5% of other operating costs (low turnover)

Finally I applied the percentage changes to the median percentage figures (e.g., 17.1% +10% = 18.8%, 17.1% –5% = 16.2%) and used the income and expense relationships above to calculate the impact on our million-dollar business of high and low staff turnover.

	w/higher turnover		w/lower turnover	
	AMOUNT	RATIO	AMOUNT	RATIO
Sales	$900,000	100.0%	$1,100,000	100.0%
Cost of Sales	328,700	36.5%	330,000	30.0%
Payroll	304,200	33.8%	275,000	25.0%
Staff Benefits	46,500	5.2%	42,100	3.8%
Other Operating Expenses	169,200	18.8%	178,200	16.2%
Operating Income	$51,400	5.7%	$274,700	24.9%

I was interested to note the difference in operating ratios correlated closely with the higher and lower quarries in the *Restaurant Industry Operations Report*.

This example suggests higher turnover could lower operating income by more than $100,000 from the median figures while lower turnover improved the bottom line by more than $120,000. The difference in indirect costs between an operation with high turnover and one with low turnover could be more than $220,000 a year in lost profits!

Add to that the $142,500 in direct costs we calculated and the potential impact of the revolving door will keep you awake at night! The good news is you already hold in your hands a prescription from the Doctor that can help you stop this bleeding.

Hospitality is powerful medicine

The Cost of Recovery

I almost called this section "The Cost of Being Chintzy" because that's typically what generates the expense. Let me explain with a recent example from an article I wrote in my weekly e-letter:

The Issue Arises

One of my favorite places to eat in Las Vegas is [an unnamed] Steakhouse. Their a la carte menu makes for an expensive evening, but I've always had a good time and a great meal, so it's been my go-to restaurant in Las Vegas for the past six or seven years. In fact, during a recent trip, I booked tables there two nights in a row with two separate groups.

The first night there were five of us. In addition to the typically great steaks, we had an array of seafood appetizers and tapped their extensive wine list for three bottles of one of my favorite wines, The Prisoner by Orrin Swift, a syrah/zinfandel blend that curls my toes. It was $90 a bottle, but hey, it's Vegas!

The waiter offered to make us a special combination appetizer with crab cakes, shrimp and stone crab claws. It sounded good so we went for it. When we got the bill, it turned out we had not received a combo deal but rather three separate appetizers with a total price of $140! Gotcha!

The next night I was back with two clients from Australia. (I didn't ask for the previous night's waiter!) In conversation, I told them the tale of my appetizer experience the night before. When our waiter asked what we would like to start with, we all took a pass.

Then it was time to order the wine. When the three of us had dined together in this restaurant the year before, I'd introduced them to The Prisoner and they wanted it again. Two bottles of wine seemed about right ... but there was a problem: the restaurant only had one 750ml bottle of the wine left in stock.

However, they had the same wine in a magnum for $225 and we had been thinking two bottles anyway. Since it wasn't my fault they were out of stock, I asked if they'd sell us the magnum for the price of two smaller bottles . It was $45 less than they wanted for the magnum but still a $180 sale and, I thought, a reasonable guest-oriented solution.

The waiter said he had to check with the sommelier. The sommelier said he had to ask the manager. Five minutes later the manager told us definitely not. Our spirits properly dampened, we only ordered one bottle.

My Take on It

People are entitled to screw up their businesses any way they like and it's certainly not my place to tell them how they should run the restaurant. I will tell you, though, that if the operation were mine, both situations would have been handled quite differently:

1. The first waiter would have been more clear about what he was actually offering for appetizers and not oversold the table. Had he been forthcoming, I would have requested to be seated in his section the following night.

2. The answer to my wine offer the second night would have been, "Of course!" The house would have made a little less on the large format bottle but doubled the wine sale. We would have been delighted rather than disappointed and would likely have tipped more generously as well.

I don't know if these lapses were the result of a corporate policy change, new management, poor ordering or pure chance, but they seemed totally out of character with my experience of prior visits to this restaurant. Still, the way things played out will make me think before I automatically make reservations next time. The bubble has popped.

I'm thinking it may be time to discover a new favorite place in Las Vegas, one that takes a longer view of hospitality. I know that's not fair ... but it's the way things work in the real world.

Post-Mortem

Because I thought they should know, I sent the restaurant a copy of my article without asking for anything in return. They called back expressing their proper horror at what happened, apologized profusely, and sent me $200 in gift cards.

That was a generous response, but let's do the math here:

The way they handled the appetizers probably made them a few dollars more than if they were more up front about what we were getting, but they lost the appetizer sale the following night because of it, so perhaps it's a wash.

The first waiter turned off a party of five, all of whom entertain clients often in Las Vegas. There are lots of other dining options in Sin City. He also lost his chance at a $75 tip the following night.

The restaurant lost again with their response to the wine issue the second night. Had they accepted my compromise offer, they would have made $45 less on the magnum and had a wine sale of $180 rather than a $90, so they're down a net $45 on that score.

Of course, the big loss would have come from the eight people involved who left with less than a favorable impression of the place. What might that cost them over time? What would it cost just to lose *my* loyalty?

I was responsible for bringing them over $1200 in sales on those two nights and I'm only in Las Vegas once or twice a year. Imagine the long term impact if I was a local regular!

After the fact, it cost manager's time and another $200 cash for damage repair. I admit their response was overly generous and I will probably go back at least once to use the gift cards, but it will be with a very critical eye. They'll have to prove themselves all over again. If my next visit isn't flawless, I'm history.

Wouldn't it have been cheaper, easier and made more sense just to do the right thing in the first place and not risk popping the bubble? People are creatures of habit and if you allow them to break the habit of patronizing your place, you may never see them again.

If you're going to comp something in the end anyway, just do it right up front and avoid a lot of hassle for everyone. The cost of keeping a guest is always far less than the cost of losing one. As "Coach" Don Smith always preaches, "The answer is yes, what's the question?"

Dollars and Sense

A hotel in Colorado called me in because their in-house restaurant had been losing 40 cents on the dollar for a number of years.

The rooms department of a hotel is quite profitable and having an on-site restaurant helps fill rooms, so the owners had been willing to live with the subsidy, but they were getting fed up with writing checks and had reached the point where something had to be done.

My task was to stop the bleeding. The real challenge, though, was to figure out how to sensitize the staff to the situation without creating mass panic or revealing figures that would likely end up in a feature article in the local paper. It was time for a full F&B staff meeting to discuss Restaurant Economics 101.

As a start, I asked the crew to write down the percentage of the sales dollar they thought was profit. After collecting their guesses, I gave them each a cup containing $1.00 in change and we started talking numbers. The change represented a dollar in sales (they understood that) and they also understood it wasn't all profit – there were some expenses against it.

Referring to the *Restaurant Industry Operations Report*, we started "paying the bills" using median figures for full service restaurants: 30 cents to food, 28 cents to labor, three cents to benefits and so on, dropping the coins into the cup as we went. They were shocked to end up with three cents ... and that was before they paid their taxes!

Then we repeated the process using the results from their restaurant, starting with 50 cents for food and 50 cents for labor. Then I said, "OK, now we have to pay the rest of the bills. Reach into your pocket and give me another forty cents. You can't stay in business if you don't pay your bills." Their eyes went wide with panic.

I gave the situation about 30 seconds to settle in before pointing out that when the income doesn't cover the expenses, you have to use your own money to keep the doors open. That's what the owners had been doing for the last three years and they were tired of it.

The staff got the message loud and clear and started asking what they could do to help get the costs under control. I did some training, helped them implement a few simple systems and the restaurant was close to break even in less than a month!

In my experience, unless you educate them to the contrary, your staff thinks you make 25-50 cents on the dollar! All they ever see is the money coming in, not the checks you have to write.

If you are raking in the profit they *think* you are, then taking home a few steaks seems only fair. How will they ever learn how the business works if nobody takes the time to explain it to them?

**To survive and prosper,
you must be a good restaurant
AND
you must be a good business**

The two require very different skill sets

9
Monitor Your Progress

Monitor Your Progress

No matter what game you're playing, it is impossible to know where you are or how you're doing if nobody keeps score. Sporting events would certainly be less enjoyable, perhaps even boring, if no one knew the score. Foodservice is no different.

Scoring provides the feedback that keeps you and your staff members involved in the quest for exemplary service, tells you if your efforts are having the desired results, and show progress (or lack of it) toward company and individual goals.

I'm not suggesting you should make the numbers your sole reason for being, but you won't know what is working (and what isn't) without a practical way to measure your results.

1. Keep Score on Service

The idea behind keeping score on service is that it enables you to identify – and hopefully fix – the weak parts of your operation before they create problems that kill profits and drive your guests away.

Carl Essert, General Manager of Christopher's and Christopher's Bistro in Phoenix, Arizona is convinced that the key to success in this business is to find out the truth from your guests and then act on it immediately. "What counts is the results we get, not our actions or our intentions," he says. "I cannot play the game to win if I don't know how we're doing with our guests."

If, as Carl suggests, results are what counts, the logical question is how you find if you are, in fact, giving your guests what they want. In other words, how do you keep score on your service?

It is dangerous to think that you are delivering a high level of guest satisfaction just because you have not heard any complaints. We mentioned earlier that only 4% of its dissatisfied guests will tell you of their problems.

Statistically, this means for every complaint you hear about, there are probably two dozen more that got away. As Jeff Jacobs, co-owner of Carroll's Creek Café in Annapolis, Maryland so neatly put it once, "No news is only bad news you haven't heard yet!"

The cost of failure is high. In Chapter 7 we calculated how a bad experience for a party of four could easily exceed $200,000 in lost business. This underscores the need to find out where your systems are breaking down and make adjustments promptly.

The search for the truth is an elusive quest and there is no single path to success. Scoring service requires input from people (your guests) and because people are all different, it takes a multi-pronged approach to be sure the picture you develop is accurate.

Some guests will talk while they are in the restaurant, some are more inclined to share their thoughts after they have left. Some will put things in writing they would never say to your face. The observations of the management and staff can be verified by the shopper's reports.

In those operations committed to exemplary service, the process is natural and ongoing. It is also time-consuming and inconvenient, but feedback is critical to your success. If you start to think it isn't worth the effort, remind yourself of the cost of a lost guest, remember that your reputation is only as good as your last meal, and realize you don't have to be bad to get better.

Mystery Shoppers

Mystery shoppers are individuals who dine anonymously in the operation at the request of management and report on what they find.

Mystery shoppers (most don't really like the term, by the way) are really guest service auditors. They provide a valuable service to management by giving you an impartial "guests-eye view" of your operation. A mystery shopper is not a critic. The shopper's proper role is to be objective and observational rather than judgmental.

Mystery shoppers are most appropriate when you need impartial documentation. The objective in engaging a shopper is to close the feedback loop by providing honest information as to what is actually happening in the operation.

Shoppers are reporters. It's not their role to tell management what *should* be happening in the operation. Shoppers do their most effective work when they know what you want to happen and what they should look for. The key to the success of a shopper program is clear standards.

Whether the shopping is done by a professional service, friends or even other guests, there should be standard factors you want each shopper to observe, allowing you to make valid comparisons over time. On the next page is a sample evaluation form for a coffee shop operation as an example.

The format should list the points of evaluation and assign a value to each based on the impact you feel each point has on the dining experience. These should relate to steps in your Service Sequences.

Scoring Shopper Reports

Shopper reports should be scored by management, not the shopper.
You determine how to interpret the observations of the shopper.

The late Sam Arnold, owner of The Fort Restaurant in Morrison, Colorado had an interesting variation on the mystery shopper idea. Periodically, he chose twenty people he believed would be bright and impartial – typically friends and regular guests – for a special offer.

He sent each a letter containing $100 along with a request to spend $50 in the restaurant and give the other $50 to the staff member who most showed their gratitude for the guest's patronage and provided the most responsive service.

The staff didn't know who these people were or when they would appear. Sam always said it sounded crass to say, but bribery works – his staff really responded to this sort of instant recognition.

He also said it really got a server's attention when their *busser* was the one consistently receiving the $50 reward!

He said the program was a good way to keep his preferred guests involved with his restaurant and was excellent PR. He also noted it was not as expensive as it may seem.

Half the money was spent in the restaurant so he didn't count that as a cost. The money that went to reward exceptional caring was insignificant when compared to the very real cost of *not* providing that level of service.

If the shopper's report is to be used as part of a bonus program or evaluation, management and the person involved should score the report separately, then mutually agree on the score that will become part of the permanent record. It also helps to post a blank copy of the shopping form so everyone on the staff knows what you consider important and what the shoppers will be watching for.

Coffee Shop Service Evaluation

DINING ROOM

SERVICE INFORMATION
Host/Hostess – Name or Description:

Server – Name or Description:

Manager – Name or Description:

% of Tables Filled:

TIMES
Time of Arrival:
Time Seated:
Beverage Offered:
Food Order Taken:
Food Order Served:
Dessert Ordered:
Dessert Served:
Check Presented:
Total Staff on Duty;

GUEST SERVICE

1. Who greeted at arrival? (5) _____
2. Describe greeting message: (5) _____
3. Was greeting wait reasonable? (5) _____
4. What did host or hostess do and say while seating you? (5) _____
5. What did server say upon arrival? (5) _____
6. Did server immediately offer coffee or an alternative beverage?
   Yes ❑ No ❑ Comment: (25) _____
7. Did server make suggestions, offer higher quality/price values?
   Yes ❑ No ❑ Comment: (25) _____
8. Did server project a special sense of enthusiasm and guest importance?
   Yes ❑ No ❑ Comment: (25) _____
9. Was server courteous, pleasant and professional?
   Yes ❑ No ❑ Comment: (10) _____
10. How long until the server's first call-back?
    Min ____ Sec ____ Comments: (25) _____
11. Was check presented after dessert was suggested or served?
    Yes ❑ No ❑ Comments: (25) _____
12. Did the server direct the guest where to pay the check?
    Yes ❑ No ❑ Comments: (5) _____
13. Was the table kept clean/cleared during the meal?
    Yes ❑ No ❑ Comments: (5) _____
14. Did the server thank you and invite you to return?
    Yes ❑ No ❑ Comments: (5) _____
15. Were all place settings neat and properly arranged?
    Yes ❑ No ❑ Comments: (5) _____
16. Was the manager visible? Yes ❑ No ❑
    What was his/her activities? (15) _____
17. Did you see a manager visit any of the tables?
    Conversation ❑ Eye Contact ❑ Comments: (15) _____

HOSPITALITY

18. Rate the staff's hospitality in the following areas from Very Poor 1 2 3 4 5 Very Good

    Personal and sincere greetings _____
    Undivided attention given to guests _____
    Good posture _____
    Guest recognition _____
    Comments:

    Staff enthusiasm _____
    Friendly smiles _____
    Music acceptable _____
    Eye contact _____
    (40) _____

    TOTAL (250) _____

Source: J&K Shopping Service, Inc., Denver, CO

(Download a full-sized copy of this form at www.restaurantdoctor.com/shopper.pdf)

Guest Feedback

Some guests are more inclined to express themselves in writing after they leave than they are in person. This makes comment cards and online surveys a valuable tool to solicit feedback and suggestions.

Surveys come in all shapes and sizes, from four color cards on coffee shop tables to engraved cards presented with the check at an upscale dinner house. Many chains (and my Gold Group members) use an online feedback system, but the principles are the same.

Dr. Steve Madenberg, Director of Organizational Research for Morehead Associates in North Carolina, designs operational surveys for restaurants and other businesses, including a detailed guest analysis system utilizing comment cards.

His research into survey design found most people wouldn't spend more that two minutes to complete one, (Aren't you always excited to receive four-page research questionnaires!) Keeping the questions simple and easy to answer, he's been able to ask as many as seventeen questions without losing interest, but I suggest we amateurs should limit ourselves to eight at most.

The trick lies in asking the right questions. "How was the service?" will take too much thought to answer and is unlikely to provide any actionable information. You'll do better to break complex questions into more manageable segments.

Service, for example, has sub-elements (length of time before an order was served, friendliness of the staff, and so forth) which can form the basis of several different survey questions.

Rewards and Punishments

However tempting, it can often be counterproductive to tie survey comments to any sort of rewards or punishment. It's always nice to get good comments and it's important to acknowledge the news (good and bad) and share it with your crew, but placing too much emphasis on positive comment cards may encourage your staff to "stack the deck" with fictitious comments.

Punishment only assures you will never see many negative comments. In one penalty-minded restaurant company, the servers could "buy" negative comment cards from the office secretary. For a fee, she'd pull a derogatory comment card before it got to the Managing Partner!

You are better advised to use the feedback strictly to gain additional perspective on your service system. If you identify a problem, address changes in the system before focusing on the behavior of individuals.

213

To preserve the team's sanity, resist any urge to change your systems based on isolated comments. Wait until you see a clear trend before altering your operation or you risk confusing both staff and guests. Handle guest comments immediately and personally, but make operational changes only after much more deliberation.

[Note: If you choose to build a reward structure on survey results, you should call a few random respondents to discuss their comments and further explore their experiences. That's not a bad idea anytime!]

Survey Design

Here are a few suggestions when designing comment cards:

Limit the Number of Questions

Limit the number of questions to those that can be answered in two minutes. When in doubt, make the card shorter rather than longer. If you have more questions to ask than can be answered in two minutes, have a selection of cards that include additional questions.

You are not limited to only one comment card. In fact, having several different cards might be a good idea anyway. Cards of different colors asking different combinations of questions might encourage repeated feedback from regular diners, many of whom could take a "been there, done that" attitude toward your cards if they were always the same.

Have Multiple Reply Mechanisms

Have a locked box at the exit for comment cards that may be filled out at the table. Many people won't take the time to fill out a card before they leave, so cards should be also be postage paid and addressed to owner or General Manager at an address other than the restaurant. This is also part of the case for using an online system to augment onsite comment cards. This helps assure that negative comments will not be removed before you can see them.

K.I.S.S.

Keep the questions clear and simple. In general, questions that lend themselves to a yes or no response usually work best, although they give you less information. Also, if you ask better questions you are more likely to get better answers. You can (and must) do better than asking about the standard food quality/service quality issues.

Give it some thought. Have some fun. Page 216 suggests a range of possible questions to get you started.

Use a Response Scale

Even if a question can be answered yes or no, use a response scale. Things are seldom black or white and a scale helps separate those items that are clear hits from those that are less positive to the guest, even though both responses might otherwise be positive.

Making the distinction allows you to assign a grade to the responses and graph the trends in various categories over time. Your measurement scale must be obvious. Be sure the scale includes a choice of N/A (not applicable). A scale from "Poor" to "Excellent" is common although the terms themselves have different meanings to different people.

Asking guests to grade an item on a scale of 1-5 tells you nothing unless it's clear whether a "1" stands for "the best" or "the worst." Steve Madenberg uses the following scale which is clearly self-evident (and more fun!)

 **N/A**

Gary Smyth of Cinema 'n Drafthouse in Coconut Creek, Florida picked up on this idea in one of my seminars and reported great luck with a blank "face" where his guests drew in an appropriate facial expression themselves!

Avoid Negative Questions

It's difficult to find a good way to ask people their opinion of the smell in the restrooms! In general, you should use questions to find out how people feel about what you *did*. An open-ended question at the end of the card will give them an opportunity to comment on what you *didn't* do!

Collect Actionable Data

Ask for information you can actually *do* something with. Asking if your restaurant is conveniently located is a waste of time! The goal of guest surveys is to help identify shortcomings in your systems and you can't do that with sweeping generalities. If your survey just asks guests to rate your food or service from 1-5, what action can you take as a result of that? Only ask questions specific enough to allow followup action based on what you learn.

Ask at Least One Open-Ended Question

Allow a place for the guests to provide specific comments or express themselves. One or two open-ended questions like "How can we do a better job for you next time" will prompt suggestions that would otherwise be lost.

This will also allow guests to become more personally involved with the restaurant than might result if they only responded to questions posed by management.

Ask for Contact Information

Provide a space for the respondent to give their name, address and phone if they wish. This information is essential if you are to respond to their comments and can provide valuable information for marketing and followup campaigns.

A word of caution, though: *never* send mail or email sales pitches to anyone who has not specifically given you permission to do so. Aside from being illegal in some states, unsolicited offers are annoying intrusions that will only guarantee guests never return.

Many people are becoming more protective of their privacy and reluctant to share such information for fear it will be misused. To cover yourself and put the guest more at ease, add this note to the bottom of every request for contact information: "Would you to be informed of cool offers and special events that will not be available to the general public?" People like to know things other people don't know and the offer of inside secrets can be attractive.

Suggested Survey Questions

To get more meaningful information from guest comment cards, ask better questions. Here are a few to start you thinking:

Background Information
Date and time of visit

Marketing Information
How often do you dine here? (first visit, ___ times per week/month/year)
How did you hear about us? (friend, advertisement, article, walk-in/drive-by)
How long did you travel to get here? (under 5 min, 5-10 min, 10-15 min, over 15 min)

Who did you dine with? (alone, family, friends, date/spouse, business associate)
Will you dine with us again? (definitely, probably, probably not, definitely not)
Will you recommend us to others? (definitely, probably, probably not, definitely not)

Operational Information
Did we give you the feeling we *really* want to serve you?
Did we answer all your questions to your satisfaction?
Have we given you reasons to see us as different from other restaurants?
Did you feel we were properly appreciative of your business?

Were you impressed with the cleanliness of our restrooms?
Did you think the hot food was really hot?
Did you think the cold food was really cold?
Did you feel we went out of our way to please you?

216

Did you feel you were treated with respect?
Were you pleasantly surprised by anything we did for you?
Did you have a great time?
Did we deliver on what we promised?

Did we get things right the first time?
Did we respond quickly to your requests for service?
Did you feel that we really listened to you?
Do you have confidence in recommending our restaurant to your friends?

Was the food as tasty as you expected it to be?
Was the pace of the meal service comfortable for you?
Was your drink order prepared just the way you asked for it?
Did the staff seem to be working well together and enjoying their work?

Can you always find something on the menu that appeals to you?
Was your food order prepared just the way you asked for it?
Did one of our managers visit your table during the meal?
Did you feel well cared-for from the time you walked in until you left?

Open-ended Questions

What pleased you most about dining with us?
What would you change about our restaurant?
How can we do a better job for you next time?
What would it have taken to make things absolutely perfect?
I would come here more often if _____

The Need to Respond

The key to creating value from guest surveys is a prompt and conscientious response

This is true whether comments are positive or negative and confirms the notion that people will talk based on how well they feel you are listening. Since everyone values their own opinion, responding to guest survey shows you are paying attention to their ideas.

Your response can also help tie guests closer to the operation, cause them to think of you more fondly and return more often. Without a response, comment cards may give you an idea of how you are doing but they will have limited marketing value and can actually work against you by suggesting you are not interested.

Responding to Criticism

Particularly with negative comments, it's important that the diner receive an immediate response by telephone, snail mail or email. Acknowledge their comments and cheerfully resolve the situation *in the guest's favor* immediately without an argument. Remember it's not about who is right or wrong but about the value of this guest's patronage over time and the damage they could do by bad-mouthing you to their others, either in person or online.

It is always wise to give critical guests a reason to return, especially if they experienced a problem. This usually takes the form of a gift certificate. If they redeem the certificate you get a second chance to get it right. If they don't bring the certificate back, you haven't lost anything and if they give it to someone else, you will get a trial from a potential new guest.

It's good to successfully resolve a problem, but it is even better (and more important) that those guests have an experience of dining in your establishment when everything goes perfectly.

A gift certificate says "please give us a chance to show you we can do a better job." Most guests will take you up on it.

We are creatures of habit and it is not in your long term interest to give patrons an opportunity or excuse to try another eatery. You don't want to give the competition a chance to win them away, do you?

Responding to Compliments

Some operators only feel the need to reply to negative comments but I believe it's equally important, although not quite as compelling, to reply to favorable comments as well. It takes interest and effort to complete a survey in the first place. If someone cares enough to take that time you should care enough to acknowledge them for it.

In a Nutshell

Your timely response helps establish trust with your patrons and trust is the key to creating loyalty over time. Lose that trust and you risk losing the guest. Whatever your other commitments, if you want to profit from guest feedback, get serious about responding as soon as you receive it. That impresses people.

2. Monitor Your Stats

We've already talked about finances, so let's look at how you can keep tabs on your operation day to day. My "Rule of Seven" is to limit your daily report to no more than seven numbers. More than that will actually lead to less action, so beware of data overload.

The idea behind limiting the report to seven numbers is to let you quickly grasp where you are. If all your numbers look to be within bounds, you can work on other projects with a clear conscience.

If one of the numbers causes concern, drill down into more detail to unearth the cause. The idea is to be able to make the right moves at the right time for the right reasons, not to micro-manage your business down to the last decimal point every day. It's a much more efficient use of your time and talent.

The Assistant Coaches in charge of each operational area will want more detail on what is happening in their specific realms, but the Rule of Seven still applies there as well.

So while the Head Coach may just want to see yesterday's cover count (number of people served), the Assistant Coach in charge of the front of the house might want to break that number down by server to track how evenly the Floor Manager is balancing the stations and how well each staff member is meeting their various timing standards.

Once a week, I recommend graphically plotting the trend line of your various numbers over the previous 30 days. Once a month, look at the trends over the past twelve months. More so than mere columns of numbers, trend lines help you quickly see what is improving and what may be slipping.

It is also revealing to compare yesterday's numbers with the same day last year and to your budget or daily forecast. (The comparison numbers aren't included in my Rule of Seven.)

In no particular order of priority, here are statistics you or someone on your coaching staff should be monitoring to keep the operation on track and verify that the herd is, in fact, moving roughly west:

Daily Sales

Everybody wants to know sales and it is an easy number to get from your point-of-sale (POS) system. Compare this number to your daily sales forecast and to the same day last year. Remember "same day" means the same day of the week – the third Friday in March – not the actual date. Comparing February 4th, 2013 (a Monday) with February 4, 2012 (a Saturday) won't be meaningful.

Daily Payroll

If your staff clocks in and out on your POS system, the computer will also give you a daily payroll figure. Express this number as a percentage of sales. The Head Coach may look at total payroll. Area coaches will want numbers for just their area, separated by job function. These will show how efficiently you are scheduling your staff and provide data for more accurate future forecasting.

Food Cost From Purchases

It is impractical to take (and cost) a full inventory every day, but if you only know your food cost when you get your monthly P&L, you could be bleeding for five or six weeks and not even know it.

An effective way to keep tabs on food cost is to calculate food cost from purchases. Divide the total value of food products purchased in the previous two weeks by the sales during those two weeks and you will have a surprisingly accurate estimate of your food cost.

I created a computer program that makes this possible in about two minutes a day and included it in the support material for my Gold Group members. You can do the same thing on an Excel spreadsheet provided you are *really* careful when adding and deleting cells.

Prime Cost

Prime cost is the total cost of food, beverages, payroll and payroll-related expenses, expressed as a percentage of sales. In most for-profit foodservice operations, the target is 55-60%. Any higher than that and your other operating expenses (utilities, marketing, rent, etc.) will severely erode the possibility of turning a profit.

Cover Count

The term is industry jargon for the number of guests served. It is a more meaningful indication of how busy the restaurant is than just daily sales. A revenue bump could come from higher menu prices but hide a declining number of guests.

Tracking head count is important in any type of foodservice operation and provides valuable information to assist forecasting, purchasing and scheduling.

Call Parties

A call party is someone who asks to be seated in a specific server's station. It is a measure of how well that server is doing at making connections with your guests. This is important because ultimately people are more loyal to people than they are to places. ("It's a great restaurant but I go there because Mary Ann always takes such good care of me.")

Check Average

This statistic is the daily sales divided by the cover count, expressed as dollars per person. The figure will vary by meal period (breakfast obviously has a lower check average than dinner) and will tell you how effectively the staff is promoting the menu. Some very sharp operators only calculate this figure periodically for diagnostic purposes, preferring instead to track head count and call parties.

Ticket Times

This is the amount of elapsed time from when an order is received in the kitchen until it is delivered to the table. The POS system will note the time the order was entered and a time clock can tell you when each order was ready for pickup.

First-Time Guests

If the Floor Managers follow the service sequence I outlined earlier, they'll ask guests if they've been in the restaurant before, how they heard of you or how long since they were last in ... and record that information. First-timers are essential to replace guests who move or lose interest and keep the business growing.

Repeat Guests

Repeat patronage is the key to building a sustainable business so it is also good to know what percentage of the cover count are repeaters and how long it has been since their last visit. If you can increase the frequency of their visits, you'll increase sales, often dramatically, without the expense of attracting first-time diners.

Bank Balance

You should always know the balance in the checking account. Many operators get in trouble because they deposit sales tax receipts in the general account, inflating the balance. This leads to a false sense of plenty and problems when it's time for sales tax returns.

The solution is simple: just have a separate tax account. Write a check every week for the taxes collected and deposit it in the tax account. The balance in the general account will always reflect real cash on hand and you'll never have to worry at tax time.

Promotion Response

When you run promotions or special events, you need to know how successful they were. Since most restaurants offer their regular menu while a promotion is running, stats like these will tell you if the response justified the cost of the promotion and give you a basis for planning the next one.

Non-Commercial Statistics

Non-commercial operations may not have a dollar sales figures to calculate some of the ratios referred to above. In that case, most relationships can be expressed as a cost per meal. For example, I managed the Olympic Training Center foodservice based on food and labor cost per meal.

If you don't keep your eyes on the road while driving, you'll never reach your destination safely.

3. Watch the Big Picture

One of the monitoring devices to maintain certification as A Place of Hospitality is the Peer Impressions Report, essentially a shopper checklist that looks at the operation as a whole from the hospitality perspective. The inspection is done randomly and anonymously by a third party restaurateur or members of their staff.

What gets inspected is what gets done and this is one way we keep everyone's feet to the fire so they won't slip into complacency. I include a copy here in the hope you will find it helpful in keeping tabs on your own operation.

Not all items will apply, of course, so just mark those you don't offer or couldn't observe "N/A" and they won't figure into the final score calculation. As with the Screening Interview, scoring is two points for a Yes, one point for a Maybe and no points for a No.

To compute your score, take the number of applicable questions times two – that will show you the maximum number of points available. Then divide that number into the total number points you received to get a final grade. In case you're curious, the minimum score for first level certification as A Place of Hospitality is 75%.

(download a copy at www.aplaceofhospitality.com/peerimpressions.pdf)

Y	N	?	N/A	**OUTSIDE IMPRESSIONS**
❑	❑	❑	❑	1. Parking area was clean – no bottles, cans, broken glass, trash or debris
❑	❑	❑	❑	2. Parking area was adequately lighted and felt safe
❑	❑	❑	❑	3. Parking area was in good condition – no broken pavement, potholes, etc.
❑	❑	❑	❑	4. Exterior of the building was clean, well-lit and inviting – no burned-out bulbs
❑	❑	❑	❑	5. Walkways were clean and clear – no dirt, debris or puddles
❑	❑	❑	❑	6. Landscaping was well-tended and free of trash
❑	❑	❑	❑	7. Trash cans and dumpsters were out of sight or kept neat and orderly
❑	❑	❑	❑	8. Entry doors were clean and free of fingerprints
❑	❑	❑	❑	9. Door hardware was secure, doors opened easily
❑	❑	❑	❑	10. Valet was well-groomed, courteous and attractively dressed

Y	N	?	N/A	**GREETER/FIRST IMPRESSIONS**
❑	❑	❑	❑	11. Greeted warmly within 30 seconds of entering – real smile, no script
❑	❑	❑	❑	12. Well-groomed and attractively dressed
❑	❑	❑	❑	13. PRESENCE - not distracted when speaking
❑	❑	❑	❑	14. Reception area was neat, clean and attractive
❑	❑	❑	❑	15. Quoted waiting time was LONGER than actual – (got seated "early")
❑	❑	❑	❑	16. Found waiting guests a place to sit
❑	❑	❑	❑	17. Offered waiting guests a menu and something to eat or drink
❑	❑	❑	❑	18. Kept waiting guests informed of the status of their wait
❑	❑	❑	❑	19. Conversed with guests on the way to the table (or at least kept pace)
❑	❑	❑	❑	20. Reasonable requests for choice of table were honored

Y	N	?	N/A	**BAR IMPRESSIONS**
❑	❑	❑	❑	21. Orderly, clean and attractive – no strange sights, sounds or smells
❑	❑	❑	❑	22. Drink order was taken promptly (within one minute)
❑	❑	❑	❑	23. PRESENCE - server/bartender was not distracted when speaking, listened well
❑	❑	❑	❑	24. The lighting level in the room was pleasant
❑	❑	❑	❑	25. The noise level in the room was comfortable
❑	❑	❑	❑	26. Drinks arrived promptly (within three minutes)
❑	❑	❑	❑	27. Bar snacks were available
❑	❑	❑	❑	28. The bar offered an unexpected extra
❑	❑	❑	❑	29. Drinks were properly made and attractively presented
❑	❑	❑	❑	30. Staff were clean, well-groomed and attractively dressed

Y	N	?	N/A	**DINING ROOM IMPRESSIONS**
❑	❑	❑	❑	31. Table top was neat, clean and attractive
❑	❑	❑	❑	32. Serviceware and glassware were spotless and properly aligned
❑	❑	❑	❑	33. Menu was clean (no stains), easy to read and understand
❑	❑	❑	❑	34. Room was clean and orderly (no strange sights, sounds or smells)
❑	❑	❑	❑	35. Lighting level was pleasant and adequate – no dark spots or burned-out bulbs
❑	❑	❑	❑	36. Noise level in the room was not intrusive – conversation was easy
❑	❑	❑	❑	37. Seating was comfortable, clean and sturdy
❑	❑	❑	❑	38. Did not feel excessively crowded by other diners or physical elements
❑	❑	❑	❑	39. No distracting noise coming from the kitchen
❑	❑	❑	❑	40. Tables were cleared and reset promptly and quietly

Y	N	?	N/A	**SERVER IMPRESSIONS**
❑	❑	❑	❑	41. Welcomed warmly w/in one minute of seating – real smile, no script
❑	❑	❑	❑	42. Started the service promptly after seating (typically within three minutes)
❑	❑	❑	❑	43. Did NOT lead with a canned introduction ("Hi, I'm ___ and I'll be your waiter.")
❑	❑	❑	❑	44. PRESENCE - not distracted when speaking, listened effectively
❑	❑	❑	❑	45. Was clean, well-groomed and attractively dressed – personable, not intrusive
❑	❑	❑	❑	46. Was knowledgeable about the menu, wine list and beverage offerings
❑	❑	❑	❑	47. Was attentive to (and responsive to) the needs of the table
❑	❑	❑	❑	48. Stayed relaxed and smiling throughout the meal
❑	❑	❑	❑	49. Handled special requests or complaints promptly and without judgement
❑	❑	❑	❑	50. Made an effort to support and guide the experience (vs. just "sell stuff")

Y	N	?	N/A	**FOOD AND BEVERAGE IMPRESSIONS**
☐	☐	☐		51. Hot food was really hot, cold food was really cold
☐	☐	☐	☐	52. Plate presentations had a WOW factor
☐	☐	☐	☐	53. Food was properly seasoned, perfectly prepared – matched menu descriptions
☐	☐	☐	☐	54. Bread and rolls were hot, fresh and moist
☐	☐	☐	☐	55. Timing of the courses matched pace of the party
☐	☐	☐	☐	56. Things that SHOULD be crisp were, things that SHOULDN'T be crisp, weren't!
☐	☐	☐	☐	57. Quality and freshness of the produce was impressive
☐	☐	☐	☐	58. Portion sizes were sufficient and consistent
☐	☐	☐	☐	59. Butter was served at a spreadable temperature
☐	☐	☐	☐	60. Wine service was smooth and unobtrusive

Y	N	?	N/A	**END OF MEAL IMPRESSIONS**
☐	☐	☐	☐	61. Server offered desserts with enthusiasm, sincerity and good humor
☐	☐	☐	☐	62. Dessert choices were varied and interesting
☐	☐	☐	☐	63. Desserts were reasonably priced
☐	☐	☐	☐	64. Coffee was full-flavored and memorable
☐	☐	☐	☐	65. Server suggested something different (unusual and fun) to end the meal
☐	☐	☐	☐	66. Check was delivered immediately when requested
☐	☐	☐	☐	67. Check was settled quickly and accurately (two minutes elapsed time)
☐	☐	☐	☐	68. Server did NOT ask if guest wanted change back
☐	☐	☐	☐	69. Server did NOT look at the tip or show a reaction to the amount
☐	☐	☐	☐	70. Guests were invited to return on a specific day for a specific reason

Y	N	?	N/A	**RESTROOM IMPRESSIONS**
☐	☐	☐	☐	71. Men: Cleanliness was impressive
☐	☐	☐	☐	72. Men: Supplies (soap, TP, towels, etc.) were fully stocked
☐	☐	☐	☐	73. Men: Fixtures were working and in good repair
☐	☐	☐	☐	74. Men: No clutter, mess or strange smells
☐	☐	☐	☐	75. Men: Unexpected amenity (after shave, hand lotion, kleenex, etc.)
☐	☐	☐	☐	76. Women: Cleanliness was impressive
☐	☐	☐	☐	77. Women: Supplies (soap, TP, towels, etc.) were fully stocked
☐	☐	☐	☐	78. Women: Fixtures were working and in good repair
☐	☐	☐	☐	79. Women: No clutter, mess or strange smells
☐	☐	☐	☐	80. Women: Unexpected amenity (flowers, hand lotion, kleenex, etc.)

Y	N	?	N/A	**GENERAL IMPRESSIONS**
☐	☐	☐	☐	81. Staff never said what they COULDN'T do for you, only what they COULD
☐	☐	☐	☐	82. Staff engaged in non task-related conversation (if appropriate)
☐	☐	☐	☐	83. Sanitation awareness was obvious – frequent handwashing, hygiene, etc.
☐	☐	☐	☐	84. Manager made contact with the table – personable, not intrusive
☐	☐	☐	☐	85. Manager was PRESENT - not distracted when speaking, listened effectively
☐	☐	☐	☐	86. Staff educated guests on points of difference in decor, service, menu, etc.
☐	☐	☐	☐	87. Service was appropriate for the occasion
☐	☐	☐	☐	88. No feeling of being rushed or pressured
☐	☐	☐	☐	89. Staff members appeared to be working together and enjoying their work
☐	☐	☐	☐	90. Kitchen staff, when visible, appeared clean, happy and well-dressed
☐	☐	☐	☐	91. The tone (feeling) in the restaurant was upbeat and positive
☐	☐	☐	☐	92. Received some unexpected extra – presented as a gift, with joy
☐	☐	☐	☐	93. The restaurant offered something unique in the marketplace
☐	☐	☐	☐	94. Staff was natural and friendly, even with unfriendly guests
☐	☐	☐	☐	95. Telephone manner was cheerful, helpful and professional
☐	☐	☐	☐	96. Staff helped guest with their coats
☐	☐	☐	☐	97. Servers showed gratitude (smile, sincere thank-you, warm tone of voice)
☐	☐	☐	☐	98. Greeter showed gratitude (smile, sincere thank-you, warm tone of voice)
☐	☐	☐	☐	99. Valet showed gratitude (smile, sincere thank-you, warm tone of voice)
☐	☐	☐		100. Staff or management went beyond basics to do something memorable

10

Develop Your Staff

Develop Your Staff

"A lot of managers trying to solve problems miss the forest for the trees by forgetting to look at their people – not at how much more they can get from their people or how they can more effectively manage their people. I think they need to look a little more closely at what it's like for their people to come to work there every day." —Gordon Bethune, Continental Airlines

Applying the principles we've discussed will help improve the quality of your operation and draw more guests who will stay loyal to you for a longer period ... but none of that can happen without your team. If you could do it by yourself, you probably would, but since foodservice is a team sport, how you deal with your staff determines what they can do for you ... and how inclined they are to do it.

In the more enlightened corners of our industry, the awareness is shifting from *training* people to *developing* people (of which training is a part.) The difference is at once simple and profound. Rather than focus just on job skills like most training does, development offers each individual what they need to reach their full potential. This goes past just job skills to people skills, financial skills ... even life skills.

It signifies an acceptance of each staff member as a total functioning human being, not just a two-legged machine to be programmed. It requires a high degree of respect and a deep sense of service. This notion is worth a bit of reflection.

The Best Employer in Town

In Chapter 4 we talked about how you could screen applicants to identify those with the best chance of success ... but what will draw these people to your door? Perhaps more important, what will make them stay with you for the long term?

Foodservice success comes from consciously designing every element of the operation to properly serve your guests. Becoming the best employer in town requires that same passion and concern for the needs of your staff because your crew creates the guests' experience. Ultimately, the key to creating a quality staff is to develop the sort of organization quality people want to become – and remain – part of.

Think about how different the business environment is now than it was when we first started working. For one thing, the nature of the work force has changed. Workers are more sophisticated, better informed, (less educated?) and have more options than ever before. If you can't find people who want to work, it may only be that there are fewer people willing to put up with the way you do business.

Could you hire someone today who would accept the conditions you endured when you first started in foodservice? I surely couldn't. In the same way that you must always look at your business from the guest's perspective, you also need to keep an eye on your business practices from the staff's point of view.

Your guests' expectations have changed, too. How many of your current guests can you satisfy with the same level of service they would accept even two years ago? Yet how much have your service systems, staff training and basic business orientation really changed to address and keep pace with your guests' new standards?

In spite of these fundamental shifts, most operators, knowingly or not, still do business the way they've always done it. They never critically question the way they learned to run a foodservice operation.

The problem is that the people who taught you in the 90s were taught in the 70s by people who learned it in the 50s. Tradition is wonderful, but not everything we learned is still relevant. Many of our current personnel practices are ineffective ways to deal with people, but we do it that way because that's the way we've always done it.

Many of these unconscious practices developed when we had an abundance of workers who would eagerly accept minimum wage jobs and repressive working conditions. When we'd wrung all we could from them, we just replaced them with someone else. It was an era of disposable labor with little real incentive to question these practices ... but you'd be in jail if you tried to operate that way today!

To create what my colleague, Mark Mayberry, calls, "The Dream Workforce," there must be a strong enough attraction to pull people into your sphere of influence. Working for you has to be attractive and worth the effort the job requires. Even the most clever scheme will not make people want to apply if you if you've earned a reputation as a terrible place to work.

If you agree that attracting the best available workers is a worthwhile goal, perhaps we should look at what it takes to earn a reputation as the best employer in town:

Good Reputation

People with high standards want to work in operations with high standards. This means you have to be known as providing a top quality food and service. This may also mean you visibly support worthwhile causes, participate in recycling programs and give something back to the community that supports you.

Participatory Climate

Today's workforce grew up in an environment where they had a voice and a vote in how things were done. If their parents asked for their input at home, what expectations do you think they have when they come to work?

The new workforce requires a different work environment to really be effective, an environment where your staff really does have a voice in the decisions that affect their lives. It doesn't work if you only try to make them *think* their opinions are important.

Fair Wages

Most managers think wages are the most important consideration to their workers. In reality, surveys show workers place wages fifth on their list. Money is a factor, but high wages are not a satisfier as much as low wages are a dissatisfier.

The most successful operators pay above the prevailing standards in their markets to make a statement about the value they place on their staff. They also demand a high level of performance from their teams. Labor is a profit center. Don't think of it simply as a cost.

Appreciative Management

Surveys suggest workers' top desire is to receive appreciation for the work they do. This gratitude is a natural consequence of shifting away from a "cop-like" management style to more of a coaching approach. Hospitality and personal connection are important here as well. People like people who like them.

Extensive Training

If you can't pay the highest wages in town (and even if you do), you can provide a great vocational training program! For many people, the education is worth more than the salary. Excellent workers are motivated by opportunities to expand professional skills. Savvy operators recognize that, ultimately, their only real job is to learn as much as they can and pass as much as they can along.

229

Meaningful Jobs

The people you are looking for want something more than just a full schedule and a paycheck. I believe that increasingly, the good workers seek out positions with meaningful content.

How much more involved might your staff be if they understood why their jobs are important? How much more meaningful would their jobs seem if they knew what contribution their work makes to the well-being of others?

PAY MORE, SPEND LESS

Several years ago, my nephew, then about 25, was working in a small pizzeria on Cape Cod ... and loving it. On one of my trips back east, he and I were talking about working in restaurants (imagine that!)

He went on at length about how much he enjoyed working at this pizzeria and how well he was being paid. I liked his enthusiasm, particularly his comments about wages since small independents are usually known for minimum wage jobs.

I started asking him questions and he asked if I would to meet his manager. I jumped at the idea. So the next afternoon I found myself sitting down for a cup of coffee with Bruce Lee (not *that* Bruce Lee!), owner of the shop.

After some small talk, I said, "Jared tells me you pay your crew about 25% more than anyone else in the area. Can you tell me more about how you manage to do that?"

"I don't have any turnover," he said. "On average, my guys have been with me for over two years so they've got the work down cold. Because I don't have the turnover and don't have to constantly be breaking in new people, I run this store with five people when it would take anyone else at least eight to put out the same volume.

"It's true that my hourly rates are higher, but as a percentage of sales, my payroll is far less than most pizzerias. That's more money for the crew ... and more money for me.

"These are all young guys. They're not going to be here forever. But when they leave, they always bring in a friend to take their job -- it's like a legacy that gets passed down from one to the next. And they don't bring in slackers because they wouldn't do that to their friends [co-workers]."

"So all these guys are friends?" I asked. He nodded. "Please explain how that works out for you, because the common wisdom in the industry is that you don't want too many friends working together."

He said, "To the extent that there's a 'them-and-us' relationship between staff and management – and there's always a bit of that no matter what you do – they may be tempted to screw me over, but they won't screw over their buddies."

"A crew member never calls off without a valid reason. If they did, the guys would take him out back and 'bring him to Jesus.' I never have to deal with issues like that. I spend all my time growing my business, not filling shifts and training rookies.."

Interesting way to run a restaurant, eh?

Productive Positions

To measure the performance of your crew, you need to do a better job of defining your jobs. Position descriptions are like a road map to your organization. Properly constructed, they help workers to better understand the game you're asking them to play ... and allows you to better measure how they are doing. Labor litigation also provides real incentives for operators to document the content of each position. The problem with most job descriptions, though, is that they're little more than lists of activities.

When I worked with typical activity-based job descriptions and had to do a performance appraisal for an under-performing worker, they invariably defended their performance by showing how they had performed every task on their job description. This is akin to claiming to be the world's greatest lover because you memorized the manual. It's also about as effective!

Marvin's Law of Creative Laziness says you never do any more work than necessary to get the results you want. Since the results are what counts, why not just define positions in terms of results instead of activities? Defining results allows people to interpret their jobs in a way that works for them. The immediate advantage is increased productivity, enhanced guest service, improved morale, reduced turnover ... and more constructive performance appraisals!

A Results-Based Position Description has four sections which should be self-explanatory:

POSITION SUMMARY
... a succinct statement of the reason the position exists at all!

ESSENTIAL PROFESSIONAL FUNCTIONS
... activities required in the successful performance of the position.

RESULTS UPON WHICH PERFORMANCE IS EVALUATED
... results by which successful performance will be measured.

QUALIFICATION STANDARDS
... basic physical requirements of the position in compliance with ADA guidelines.

Position descriptions don't have to be static HR documents gathering mold in a filing cabinet. One operator I know actually used Results-Based Position Descriptions as his primary pre-opening training for a new restaurant.

He spent several days reaching a consensus with his new crew on their jobs. They discussed the critical results by which they would evaluate each position and agreed on the means by which they could tell if they were on track or not. He said he was gratified to learn his new staff had standards that equaled or exceeded his own.

The ability to define and measure results as the primary means of performance appraisal makes Results-Based Position Descriptions unique. On Page 237 I include a sample to give you an idea of what one looks like. Be sure your positions don't call for standards you're not prepared to uphold. Better yet, review them with your staff and agree what is possible!

Position Titles

As the structure of jobs change, position titles should change as well. Foodservice job titles haven't changed very much in 100 years! Here are the rough equivalents between traditional job titles and the updated structure I am suggesting:

SUGGESTED TITLE	TRADITIONAL TITLE
Head Coach	General Manager
Assistant Coach	Assistant Manager
Beverage Manager	Bartender
Assistant Beverage Manager	Cocktail Server/Bar Back
Production Manager	Chef/Sous Chef/Cook
Assistant Production Manager	Dishwasher/Prep Cook
Floor Manager	Greeter/Host/Hostess
Service Manager	Waiter/Waitress/Server
Assistant Service Manager	Busser

You'll notice I eliminated the title of Manager at the supervisory level. Call someone a manager and they may try to manage *people*. Often, this is little more than manipulation. When you think about it, our management model is closer to law enforcement than to enlightened leadership. If being a cop appeals to you, apply to the Police Academy!

The only effective way to get results through others is to lead them which is why I prefer the title of Coach to that of Manager. I don't think it's possible to *manage* people – you must lead and inspire them. Besides, managers look for problems, coaches look for strengths.

Coaches do their work with an eye toward how they can use the available talent to best accomplish their mission. Approaching your job as a coach is not only more productive, but a lot more fun as well.

In my organization, the Manager title exists at the hourly level because it *is* possible to manage activities ... and who better to manage them than the person doing the job? Service Managers manage the service delivered to guests. Production Managers manage production in the kitchen. Floor Managers manage the wait and the flow of traffic in the dining room. Beverage Managers manage bar and drink service.

In addition, each acts as a mentor to their assistants. So, for example, the task of the Assistant Service Manager is to learn the Service Manager's job; the Service Manager's job is to teach it to them. Think what this will do to create a supportive work environment!

Because we're so accustomed to thinking of foodservice positions in the same old terms, a brief discussion of the function and content of these restructured positions might help.

Coaches

When you look at the person in charge as a coach, the job changes. The success criteria shift away from problems they've solved and toward the degree of success their staff enjoys. Perhaps the job of the coach job could be better defined as "achieving success through developing the talents of others."

Some whose jobs currently carry the Manager title may approach their work with a coaching mentality, but too many more do not. If the subtle distinction between a Coach vs. a Manager sounds like splitting semantic hairs, remember that language is powerful. When the top spots in your operation carry the title of Coach, I think people approach their work from a fundamentally different direction.

> **THE COACH MAKES THE DIFFERENCE**
>
> Donald I. Smith, former football coach, longtime industry leader and mentor always taught that the coach makes the difference. Here are some of Don's thoughts on coaches and coaching that are worth considering:
>
> *Great coaches are noticed by their uncanny ability to produce championship teams. However, to be called Coach, a leader must be measured by more than balance sheets, battles won or lifetime win-loss records.*
>
> *Great coaches have one more gift. They change the lives of those they touch. I suggest that great coaches can be measured by the number of success stories they leave in their wake. For once they give their players a taste of sweet success, they will have more.*
>
> *They leave behind a legacy of winning which becomes a lifetime habit. Players ultimately become champions of the coach's values, beliefs and passions for the rest of their lives.*

233

Service Manager

The Service Manager has more responsibility and authority than the typical server/waiter/waitress. If someone is managing the service, they must have a broad understanding of the end result and the latitude to do what they think is appropriate to assure guest delight.

The buzzword for this is empowerment, but it's simply recognition that the one on the scene probably knows what's most appropriate to do at any given moment. As with the other managers, exceptional candidates must display not only professional competence, but the willingness and ability to share their knowledge with others.

Assistant Service Manager

The busser position evolves into the Assistant Service Manager post. This person assists the Service Managers in delivering legendary service to the guests. Their entire perspective changes from doing "grunt work" to a realization that they are becoming an increasingly important part of the guest gratification system. The change in structure may or may not increase the length of time a worker remains with you, but it *will* change the level of enthusiasm and interest they bring to the job during their tenure.

Floor Manager

The job of the Floor Manager is to manage the flow of traffic on the floor. This includes creating positive first (and last) impressions, managing the wait and properly seating the dining room so stations are balanced and the room always looks comfortably full.

When you structure it this way, the position has greater importance and responsibility than the typical Greeter/Hostess job. Now it calls for more than a pretty face to take names and walk guests to a table. It requires interpersonal skills, sensing where waiting guests are in the process, monitoring the status of the dining room and the ability to keep it all flowing smoothly.

Production Manager

Call someone a cook and they may think they've done the job if they just cook. On the other hand, describe the position as "Production Manager" and their job clearly becomes managing the flow of food production in the kitchen, a different mindset than simply cooking.

In most mid-scale operations, it also sidesteps the controversial distinctions between who can legitimately be called a chef and who can't. The structure of this position encourages workers to learn all aspects of kitchen operation rather than just filling a slot on the line.

Because the position requires the ability and willingness to teach, you'll be looking for qualities beyond simply the candidate's ability to produce palatable food.

Assistant Production Manager

A common foodservice staffing problem seems to be finding and keeping dishwashers, probably because few people really want to be dishwashers. My solution involves a subtle restructuring of the way the kitchen operates.

Assistant Production Managers clean and wash dishes, of course, but since they are also in training to become Production Managers, they must learn receiving, storage and food preparation as well. When the rush hits or a Production Manager is out, the Assistant can temporarily fill in on the line to get you through.

The job content is greater, so the post merits a higher wage than a dishwasher. The job also requires a different sort of motivation in the applicant. When this is the entry level kitchen position, it will tend to draw more motivated prospects while making the job less attractive to those just looking for an easy path to a paycheck.

Beverage Manager

The bartender's job also takes on more depth when the title changes. Besides the responsibility for making and serving drinks, the Beverage Managers teach their assistants (bartenders, bar backs and cocktail servers) about bar operations. They are also tasked with teaching the service staff about beverages and beverage service.

Job responsibilities could include control of pouring costs, ordering, inventory control, beverage merchandising and other activities usually reserved to higher management. The teaching content of the position requires more than simply a good bottle mechanic.

Assistant Beverage Manager

Assistant Beverage Managers assist the bartender and serve cocktails. In addition, they are evaluated on how quickly they are learning bar operations. For typical cocktail servers, learning to tend bar is a skill upgrade they can get excited about.

For example, during slow periods a cocktail server could tend bar with a smile as opposed to a bartender grumbling about having to cover the tables. More than just simple competency, this position, too, requires a desire to learn and expand professional skills.

If these title changes sound a bit radical, I'm pleased. That means you are at least thinking about the subject. That's always a good start.

Doing more of what you've been doing will only get you *less* of what you've already got! There's an entirely different game going on out there and it calls for a fresh approach. At worst, more comprehensive jobs will help you stand out from the competition ... and that's the first step to becoming the employer of choice.

To help you understand how to put something like this together for yourself, there's an example of a Results-Based Position Description for a Service Manager on the next page. Feel free to modify and adapt it to fit your own unique circumstances.

Performance Appraisals

Appraisals are the way you measure performance and provide feedback to your crew on how they are doing. In case you haven't figured it out, everybody hates your performance appraisal system.

Don't take it personally. That's just the way it is in most companies. Your managers hate it because it requires them to be judgmental and either painfully honest or pull their punches in the interests of keeping peace in the family.

Your staff hates it because they rarely feel they are getting the honesty or support they really need from the leadership. They know they are doing the best they can and don't like finding out their efforts are either misunderstood or unappreciated. They may also feel your performance appraisals reflect the degree to which someone has managed to stay on the good side of the boss, not the level of their professional performance.

Many independent operators try to sidestep the issue by not engaging in performance appraisal at all. This is even more destructive to staff morale. The practice of "I'll let you know if you're screwing up," leaves workers in the dark as to whether they are doing things right. They live in fear that suddenly being blind-sided, fired for mistakes they didn't even know they were making.

If that happens, they'll spend a lot of energy that could otherwise be going into the work continually looking over their shoulder for the attack they feel sure is coming.

Position Description

Position: Service Manager
Mentor: Assistant Head Coach
Trains: Assistant Service Managers

POSITION SUMMARY:

Delights restaurant patrons with responsive food and beverage service

ESSENTIAL PROFESSIONAL FUNCTIONS:

- Sells and serves food and beverages to guests in the dining room and bar
- Presents menus, answers questions, makes suggestions regarding food and beverages
- Writes orders on guest checks
- Relays orders to the service bar and kitchen
- Serves courses from service bar and kitchen
- Observes guests, anticipates needs and responds to additional requests
- Accurately totals guest checks, accepts payment and makes change
- Clears and resets tables
- Cleans the service areas as necessary
- Inspects restrooms every 30 minutes and cleans as necessary
- Conducts daily inspections of service areas
- Creates effective training program for assistants
- Recognizes and reports all necessary maintenance promptly
- Fills in where needed to ensure efficient operations
- Suggests improvements to the operating format

RESULTS UPON WHICH PERFORMANCE IS EVALUATED:

- Guests are acknowledged within one minute of being seated
- Food orders are delivered within 1 minute of completion
- Average check meets or exceeds posted goals
- Hot food is consistently served hot and cold food is consistently served cold
- Guests have a spontaneous positive reaction when plate is presented to guest
- Health department scores exceed 90 with no major violations
- Assistants are steadily improving their skills as measured by quarterly tests
- Service staff vacancies are filled by internal promotions
- Regularly attends training seminars
- Stories of legendary guest service abound
- Contributions are recognized by co-workers on peer appraisals
- Guests comment favorably on the tastiness and presentation of meals
- Service areas are always neat and clean
- Guests have a great time every time as measured by repeat patronage of 80-85%
- Resolves guest problems (in favor of the guest) immediately
- Knowledgeable on menu items, drinks and wines
- Guests regularly ask for this staff member to serve them
- Guests make unsolicited comments on the cleanliness of the restrooms

QUALIFICATION STANDARDS:

- Able to operate a cash register or electronic POS system
- Walks and stands during the entire shift
- Reading and writing skills required
- Reaches, bends, stoops, and wipes
- Carries 30 lb. tray from kitchen to dining room about 24 times per shift
- Interacts verbally with patrons
- Hazards may include, but are not limited to, cuts, burns, slipping and tripping

(Download a full-sized copy at www.restaurantdoctor.com/description.pdf)

You can see how fear and anxiety can make workers feel insecure, lowering their state of mind which, in turn, lowers their productivity and sense of service while increasing their general dissatisfaction with both the company and their jobs.

Understand that the basic problem may be structural. Performance appraisals have a much poorer chance of success in the cop school of management. Since cops look for problems to fix, the appraisal process can easily become negative, heavily weighted in favor of identifying shortcomings, setting deadlines and instilling fear.

You can't play to win if you don't know the score and performance appraisals are an essential element in any staff development system. Fortunately, a shift to Results-Based Position Descriptions makes the process almost painless by putting the Coach in the position of reporter and facilitator rather than that of a judge.

Because you identified the results you want each position to achieve, it becomes possible to coach. It allows you to create more of a feedback system than a typical performance appraisal system.

Feedback is important, but the basis should be some form of data collection rather than just the subjective opinions of those in charge. Feedback based on established standards is less threatening to the staff, more positive for the coaches and helps contribute to a productive working environment.

The Coaching Report

What follows is a sample Coaching Report (performance evaluation) that follows the structure of the Results-Based Position Description. It makes performance review as positive (and painless) as possible. You should find it a straightforward document, but here is a bit of guidance to help you understand how this valuable tool is used:

The first page lists the Essential Professional Functions (from the position description). Page 2 does the same with the key points from the "Results Upon Which Performance is Evaluated" section.

The coach then notes the results desired and the results observed. Desired results can come from the service sequences, the position description, counseling during the confirmation period or at their last performance appraisal.

The comments section on the first two pages notes points you want to discuss in the session and the last page gives the staff member an opportunity to add their own comments. The Peer Appraisals on the third page are discussed starting on Page 242.

Remember your goal is professional development, not fault-finding.

COACHING REPORT — Page 1

NAME: Susan Service Manager
PERIOD COVERED: August 15 - February 14
PREPARED BY: Coach Pete

ACTIVITIES	RESULTS DESIRED	RESULTS OBSERVED	COMMENTS/SUGGESTIONS
Sells and serves food and beverage	smooth, seamless service	generally competent service	service can be uneven when rushed, relax and stay focused
Presents menus	menus open, right-side up	menus open, right-side up	eye contact and a smile when presenting menus - excellent!
Answers guest questions	never hear "I don't know"	some confusion on new items	study new items, work with mentor to fill in voids
Makes suggestions	personal recommendations	some descriptions memorized	doing much better, be sure to taste and talk from experience
Writes orders on guest checks	neat, legible, proper codes	neat, legible, proper codes	checks are perfect, makes it easier for the kitchen - super!
Relays orders to service bar and kitchen	orders get there w/in 60 seconds	OK during week, 2 min Fri/Sat	ask for help when getting behind
Serves courses from service bar and kitchen	service pace matches guest needs	generally appropriate pace	the key to reading the table is to drop distractions
Anticipates needs, responds to requests	guests never have to ask	improving	the key to reading the table is to drop distractions
Accurately totals guest checks	math is 100% accurate	all audited checks were perfect	exceptional math skills
Accepts payments, makes change	100% accuracy	accuracy good, style is still rough	face bills, count each back to guest
Clears and resets tables	tables are reset within 3 minutes	average reset time: 4.25 minutes	note table status, time should improve as other skills are mastered
Cleans the service areas	always neat and clean	exceptionally clean service areas	does a great job of cleaning service areas
Inspects restrooms and cleans as necessary	positive guest comments	adequate job of cleaning	with a little extra effort, could make them sparkle
Conducts daily inspections of service area	always stocked and complete	some unnecessary shortage noted	it is time to work on anticipating supply needs
Creates effective training for assistants	assistants are advancing	not applicable	ready to take on training responsibilities
Recognizes/reports necessary maintenance	no unreported problems		no specific comments
Fills in where needed	supervisor never has to ask	misses opportunities to help	remember that we are all in this together
Suggests operational improvements	actively involved in the company	holds self out	needs to recognize the importance and value of her input

EVALUATION FACTORS	RESULTS DESIRED	RESULTS OBSERVED	COMMENTS/SUGGESTIONS
New guests promptly acknowledged	within one minute of seating	average 75 seconds	ask for help when getting behind
Food orders delivered quickly	within one minute of completion	average 90 seconds	ask for help when getting behind
Average check meets or exceeds goals	$7.50 lunch, $13.50 dinner	$7.20 lunch, $13.45 dinner	good work/remember to build loyalty, not the check average
Hot food is consistently served hot	food temperature is over 150°	late delivery makes for cool food	need to get food to the table more quickly
Cold food is consistently served cold	food temperature is under 38°	generally OK	faster service would keep chill on the food
Guests delighted w/plate presentation	spontaneous positive reaction	spontaneous positive reaction	plate presentation skills are good
Health inspection scores are excellent	over 90 with no major violation	last inspection score 86	keep working on general sanitation awareness
Helps assistants develop professionally	test scores are improving	not applicable	she is ready to take on training responsibility
Service staff ready for promotion	vacancies filled internally	not applicable	she is ready to take on training responsibility
Continues their professional education	attends training seminars	missed one seminar	understand the need for continuous improvement
Guests appreciate & notice extra effort	guests comments are favorable	comments are generally favorable	guests appear to be satisfied, now we can work on guest delight!
Service areas are well-maintained	always neat and clean	exceptionally clean service areas	does a great job of cleaning service areas
Guests have a great time every time	repeat patronage is 80-85%	repeat patronage estimate: 60%	work on improving connection with guests and inviting them back
Guest problems are resolved quickly	immediately/in favor of the guest	generally handles problems well	very conscientious to resolve difficulties quickly
Knowledgeable on menu, drinks, wines	never hear "I don't know"	some confusion on new items	study new items, work with mentor to fill in voids
Service is personal and memorable	guests ask for this server	two requests in this eval period	work on improving connection with guests and inviting them back
Guests impressed w/clean restrooms	candid comments on cleanliness	doing acceptable cleaning job	delighting guests calls for doing more than expected

Approach this process as a coach rather than a cop. This means being sure the staff member being coached know the measurement standards in advance and receives a copy of the Coaching Report when the session is completed.

240

Peer Appraisal

EVALUATION FACTORS	NEVER	SOMETIME(S)	USUALLY	ALWAYS	GENERAL PEER COMMENTS
Contributes to a positive atmosphere		7	12	14	fun to work with, can be moody, great smile
Uses time appropriately		14	15	4	ignores some guests and talks to others, long restroom breaks
Does their job right	1	8	11	13	very sharp, gets all the details
Is a good team player	1	11	12	9	makes me look good, looks out for herself first
Cares about their work		5	13	15	takes pride in what she does

Coaching Comments and Suggestions

(Download a full-sized copy of this example along with a blank form at
www.restaurantdoctor.com/coachingreport.pdf)

241

COACHING REPORT

Goals For Next Appraisal Period

Staff Member's Comments

My coach and I have discussed my performance including all the comments and suggestions above. I understand the reasoning behind all comments included in this report.

STAFF MEMBER: Susan Service Manager (signature)   DATE: February 21

COACH: Coach Pete (signature)   DATE: February 21

Peer Appraisals

Your staff can fool you, but they can't fool their co-workers, so a meaningful feedback system must also allow workers to rate each other. Here's a format for a peer appraisal I have used with success.

Peer Appraisal

APPRAISAL FOR:	Never	Sometimes	Usually	Always
1. CONTRIBUTES TO A POSITIVE WORKING ATMOSPHERE: Friendly, cooperates readily with others, flexible, makes things flow more easily, keeps a sense of humor, has a positive outlook, is patient with unexpected change				
2. USES TIME APPROPRIATELY: Reports to work on schedule, respects break time, works efficiently, does not waste time, meets deadlines				
3. DOES THEIR JOB RIGHT: Doesn't miss much, works accurately, follows proper sanitation practices, works safely, meets all company standards, controls waste, gets it right the first time				
4. IS A GOOD TEAM PLAYER: Works well with others, makes co-workers look good, steps in readily when things need to be done, speaks positively about the company and co-workers				
5. CARES ABOUT THEIR WORK: Takes pride in everything they do, maintains high professional standards, conveys a professional image to the public and co-workers				
ADDITIONAL COMMENTS:				

At appraisal time, ask co-workers to complete this form anonymously and return them to a locked drop box. Then summarize the comments and include them on the Coaching Report.

To be fair, the performance appraisal system should also allow workers to comment on the effectiveness of their coaches. This is a harder concept for many at the top to accept, probably because they're afraid to face the truth. These are likely the same managers who don't ask their guests for honest feedback on their dining experiences for fear of hearing something less than complimentary.

Since the way you treat your staff is the way they will treat your guests, asking for feedback from the crew on your own performance and finding out how you can be more effective for them will make it easier for the staff to ask for the same sort of feedback from you and your guests. Remember: you don't have to be bad to get better.

So I also suggest a format for a coach/supervisor appraisal. Handle it in a similar manner as suggested for the Peer Appraisal.

Coach/Supervisor Appraisal

APPRAISAL FOR:	Never	Sometimes	Usually	Always
1. CONTRIBUTES TO A POSITIVE WORKING ATMOSPHERE: Friendly, cooperates readily with others, flexible, makes things flow more easily, keeps a sense of humor, has a positive outlook, is patient with unexpected change				
2. SETS A GOOD EXAMPLE: Is a positive role model, holds themselves to the same standards demanded of the staff, speaks positively of the company, guests and staff, does what they say they will do				
3. IS A GOOD TEACHER: Helps me be more effective, answers my questions patiently, listens to my ideas, takes an active interest in my personal and professional development				
4. INSISTS ON MY BEST WORK: Consistently upholds company performance standards, is "tough but fair," believes in my ability to improve my performance, challenges me to excel, notices when I do				
5. CARES ABOUT THEIR WORK: Takes pride in everything they do, maintains high professional standards, conveys a professional image to the public and staff				
ADDITIONAL COMMENTS:				

Frequency

Performance appraisal can be a time-consuming – but valuable – process. With the pressures of day-to-day operations, it is also an event that can too easily be put off.

However, if you fail to conduct regular appraisals, it suggests you don't give performance a high priority and your staff will mirror your attitude toward their work.

When a written performance appraisal is just a formal adjunct to consistent one-on-one coaching, it won't need to happen as often to be effective. At the least, you should sit down with everyone once a year to document their progress. You can do it more often, but any more frequently than twice a year is overkill.

Not to be open and honest with your staff is disrespectful

Treat them as intelligent adults and most won't disappoint you

11
Yeah, But ...

Yeah, But ...

In my seminars, there are always a few who question the wisdom or practicality of the ideas I present, perhaps because they challenge conventional thinking. Personally, that's why they appeal to me, but I suspect many readers may still have a few questions – or even some reservations – at this point.

To help put things in perspective, let me address a few questions and concerns you may have after digesting all these ideas:

Yeah, I can see where a clear Purpose might help me, but how do I know what my Purpose should be?

At the outset, you probably won't have a clue, but understand there's no *should*, no right or wrong answers. The process is more about letting your Purpose find *you* than the other way around ... or you could just blow it off and settle for being just like everyone else.

As a start, ask yourself the "So what?" question. Let's say you have a profitable diner. So what? What's the greater good the community derives from you being in business? Why should they care?

Do you see a need for the community to come together to address mutual issues? Is your neighborhood in need of revitalization? Would you like to introduce the area to the wonders of Lebanese cuisine and culture? It's your life, your "impossible dream" and totally your call.

When you're ready to make your game bigger, give yourself some quiet time and reflect on what you would do if you had a magic wand. What would you change/fix/create to fill the need or solve a problem that's meaningful to you?

Reflect on something like, "Wouldn't it be cool if we could ____?" Don't censor your thoughts or struggle with it, just let ideas flow through your head until one of them sticks with you.

In the early 60s when President Kennedy challenged the country to put a man on the moon by the end of the decade, it wasn't just that nobody knew how to do it ... nobody knew if it was even *possible!* But his audacious dream mobilized the talent to do the impossible.

249

Yeah, I know training is a good thing but I don't have the time or budget to train like I should.

All you can do is the best you can do. Most managers think they don't have time to train but that's because they're trying to do everything themselves. Training is a task you can delegate to certified staff trainers (Page 71). Get them up to speed and let them take the load off you. They will be happier and take more ownership in the end result of their work.

Members of my Gold Group and Pizza Insight programs have access to 24/7 online video training courses which can also help the staff develop their skills and understanding.

As to budgets, necessity is still the mother of invention. If you can't do it the way you wanted, find another way to get it done. In the end, training will actually save you money through lower turnover and higher productivity. Make the case for the long term results.

Yeah, organizing things helps, but isn't the idea of service sequences at odds with just tapping into someone's innate hospitality?

If you follow the service sequences like a little robot, that might be true. But as much as anything, the service sequences are blueprints for training – a way for people to understand what you want, when you want it and why it's important. After that, the actual flow of service will be dictated by the person and conditions in the moment.

For example, there are lots of ways to drive from Point A to Point B. The goal is to get your passengers there safely and without breaking any traffic laws. If traffic is heavy on one street, you might take another. You might know a shortcut nobody ever thought of. In some places you must creep along, in other spots you can make up some time. As long as you arrive at Point B safely, on time, and with all your passengers delighted by the ride, you're good!

Service sequences lay out the most commonly traveled route to the destination. Hospitality is the way you drive there, the route you take and how good your passengers feel about the trip.

Yeah, the climate thing makes sense, but how can you create a positive climate when those at the top are micro-managers?

Nice as it would be, you cannot change another person (and it is disrespectful to try). All you can do is create sanity in your slice of the pie and hope that someone else may notice.

If so, they might become curious enough to ask how you get such amazing results. At the least, your spectacular results might make the brass see you as an asset and leave you alone to do it your way. At least that's the way it worked for me at the Olympic Training Center.

But it's also your life to live and you must take charge of it. If those at the top insist on second-guessing your every move – particularly when their "solutions" only make the problem worse – you don't have to sacrifice your peace of mind. If you reach a point where you can't live with the situation, leave the place in as good a shape as possible and hire another employer.

Yeah, more responsibility is fine, but if I let my crew do whatever they think is right to make guests happy, they'll give the place away!

Without exception, managers I know who have given their crew the authority to do what they need to do at the table, at the time, to resolve a guest's complaint say the biggest problem is actually getting them to do it! Most report their servers are more reluctant to comp an item than the managers are.

Before turning them loose, I'd certainly have a discussion about what might be appropriate under various circumstances. For example, if a guest complained about cold soup and you not only replaced it but told them their meals would be free for the rest of their lives, that overkill would likely make them feel uncomfortable about returning.

Once you've had the discussion and they understand their job is to write a great last chapter to the meal, I fully support whatever their own best judgement leads them to do. If a server does go too far, we can discuss it in private the next day.

Yeah, happy guests are fine, but if we're all about delighting guests and solving problems without a hassle, they'll take advantage of us.

You can count on there being people who'll take advantage of you if you take this stance. But it is never as bad as you fear.

For example, the Hampton Inn hotel chain has a guarantee that says that if you don't like the room, it's free. "What a scam," you'd think. "Let's travel across the country, stay in Hampton Inns, tell them we didn't like the rooms and stay for free!" Is that what you mean?

My friends at Hampton Inn tell me the people who actually invoke the guarantee amount to 3/10 of one percent – three in a thousand ask for the free room!

251

I don't know if those numbers hold for restaurants, but assuming they're close, it means if you serve 1000 people, you're likely to run into three problems. If you comp the meals for these three, it's like selling at a 0.3% discount. Could live with that? How many 10%, 20% and two-fer discount coupons do you have in circulation?

There is a tendency to make rules to control the three opportunists and forget the other 997 diners who will be thrilled that you're so unconditionally committed to their well-being.

Yeah, making it right for the guest will take some pressure off, but aren't you just trying to comp your way to success?

The goal isn't to give away food but to make sure guests have a great time every time they dine with you. If giving away food will fix a problem, I will do it. Then I'll find out *why* I had to do it – where the system broke down – and fix it so I never have to give food away for that reason again.

You also have to be careful that comping the food doesn't become an acceptable alternative to doing it right the first time. If you allow an attitude like, "OK, we screwed up. Here's your free dessert. Now stop whining and get off my case," it won't make anyone feel well-served or anxious to return, it will make things worse.

People don't want bad food for free. Besides, it isn't the free food that solves the problem. It's the personal gesture of offering to make up for a lapse in service. Guests don't expect everything will be perfect every time, but they sense when their experience is important to you.

Yeah, this all sounds good, but I'm in military feeding and much of what you're teaching doesn't apply to my situation.

It sounds like your mind is only picking up on the specifics from my examples and not grasping the principles that led to those particular actions. So how, exactly, is a military situation really all that different from a typical civilian sit-down restaurant?

- Both operations feed people. The menus and styles of service differ, but that's true of any two restaurants.

- The military doesn't have greeters, but there is still someone on the door and procedures to follow when people enter.

- All foodservice operations have specific steps in the service of their food and all of them must train their staff in how to perform the desired processes.

- People are still people whether they wear suits or BDUs, so the information about climate and hospitality still applies. You're still a major factor in troop morale.

Granted, you don't get any more pay if you feed 1000 more people, nor are your promotions affected by whether those you feed are thrilled with your food (or just not unhappy with it). Money can be a nice reward, but it's not the only incentive to go above and beyond.

Case in point: I was a young Navy ensign fresh out of Supply School when I took over the enlisted feeding at NAS Sangley Point in the Philippines. We had a great division but my crew was discouraged. Even though the food was really good, everyone was griping about the meals. (Sailors are known to do that!) I knew we didn't have a food problem, we just needed to address an attitude problem.

So I started talking with the sailors one on one (it freaked them out that an officer would actually do that!) In conversation and through regular questionnaires, I got some great ideas from them and we implemented as many as we could.

Six months later, everybody loved us. Those who were once my biggest critics came in on their off duty time to install a sound system for us and every duty officer on base was making the case as to why they should be allowed to eat in the General Mess rather than the Officers Club. My cooks were happy because the sailors were happy and I was happy to see it all working smoothly.

Excel and the rewards will follow ... and if they don't, you still get to live a happier, more fulfilling life.

Yeah, I can handle most complaints but what do I do about a few regulars who seem to gripe about everything?

As a start, re-read the section on dealing with difficult people on Page 170. Understand that if you get caught up in their drama, then both of you are lost. It may also help to realize that their whole life may be like that (whining and complaining) and compassion may move you to cut them some slack.

If the chronic complainers are still regular guests, they obviously like your restaurant and may just enjoy complaining(!) but that still leaves the question of how best to deal with them.

I can't possibly give workable answers to every situation you might face, but let me suggest four approaches that might fit the bill and a few stories to help illustrate the application of these notions:

253

Leave Them No Option

The late Mike Hurst of 15th Street Fisheries told of a particular guest who was always such a problem that servers actually paid the greeter not to seat him in their stations! Mike found out what was happening and proved the best defense is a good offense.

He met the guest – call him "Dr. Stone" – at the door with a warm welcome. Things went roughly as follows:

"Doctor, I'm so pleased to have you at the Fisheries tonight. I understand that we've had some problems in the past but I can personally assure you that tonight is going to be the finest meal of your life!

"I have personally seen to all the details myself. I saved you our best window table overlooking the Marina and I assigned my very best waiter to your party – in fact, he's my son.

And I personally inspected all the fish that came in today to assure that what you'll receive will be the very finest and freshest we have."

The entire evening went like this, with constant reassurance and personal attention that left no "wiggle room" at all. At the end of the meal, Mike went to the table and asked, *"Now tell me, the truth, Doctor. Was this, in fact, the finest meal of your life?"*

Mike said there was a long pause, then the doctor broke into a big grin and blurted, *"Well, yes. By God, it was!"* He said Dr. Stone was a regular (and well-behaved) guest ever after!

Underneath the gruff exterior, most tough guests are really teddy bears. Show a little extra personal attention, let them see you have their best interests at heart and most of them will come around.

Offer No Resistance

I love this story from the Domino's franchise in Washington, DC. At the time, Domino's had a policy that said if a guest didn't like the pizza they'd get their money back. One particular customer was always returning the pizzas, so the franchise owner called him on the phone.

"I notice you're always sending back the pizzas so it's apparent to me we must not know how you want your pizzas done. If we sent a car for you, would you come down to the shop and show us exactly what you want? We'll make notes so when you call the next time we can do it perfectly for you."

The guest agreed. They drove him to the store and he showed the staff exactly how he wanted his pizza. They dutifully made notes and started preparing to his exact specification when he ordered. He continued to send the pizzas back.

At that point, I admit I would have been tempted to write this guy off as a complete jerk, but here's where things really became brilliant. The franchise owner called the guest back.

"Look," he said, "this is too much work. You call, order a pizza, we make the pizza, drive it over to you, we give you the pizza, you give us the money, we drive back, you call us up again, we bring you back the money, you give us back the pizza ... way too much work!

"How about if we just make it easier on everyone? From now on your pizzas are free – free! – until we get it right! Tell us when we get it right and we'll start charging you again!"

Two pizzas later, the guest said, *"You've got it!"* When there's no system to beat, it takes the sport out of angling for a freebie. If you would comp them anyway, what have you got to lose?

Enlist Them as a Shopper

Say you have a guest – call him Murray – who always complains. Some whiners aren't worth the effort, but let's say you want to retain Murray's business. The approach could go like this:

"Murray, you drive me crazy! Your standards seem impossibly high, but I know you're right most of the time. I also know that if I can make you happy, we'll be the better for it.

"Instead of us always being at odds, would you be a shopper for me? It's sort of like a spy. Don't tell anyone about our deal but come in like you always do and pay for your meal as usual.

We'll get together afterward to discuss your experience. I will reimburse you for your meal, give you a few extra dollars for your trouble and see where you think we can improve."

This changes the relationship from adversarial to cooperative. If you would otherwise pick up Murray's meals, you haven't lost anything ... and you might just improve in the process! You will also eliminate one more hassle from your life.

Pass Them off to a Competitor

If you have a guest you cannot please and whose patronage you *don't* want to keep, resist the urge to put them in their place. As cathartic as the put-down may seem at the time, you don't need enemies wandering around the streets. If you challenge a chronic complainer, count on them to try to get even. If you have such a guest, try an approach like this:

"Jack, you've been in here a lot and it seems we still haven't been able to satisfy you. If we've failed to make you happy after five tries, the odds are that we just won't be able to do it.

But it's important to me that you get what you want, so let me buy you dinner at [a competitor's]. They're great people and I'm sure they will do a better job for you than we have!"

This may be a little unfair, but let your competitor worry about Jack for a while! Sometimes you just have to fire a guest.

Yeah, I hear you about motivating and coaching, but where do you start with a crew that seems totally disinterested?

Been there, done that. While the problem seems tough when you look at it from the old understanding, it gets really easy when you apply the principles we've been talking about. Whenever you don't know where to start, the best thing to do is get input. That's a fancy way of saying to quiet your mind, ask good questions and listen.

Here's a simple sequence of steps that will vastly improve your skill as a listener (and a learner!) ... if you have the courage to actually put it into practice:

1. Quiet Your Mind

We get all speeded up in the normal course of life, so the first step in learning to listen is to slow down. Start to notice your busy-minded thinking and just let it go. A few deep breaths can help, maybe shake the tension out of your arms and shoulders. You'll get better at this as you become more self-aware.

2. Drop Distractions

As your mind quiets, you'll start to notice the mental baggage you are carrying around. Let go of those thoughts as well. Your purpose in listening is to really *be* with the other person and to learn something new about who they are or how they think.

Stray thoughts make the process harder. The other person will know when you're thinking about something else. They won't feel you are truly interested in them and they won't tell you anything significant. Don't let stray thoughts get in the way of the learning ... or the relationship.

3. Ask and Answer Questions

You won't get yourself in much trouble if you're either asking or answering a question. It's when you start making unsolicited statements that you tread on thin ice. Slow down. Know less. Learn more.

If you want to learn, you have to ask good questions ... and be intently interested in the answers.

256

If the other person asks a question, feel free to answer it, but then turn the conversation right back to them. Remember your only purpose is to learn, not to impress or inform.

4. Encourage and Explore Differences

There's a lot that you don't know ... but you don't know what it is! Usually we listen for things we agree with and discount everything else, but your purpose in listening is to learn something new from (or about) the other person, so be listening for ideas that are different from the way you see things.

Even notions that sound "crazy" to you make sense to the other person. Respect their point of view and ask questions to help you better understand why they see things the way they do.

Be curious. You don't have to agree, disagree or have an opinion one way or the other about what the other person is telling you. Being judgmental will only hamper your learning.

5. Listen for Insights

Insights are the pot of gold at the end of the listening rainbow. You won't know exactly what you're listening for ... but you'll recognize it when you hear it! If you're willing to hang out in "I don't know," it will keep your mind quiet and open you up to fresh possibilities. At the least, the person you're listening to will feel well-heard, understood and valuable.

The procedure I suggest is this: at least once a month, sit down with each member of your crew one-on-one for 10-15 minutes. This needs to be totally uninterrupted time – no phone calls, no distractions, no re-scheduling because "something important" came up.

Expect people to be a little suspicious of your motives, particularly if you don't regularly do something like this. Pay attention and put them at ease by not being judgmental.

Your only goal is to listen and learn something new. If you get stuck when you sit down with a staffer, here are some questions to help open up the discussion or keep the dialogue flowing:

- What do you like most about working here?
- If this was your place, what would you change about it?
- How can we help you be more successful on the job?
- What are we doing that makes no sense to you?
- If you weren't working in this kind of business, what would you be doing?
- What is it about this work that appeals to you?

257

- What are you do with your time off these days?
- What have you done lately that you're particularly proud of?
- How can I help you achieve your goals in life?
- What else should I know about you as a person?

Yeah, the Assistant Production Manager idea sounds good, but who's washing the dishes?

When the rush is on, Assistant Production Managers are on the line helping to get the meal out, because that's what it takes to make the guests happy.

That could leave the dishroom empty, of course, but in most operations there's no real reason other than force of habit or lack of inventory why dishes have to be washed during the rush.

As dishes come in during busy times, load them into bus tubs and pack the tubs into rolling racks. You can fit a lot of racks in an empty dishrooml. When the pace slows, put two or three people in there, wash all the dishes in an hour and start prep for the next meal!

To make this idea work, you'll probably have to invest in additional serviceware, a few more bus tubs and some racks, but that's a lot less expensive than buying years of hourly labor!

High-volume operations may still have to wash dishes during the meal. In that case, the Assistant Production Managers could spend part of their shift on the line and part of it in the dishroom without compromising the intent of the position.

Yeah, but if being negative brings the mood down, how can I enforce rules people don't like without lowering the climate?

The short answer is to be certain, not stubborn. This is an important point, so let me explain that with a brief story: I tend to drive a little fast, and in twelve years of living in California, I had occasion to run into the California Highway Patrol a time or two.

Their officers were extremely courteous, personable and respectful ... but when I got stopped, there was never a flicker of doubt but that I was going to get a ticket! The possibility of talking my way out of the ticket was so not in the officer's consciousness, it never crossed my mind to even attempt it! That's what I mean by certainty.

Putting this into a foodservice context, I am absolutely certain you cannot work for me and steal from me. You can't work for me and use drugs or have poor sanitation practices. These are like gravity in my mind: zero tolerance "hanging offenses."

Don't even *think* about walking out of the restroom without washing your hands properly. From time to time I'll be waiting with a petri dish, take a swab of your fingers and incubate it overnight. If anything nasty grows, showing me you didn't wash your hands, you're gone ... no matter who you are.

Call that anal if you will, but in my mind there is no room for any individual interpretation of right or wrong in these areas. Because I was so certain these offenses were non-negotiable, my staff never argued with me about them.

I wouldn't disrespect other ideas or fail to listen to differing opinions if they were offered, but I was not open to compromise in these areas and they knew it.

Yeah, I'm starting to look at things a lot differently now, but how do I introduce these ideas to my team?

At this point, don't try. You'll only confuse them. The real lesson is not in the content of your words but in the *feeling* you create on the job. I talk about the incredible results we achieved at the OTC, but I never talked to my staff about any of the things I've put into this book. I just didn't have any words for it back then.

But just the fact that my own thinking had shifted was enough to make a visible change in the way the department operated. They didn't need to understand *why* things were different in order for things to be different.

So don't feel you need to become an evangelist – that will do more harm than good. Start with yourself and don't worry whether you will be enough to make a difference. You will be. If they ask, get them a copy of this book and they may start to see it for themselves.

How One Company Does It ...

Shake Shack is a re-imagined burger and fries concept from Danny Meyer's Union Square Hospitality Group. It's growing steadily and seems to draw a perpetual waiting line wherever it opens.

Here are a few excerpts from an interview with Shake Shack CEO, Randy Garutti. It struck me as a fitting way to end the book because if you pay attention, you'll notice Randy talks about all the key notions we've just discussed: purpose, service, climate, staff selection and hospitality, although in different words. The incredible public support for Shake Shack certainly proves that combination works.

You've said in interviews that Shake Shack was an accident. When did you decide to roll with that accident?

It was absolutely an accident. I remember it goes all the way back to 2001 when it was a hot dog cart. Then Shake Shack got created in 2004. It wasn't until the end of 2008 that the second Shake Shack opened on the Upper West Side. So it was four and a half years in between. That's the beauty of it.

People come to us all the time and say how did you guys do it? And we say, "We did it because all we wanted to do was make one great community gathering place and we did that at Shake Shack." And, of course, we had great food because that was our fine dining heritage. It's always important to remember that. We had incredible hospitality because that's the Danny Meyer way.

Did you think you'd grow as much as you have?

We never set out to have an international company. And then when the second one opened on the Upper West Side and it was as busy as the first, we said, "Whoa, wait a second. People are really resonating with this idea we've created."

It took another two years really to start opening a couple. And we've only done four Shake Shacks a year. This year will be more than that. We're going to grow quite a bit. We're going to open in Istanbul in June. And then we're going to open in London this summer. We are really excited.

How has size changed you?

That's the beauty of it. When people come into my office, there are two things on the wall. One is the original Danny Meyer back of the napkin where he wrote down what he wanted Shake Shack to be. Every time we make a decision, I point to that and say, "Would it fit with that? Are we still acting like we only have one restaurant?"

The second thing is, "The bigger we get, the smaller we need to act." It's how we make decisions. Would you make the same decision if you were just one restaurant? It keeps us being the anti-chain, keeps us thinking small and using our culinary heritage. Decisions that affect this place are made as if it's only this place. Decisions need to make sense in each specific location and that makes it hard to grow.

How do you ensure consistency at all locations?

It starts with hiring the right team. We spend lots of time hiring and developing our leaders so they can continue to hire, train and retain the best people. It sounds cliche, but it's real work. It's nonstop. We have a much lower turnover rate than any burger joint out there.

We have incredible people who work really hard to keep things consistent and we have leaders who have been with us for awhile and understand the culture. Myself and a lot of our leaders at Shake Shack were fine dining people. The people who run operations and training, they've all come from mostly fine dining positions. They instill that kind of pride and consistency.

What is training like?

It's usually about seven days of active training before we open. And then we have our trainers there for weeks after opening to make sure the new team is learning. progressing and doing things right. We spend a lot of money on training and investing in our team.

One of the cool things we do is called Shack Dollars. Each month, we take up to one percent of the revenue and give it back to the team on their paychecks as a bonus.

So if you're working in a restaurant that's busy, you want to be busy because you're getting a piece of that on your paycheck. That's cool. People like it. It's hard to work at Shake Shack. It's busy. It never stops. It's fun, but it's hot and relentless, so we want our team to feel great about supporting being busy.

Is there an end goal?

To create the best burger company in the world, for the world and for our team. We want to create a great place to work, where we train people, develop them and allow them opportunities. The number of people we've had who started in hourly positions making burgers and frozen custard and who have turned it into manager or general manager jobs and support families ... that is the best thing.

Author's Note:

Shake Shack is a great example of what happens when you operate consistent with the principles we have discussed. Their reputation precedes them into each new market, drawing curious crowds. Expectations are high ... and when those high expectations are validated by the guests' actual experience, Shake Shack quickly becomes a Restaurant of Choice. It's a beautiful thing.

The world doesn't need another place to eat

**Be remarkable
Be memorable
Be hospitable**

Be the Restaurant of Choice

Management
Resources

Management Resources

There's never enough time or space to treat every topic in the depth it deserves, so I recommend the following resources for those who wish to explore some of these ideas more deeply. Yes, all these resources are also in my personal professional library and I refer to them frequently.

Bill

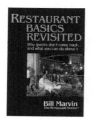

RESTAURANT BASICS REVISITED:
Why Guests Don't Come Back and What You Can Do About It
Bill's easy-to-read, common sense look at restaurant service teaches the details of good service. It explores the process by which guests form their opinions of restaurant service and gives a competitive advantage to operators.

SETTING THE TABLE:
The Transforming Power of Hospitality in Business
Danny Meyer shares lessons he's learned developing the business model he calls "enlightened hospitality." This innovative philosophy emphasizes putting the power of hospitality to work in a new and counter-intuitive way.

GUEST-BASED MARKETING:
How to Increase Sales Without Breaking Your Budget
Bill demonstrates that success doesn't come from beating the competition, but from pleasing your guests. He shows how to work from the inside out to build on your strengths and to use the intrinsic advantages you didn't even know you had.

ZINGERMAN'S GUIDE TO GIVING GREAT SERVICE
Based on the principles that made service a bottom-line at Zingerman's, founder Ari Weinzweig lays out the steps they teach their staff on how to give great service.

FROM TURNOVER TO TEAMWORK:
How to Build and Retain a Guest-Oriented Staff
Bill Marvin takes a common-sense approach to why people leave and what can be done about it. Treats such issues as rapport between staff and management, training, salary structure and wages, incentives, performance reviews and disciplinary procedures.

REMARKABLE SERVICE:
A Guide to Winning and Keeping Customers
The Culinary Institute of America offers tips and tactics on offering consistent, high-quality service in a wide range of dining establishments, from casual and outdoor dining to upscale restaurants and catering operations.

THERE'S GOT TO BE AN EASIER WAY TO RUN A BUSINESS:
How to Have a Successful Company ... and a life!
Bill shows you how to have a successful company ... and a life! He suggests common sense alternatives that will allow you to be more effective with less effort ... and get your life back!

LESSONS IN SERVICE FROM CHARLIE TROTTER
Charlie Trotters was a renowned Chicago hot spot, but his reputation was built on a subtle relationship between food, wine, ambiance, and service.

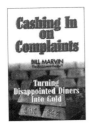

CASHING IN ON COMPLAINTS:
Turning Disappointed Diners Into Gold
Nobody likes to get complaints, but if you know how to mine it, there's gold in those gripes! Bill helps you understand how to deal with – and profit from – the complaints you are sure to receive in the normal course of business.

ZINGERMAN'S GUIDE TO GOOD LEADING, PART 1:
Building a Great Business
Ari Weinzweig examines the basic building blocks of the culture and structure now known as Zingerman's. These approaches are the behind-the-scenes "secret" stuff that goes into making a very special, sustainable business of any kind.

59½ MONEY-MAKING MARKETING IDEAS:
How to Build Volume without Losing Your Shirt
Bill explores ways to build volume that are simpler, more effective, much less risky ... and almost free! The secret is to get existing guests to come back more often and say wonderful things about you to their friends.

ZINGERMAN'S GUIDE TO GOOD LEADING, PART 2:
Being a Better Leader
The second book in the series looks at the leadership style that has helped make Zingerman's such a special place to work and to eat. The book includes their entrepreneurial approach to management and more.

HOME REMEDIES:
A House Call From the Restaurant Doctor
This is some of The Doc's best stuff, taken from the first several years of Bill Marvin's "Home Remedies" newsletter.

RESTAURANT SERVICE: Beyond the Basics
A how-to guide to the rituals and amenities that make customers feel comfortable and turn a meal into a memorable event, including guidance on table and guest service.

50 TIPS TO IMPROVE YOUR TIPS:
The Service Pro's Guide to Delighting Diners
Bill created this pocket-sized paperback to help your service staff create more personal connection with your patrons and increase their tips while improving service and guest delight. Quantity prices are available.

REVIVING WORK ETHIC: A Leader's Guide to Restoring Pride in the Emerging Workforce
Eric Chester takes an incisive look at the entitlement mentality that afflicts many in the emerging workforce and shows readers the specific actions they can take to give their employees a deep commitment to performing excellent work.

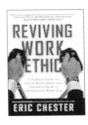

266

50 PROVEN WAYS TO BUILD RESTAURANT SALES & PROFIT

The first in a series, this book contains fifty of the best ideas from the sharpest minds in the hospitality business, capsulized in one to three pages so you can quickly pick up an idea and get back to work.

50 PROVEN WAYS TO ENHANCE GUEST SERVICE

Profitable ideas from Susan Clarke, Barry Cohen, Howard Cutson, Peter Good, Raymond Goodman, Winston Hall, Jim Laube, Bill Main, Phyllis Ann Marshall, Bill Marvin, Rudy Miick and Banger Smith.

WHAT EVERY SERVICE PRO SHOULD KNOW ABOUT PEOPLE (DVD/CD SET)

Bill offers some valuable insights that can help your service staff have more fun on the job, be more confident and relaxed when dealing with the public and be more effective at generating income for both the restaurant and themselves!

50 PROVEN WAYS TO BUILD MORE PROFITABLE MENUS

This collection explores menus and menu design with some great money-making secrets from Barry Cohen, Howard Cutson, Peter Good, Raymond Goodman, Jim Laube, Bill Main, Phyllis Ann Marshall, Bill Marvin, Banger Smith and Ron Yudd.

AT YOUR SERVICE:
A Hands-On Guide to the Professional Dining Room

From the Culinary Institute of America, At Your Service is a comprehensive guide to help professionals learn the ins and outs of running a successful front-of-the-house operation.

WAITSTAFF TRAINING HANDBOOK:
A Complete Guide to the Proper Steps in Service

The guide covers every aspect of restaurant customer service for the positions of host, waiter or waitress, head waiter, captain, and bus person.

PROTOTYPE STAFF MANUAL & HUMAN RESOURCES MANUAL (Download)

The Human Resources Manual details the company's policies relating to people. The Staff Manual contains all the basic information about the company that every member of the staff needs to be a functioning part of the company culture.

THE ENCYCLOPEDIA OF RESTAURANT TRAINING

An ready-to-use staff training program for all positions in the food service industry. This book shows how to train your employees in the shortest amount of time, and lets you get back to your own job of running a profitable enterprise.

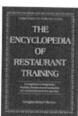

RESTAURANT MANAGEMENT AGREEMENT (Download)

Restaurant management contracts are a way to have your cake and eat it too: an experienced operator takes over a property (often distressed), retains a percentage of the profits for his efforts and passes net proceeds through to the owner.

THE RESTAURANT TRAINING PROGRAM:
An Employee Training Guide for Managers

This training manual covers safety and sanitation, food production skills and service ability, including standard industry procedures and practices with instructions for customizing to individual restaurant operations.

BRING YOUR "A" GAME TO WORK

Eric Chester reveals the seven essential work ethic values required for success in any job. Every employer sees these values as non-negotiable and yet they have a difficult time finding people who demonstrate these values on the job.

GAMES TRAINERS PLAY

These brilliant offbeat, unexpected, disarming games have one serious mission: to coax even the most reluctant groups to talk, laugh, think, and work together. Page after page of fun, easy-to-plan tear-out exercises to shake up outworn habits.

RUNNING A RESTAURANT FOR DUMMIES

If you're entering the field for the first time or switching to independent restaurants from another style of foodservice, this book can give you a reasonable idea of what you are getting yourself in for.

THE RESTAURANT MANAGER'S HANDBOOK w/CD

This massive (600 page) book will show you step-by-step how to set up, operate, and manage a financially successful foodservice operation. Helpful as far as it goes but may seem overly simplistic and a bit of an infomercial.

UNIFORM SYSTEM OF ACCOUNTS FOR RESTAURANTS

Don't go into business without it! The Uniform System lays out the standard account classification system used by most restaurant operators allowing you to compare your operating results with those of other similar restaurants.

RESTAURANT FINANCIAL BASICS

This down-to-earth guide focuses on the crucial information busy managers must know-for both day-to-day operations and long-term planning, including cash flow, pricing, budgeting, cost control, equipment accounting, and cash control.

AUDIO CDS OF LIVE SEMINARS

How to Prosper in Tough Times

There's Got to Be an Easier Way to Run a Restaurant!

Cashing in on Complaints

Why Guests Don't Come Back and What You Can Do about It

50 Money-Making Marketing Ideas

Guest-Based Marketing

The Server as an Independent Business Person

How I Cut My Food Cost by 10% Overnight

Finding the Right People

Marketing Advantages of the Independent Operator

Retention Is Better than Recruitment

Five Great Ways to Build Sales ... and One Really Lousy One!

(... and there's more on the website!)

Re-Thinking Restaurants

What if I said you could trigger a **contagious resurgence of hospitality** in your community by delivering the experience of heartfelt caring to every patron, every time?

What if I told you we had developed an **elegantly simple system** that provided the logic, methodology and support structure that enabled you to operate with **effortless excellence**?

What if I assured you this approach would give you and your staff a **fulfilling sense of purpose** and the **joyful experience** of enriching the lives of the people you serve?

What if I made this program so **irresistible** and so **easily affordable** that hospitality could truly become your competitive point of difference in the market?

Would you think I must be crazy ... or would you ask, "How can I become part of this?"

A Place of Hospitality™ is a breakthrough certification and support program to help you ...

- ▸ re-discover your roots: hospitality itself!
- ▸ instill the hospitable mindset in your team
- ▸ enjoy more balance in your life
- ▸ put the joy back into serving the public
- ▸ level the playing field when competing against the national chains
- ▸ develop a sustainable, steadily growing business model built not on discounts and hype but on personal connection and service to the community
- ▸ do all this in a way that's both operationally practical and extremely profitable!

Certification as **A Place of Hospitality** recognizes foodservice operators who have not only made a deep commitment to provide exceptional personal hospitality to every guest ... but have succeeded at it! This certification cannot be purchased and you cannot pay to keep it – you either deliver the goods every day or you lose it!

The Missing Link

It always seems ironic to me that the competitive element most responsible for success in the hospitality business ... and the piece most visibly absent ... is hospitality itself!

We're out to change that – to make hospitality the rule rather than the rare exception, to allow you to re-kindle your love of serving others, eliminate most of the stress from your life and build your business (at full price) with the enthusiastic support of your patrons.

269

The Ripple Effect

Human beings tend to treat others the way they are treated and it has to start somewhere. Who better to trigger a resurgence of hospitality in the world than the hospitality industry itself? Where better to start than inside your four walls?

When guests feel well- and personally served, they leave feeling better about life in general and are naturally more considerate of others. In this way, hospitality has a way of paying itself forward. Niceness begets niceness. Courtesy brings more courtesy.

When you are focused on nurturing relationships with your guests rather than simply trying to "sell more stuff," your patrons trust you. When you become their favorite place they will return more often, recommend you to their friends and become fiercely loyal fans. They will stick with you through tough times and rarely quibble about price! The result is higher sales, lower marketing costs, a happier staff and better tips. It is truly a win-win-win situation.

What's the Point?

In addition to the task of re-kindling hospitality in the community, the point of becoming certified as A Place of Hospitality is to grow your business ... not from endless hype and discounting, but from the voluntary, enthusiastic support of the neighborhood ... and it works!

Certified restaurants have consistently generated higher guest satisfaction scores in our online feedback system. Below is the comparative performance for three months in mid-summer 2013. While the scores for all Gold Group members (dotted line) were generally exceptional, certified Places of Hospitality (solid line) consistently out-performed them.

Strong Grades Build Strong Sales

A study by the Harvard Business Review documented that sales grow exponentially as guest feedback scores exceed 4.5 (on a five-point scale), suggesting happier guests spend more money!

Do higher feedback scores actually lead to increased sales in the real world?

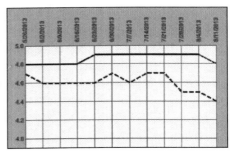

We don't collect financial information from participating restaurants, but our certified operators report annual sales increases of 10-15% ... and a few reported their highest sales year EVER! Even in a down economy, it appears hospitality is very good for business!

In fairness, I won't attribute the increase solely to their certification – these are all excellent operators. But they did feel the increased focus on hospitality was a big factor in their sales growth. (It certainly didn't hurt!)

Getting Started

The support resources that make certification as **A Place of Hospitality** practical are part of membership in the Gold Group. Here's just some what you'll have access to as a member:

270

Weekly Electronic House Call e-Letter

The Restaurant Doctor's weekly e-letter with ideas to grow your business (and assure you will always have something new to talk about in your staff and management meetings!)

Monthly Interviews with Industry Experts

An audio chat with industry leaders on topics ranging from marketing and management to menu design and operations.

Monthly Roundtable Teleconference

Members get together on the phone to share ideas and discuss items of mutual interest or concern.

Monthly Home Remedies Newsletter

A four-page newsletter with insights, trade secrets and best practices, all in a short, easy-to-digest format.

FREE Telephone Consulting

Pose your questions directly to recognized industry experts without a meter running.

Online Staff Selection System

The full Sure-Fire Staff Selection System to make the process easier and more effective, so you can get the right people ... the first time!

On-Demand Video Training

24/7 access to online training resources typically available only to chain operators.

Real-Time Online Guest Feedback System

Know – almost in real time – what your patrons think about their experience of doing business with you.

Food Cost Control System

Know your food cost every day ... without taking an inventory. (Imagine how much better you'd sleep at night!)

... and there are many more resources in development!

In keeping with my purpose, Gold Group membership is easily affordable. The program is constantly evolving so realistically, that amount may change as we refine the structure and include additional resources in the membership. But unlike most other industry support programs, we have a larger purpose than merely maximizing our own income.

To stay true to our mission of being irresistible and easily affordable, we must offer you as MUCH as we can for as LITTLE as possible! How's THAT for a fresh approach?

Have the courage to test drive the program risk-free for 90 days and prove to yourself there is, in fact, a painless process that can help you accomplish "impossible" results, put the passion back into your work and help you become the Restaurant of Choice.

Then, perhaps, you will choose to pursue certification as A Place of Hospitality, differentiate yourself from all other competitors and tap the transforming power of hospitality to grow your business even faster!

Why not give it a try? You've got nothing to lose but your struggle!

Get full details and join the Gold Group at www.APlaceOfHospitality.com.
Look under "Getting Started."

About the Author

Bill Marvin, aka "The Restaurant Doctor^{SM}" is a leading authority on how good restaurants can become great restaurants and an advisor to service-oriented organizations across North America. Bill founded Effortless, Inc., an industry consulting and education company and Hospitality Masters Press, publishers of the acclaimed Hospitality Masters Series of restaurant management resources.

He's earned the designation of Certified Speaking Professional from the National Speakers Association. is a lifetime member of the Council of Hotel and Restaurant Trainers and was one of the first to be certified as a Foodservice Management Professional by the National Restaurant Association.

Bill started in the industry at the age of 14, washing dishes (by hand!) in a small restaurant on Cape Cod and went on to earn a degree in Hotel Administration from Cornell University. He moved to Colorado in 1984 to design the foodservice system for the U.S. Olympic Training Centers. In 1993, he and his wife Margene relocated to Gig Harbor in the Puget Sound area of Washington State.

Before joining the Olympic Committee, Bill spent twelve years in the San Francisco Bay Area in a number of roles. He was a supervisor in the management consulting department of an international hospitality consulting firm, developed and operated two restaurants for his own account and started his practice an independent restaurant consultant. In typical Northern California fashion, he also became a commercial hot air balloon pilot and in the fall of 1981, became the first person in history to fly a hot air balloon in China!

He's managed a condominium hotel in the Virgin Islands, helped run a prestigious New England country club and been a consultant/designer for a national food facilities engineering firm. As a foodservice officer in the U.S. Navy, he also was responsible for operating several enlisted feeding facilities, the largest serving over 20,000 meals a day with a staff of 525 – all pieces in the puzzle of his life.

Bill is a prolific author and a sought-after consultant in the areas of concept development and organizational effectiveness. In addition to over a dozen well-regarded books focused on the hospitality industry, he writes two weekly e-mail newsletters, offers several subscription series and contributes regularly to trade magazines in a variety of industries. He still has a healthy private consulting practice and logs (way too many!) miles a year delivering corporate keynotes and training programs in North America and around the world.

Bill's final project is to trigger a contagious resurgence of hospitality in the world, starting by helping independent restaurant operators re-discover their roots: hospitality itself! Toward that end he developed a certification and support program called "A Place of Hospitality" that allows operators to enjoy more balance in their lives, put the joy back into serving the public, level the playing field when competing against the national chains, develop a sustainable, steadily growing business model built on personal connection and service to the community not on discounts and hype ... and which does all this in a way that is both operationally practical and extremely profitable!

Bill Marvin
The Restaurant Doctor

EFFORTLESS, INC. • PO Box 280 • Gig Harbor, WA 98335 USA

800-767-1055/253-858-9255 • Bill@RestaurantDoctor.com
www.RestaurantDoctor.com • www.APlaceOfHospitality.com

30984764R00157

Made in the USA
San Bernardino, CA
28 February 2016